A Collection Of Stories
Reviews And Essays

By

Willa Cather

Double 9
BOOKS

A Collection Of Stories
Reviews And Essays
by Willa Cather

ISBN: 978-93-60466-59-6
Published by

DOUBLE 9 BOOKS

2/13-B, Ansari Road
Daryaganj, New Delhi – 110002
info@double9books.com
www.double9books.com
Tel. 011-40042856

ABOUT THE AUTHOR

American author Willa Sibert Cather is well-known for her Great Plains-set books, such as O Pioneers! The Song of the Lark, and My Ántonia. Her novel One of Ours, which takes place during World War I, won her the Pulitzer Prize in 1923. When Willa Cather was nine years old, her family relocated from Virginia to Webster County, Nebraska. Afterwards, the family made Red Cloud, Minnesota, their home. Cather spent ten years in Pittsburgh after earning her degree from the University of Nebraska–Lincoln, where she worked as a high school English teacher and magazine editor to support herself. She made her lifelong home in New York City when she moved there at the age of 33, though she also traveled extensively and made frequent trips to her summer house on Grand Manan Island, New Brunswick. She lived her final 39 years with Edith Lewis, her domestic partner, before receiving a breast cancer diagnosis and passing away from a brain hemorrhage. Beside her, in a Jaffrey, New Hampshire, plot, lies Lewis. As a novelist of the frontier and pioneer experience, Cather attained prominence.

CONTENTS

Part I
Stories

Peter

"No, Antone, I have told thee many times, no, thou shalt not sell it until I am gone."

"But I need money; what good is that old fiddle to thee? The very crows laugh at thee when thou art trying to play. Thy hand trembles so thou canst scarce hold the bow. Thou shalt go with me to the Blue to cut wood to-morrow. See to it thou art up early."

"What, on the Sabbath, Antone, when it is so cold? I get so very cold, my son, let us not go to-morrow."

"Yes, to-morrow, thou lazy old man. Do not I cut wood upon the Sabbath? Care I how cold it is? Wood thou shalt cut, and haul it too, and as for the fiddle, I tell thee I will sell it yet." Antone pulled his ragged cap down over his low heavy brow, and went out. The old man drew his stool up nearer the fire, and sat stroking his violin with trembling fingers and muttering, "Not while I live, not while I live."

Five years ago they had come here, Peter Sadelack, and his wife, and oldest son Antone, and countless smaller Sadelacks, here to the dreariest part of south-western Nebraska, and had taken up a homestead. Antone was the acknowledged master of the premises, and people said he was a likely youth, and would do well. That he was mean and untrustworthy every one knew, but that made little difference. His corn was better tended than any in the county, and his wheat always yielded more than other men's.

Of Peter no one knew much, nor had any one a good word to say for him. He drank whenever he could get out of Antone's sight long enough to pawn his hat or coat for whiskey. Indeed there were but two things he would not pawn, his pipe and his violin. He was a lazy, absent minded old fellow, who liked to fiddle better than to plow, though Antone surely got work enough out of them all, for that matter. In the house of which Antone was master there was no one, from the little boy three years old, to the old man of sixty, who did not earn his bread. Still people said that Peter was worthless, and was a great drag on Antone, his son, who never drank, and was a much better man than his father had ever been. Peter did not care what people said. He did not like the country, nor the people, least of all he liked the plowing. He was very homesick for Bohemia. Long ago, only eight years ago by the calendar, but it seemed eight centuries to Peter, he had been a second violinist in the great theatre at Prague. He had gone into the theatre very young, and had been there all his life, until he had a stroke of paralysis, which made his arm so weak that his bowing was uncertain. Then they told him he could go. Those were great days at the theatre. He had plenty to drink then, and wore a dress coat every evening, and there were always parties after the play. He could play in those days, ay, that he could! He could never read the notes well, so he did not play first; but his touch, he had a touch indeed, so Herr Mikilsdoff, who led the orchestra, had said. Sometimes now Peter thought he could plow better if he could only bow as he used to. He had seen all the lovely women in the world there, all the great singers and the great players. He was in the orchestra when Rachel played, and he heard Liszt play when the Countess d'Agoult sat in the stage box and threw the master white lilies. Once, a French woman came and played for weeks, he did not remember her name now. He did not remember her face very well either, for it changed so, it was never twice the same. But the beauty of it, and the great hunger men felt at the sight of it, that he remembered. Most of all he remembered her voice. He did not know French, and could not understand a word she said, but it seemed to him that she must be talking the music of Chopin. And her voice, he thought he should know that in the other world. The last night she played a play in which a man touched her arm, and she stabbed him. As Peter sat among the smoking gas jets down below the footlights with his fiddle on his knee, and looked up at her, he thought he would like to die too, if he could touch her arm once, and have her stab him so. Peter went home to his wife very drunk that night. Even in those days he was a foolish fellow, who cared for nothing but music and pretty faces.

It was all different now. He had nothing to drink and little to eat, and here, there was nothing but sun, and grass, and sky. He had forgotten almost everything, but some things he remembered well enough. He loved his violin and the holy Mary, and above all else he feared the Evil One, and his son Antone.

The fire was low, and it grew cold. Still Peter sat by the fire remembering. He dared not throw more cobs on the fire; Antone would be angry. He did not want to cut wood tomorrow, it would be Sunday, and he wanted to go to mass. Antone might let him do that. He held his violin under his wrinkled chin, his white hair fell over it, and he began to play "Ave Maria." His hand shook more than ever before, and at last refused to work the bow at all. He sat stupefied for a while, then arose, and taking his violin with him, stole out into the old sod stable. He took Antone's shot-gun down from its peg, and loaded it by the moonlight which streamed in through the door. He sat down on the dirt floor, and leaned back against the dirt wall. He heard the wolves howling in the distance, and the night wind screaming as it swept over the snow. Near him he heard the regular breathing of the horses in the dark. He put his crucifix above his heart, and folding his hands said brokenly all the Latin he had ever known, "*Pater noster, qui in cælum est.*" Then he raised his head and sighed, "Not one kreutzer will Antone pay them to pray for my soul, not one kreutzer, he is so careful of his money, is Antone, he does not waste it in drink, he is a better man than I, but hard sometimes. He works the girls too hard, women were not made to work so. But he shall not sell thee, my fiddle, I can play thee no more, but they shall not part us. We have seen it all together, and we will forget it together, the French woman and all." He held his fiddle under his chin a moment, where it had lain so often, then put it across his knee and broke it through the middle. He pulled off his old boot, held the gun between his knees with the muzzle against his forehead, and pressed the trigger with his toe.

In the morning Antone found him stiff, frozen fast in a pool of blood. They could not straighten him out enough to fit a coffin, so they buried him in a pine box. Before the funeral Antone carried to town the fiddle-bow which Peter had forgotten to break. Antone was very thrifty, and a better man than his father had been.

The Mahogany Tree, May 21, 1892

On the Divide

Near Rattlesnake Creek, on the side of a little draw stood Canute's shanty. North, east, south, stretched the level Nebraska plain of long rust-red grass that undulated constantly in the wind. To the west the ground was broken and rough, and a narrow strip of timber wound along the turbid, muddy little stream that had scarcely ambition enough to crawl over its black bottom. If it had not been for the few stunted cottonwoods and elms that grew along its banks, Canute would have shot himself years ago. The Norwegians are a timber-loving people, and if there is even a turtle pond with a few plum bushes around it they seem irresistibly drawn toward it.

As to the shanty itself, Canute had built it without aid of any kind, for when he first squatted along the banks of Rattlesnake Creek there was not a human being within twenty miles. It was built of logs split in halves, the chinks stopped with mud and plaster. The roof was covered with earth and was supported by one gigantic beam curved in the shape of a round arch. It was almost impossible that any tree had ever grown in that shape. The Norwegians used to say that Canute had taken the log across his knee and bent it into the shape he wished. There were two rooms, or rather there was one room with a partition made of ash saplings interwoven and bound together like big straw basket work. In one corner there was a cook stove, rusted and broken. In the other a bed made of unplaned planks and poles. It was fully eight feet long, and upon it was a heap of dark bed clothing. There was a chair and a bench of colossal proportions. There was an ordinary kitchen cupboard with a few cracked dirty dishes in it, and beside it on a tall box a tin wash-basin. Under the bed was a pile of pint flasks, some broken, some whole, all empty. On the wood box lay a pair of shoes of almost incredible dimensions. On the wall hung a saddle, a gun, and some ragged clothing, conspicuous among which was a suit of dark cloth, apparently new, with a paper collar carefully wrapped in a red silk handkerchief and pinned to the sleeve. Over the door hung a wolf and a badger skin, and on the door itself a brace of thirty or forty snake skins whose noisy tails rattled ominously every time it opened. The strangest things in the shanty were the wide window-sills. At first glance they looked as though they had been ruthlessly hacked and mutilated with a hatchet, but on closer inspection all the notches and holes in the wood took form and shape. There seemed to be a series of pictures. They were, in a rough way, artistic, but the figures were heavy and labored, as though they had been cut very slowly and with very awkward instruments. There were men plowing with little horned imps sitting on their shoulders and on their horses' heads. There were men praying with a skull hanging over their heads and little demons behind them mocking their attitudes. There were men fighting with big serpents, and skeletons dancing together. All about these pictures were blooming vines and foliage such as never grew in this world, and coiled among the branches of the vines there was always the scaly body of a serpent, and behind every flower there was a serpent's head. It was a veritable Dance of Death by one who had felt its sting. In the wood box lay some boards, and every inch of them was cut up in the same manner. Sometimes the work was very rude and careless, and looked as though the hand of the workman had trembled. It would sometimes have been hard to distinguish the men from their evil geniuses but for one fact, the men were always grave and were either toiling or praying, while the devils were always smiling and dancing. Several of these boards had been split for kindling and it was evident that the artist did not value his work highly.

It was the first day of winter on the Divide. Canute stumbled into his shanty carrying a basket of cobs, and after filling the stove, sat down on a stool and crouched his seven foot frame over the fire, staring drearily out of the window at the wide gray sky. He knew by heart every individual clump of bunch grass in the miles of red shaggy prairie that stretched before his cabin. He knew it in all the deceitful loveliness of its early summer, in all the bitter barrenness of its autumn. He had seen it smitten by all the plagues of Egypt. He had seen it parched by drought, and sogged by rain, beaten by hail, and swept by fire, and in the grasshopper years he had seen it eaten as bare and clean as bones that the vultures have left. After the great fires he had seen it stretch for miles and miles, black and smoking as the floor of hell.

He rose slowly and crossed the room, dragging his big feet heavily as though they were burdens to him. He looked out of the window into the hog corral and saw the pigs burying themselves in the straw before the shed. The leaden gray clouds were beginning to spill themselves, and the snowflakes were settling down over the white leprous patches of frozen earth where the hogs had gnawed even the sod away. He shuddered and began to walk, tramping heavily with his ungainly feet. He was the wreck of ten winters on the Divide and he knew what they meant. Men fear the winters of the Divide as a child fears night or as men in the North Seas fear the still dark cold of the polar twilight.

His eyes fell upon his gun, and he took it down from the wall and looked it over. He sat down on the edge of his bed and held the barrel towards his face, letting his forehead rest upon it, and laid his finger on the trigger. He was perfectly calm, there was neither passion nor despair in his face, but the thoughtful look of a man who is considering. Presently he laid down the gun, and reaching into the cupboard, drew out a pint bottle of raw white alcohol. Lifting it to his lips, he drank greedily. He washed his face in the tin basin and combed his rough hair and shaggy blond beard. Then he stood in uncertainty before the suit of dark clothes that hung on the wall. For the fiftieth time he took them in his hands and tried to summon courage to put them on. He took the paper collar that was pinned to the sleeve of the coat and cautiously slipped it under his rough beard, looking with timid expectancy into the cracked, splashed glass that hung over the bench. With a short laugh he threw it down on the bed, and pulling on his old black hat, he went out, striking off across the level.

It was a physical necessity for him to get away from his cabin once in a while. He had been there for ten years, digging and plowing and sowing, and reaping what little the hail and the hot winds and the frosts left him to reap. Insanity and suicide are very common things on the Divide. They come on like an epidemic in the hot wind season. Those scorching dusty winds that blow up over the bluffs from Kansas seem to dry up the blood in men's veins as they do the sap in the corn leaves. Whenever the yellow scorch creeps down over the tender inside leaves about the ear, then the coroners prepare for active duty; for the oil of the country is burned out and it does not take long for the flame to eat up the wick. It causes no great sensation there when a Dane is found swinging to his own windmill tower, and most of the Poles after they have become too careless and discouraged to shave themselves keep their razors to cut their throats with.

It may be that the next generation on the Divide will be very happy, but the present one came too late in life. It is useless for men that have cut hemlocks among the mountains of Sweden for forty years to try to be happy in a country as flat and gray and as naked as the sea. It is not easy for men that have spent their youths fishing in the Northern seas to be content with following a plow, and men that have served in the Austrian army hate hard work and coarse clothing and the loneliness of the plains, and long for marches and excitement and tavern company and pretty barmaids. After a man has passed his fortieth birthday it is not easy for him to change the habits and conditions of his life. Most men bring with them to the Divide only the dregs of the lives that they have squandered in other lands and among other peoples.

Canute Canuteson was as mad as any of them, but his madness did not take the form of suicide or religion but of alcohol. He had always taken liquor when he wanted it, as all Norwegians do, but after his first year of solitary life he settled down to it steadily. He exhausted whisky after a while, and went to alcohol, because its effects were speedier and surer. He was a big man with a terrible amount of resistant force, and it took a great deal of alcohol even to move him. After nine years of drinking, the quantities he could take would seem fabulous to an ordinary drinking man. He never let it interfere with his work, he generally drank at night and on Sundays. Every night, as soon as his chores were done, he began to drink. While he was able to sit up he would play on his mouth harp or hack away at his window sills with his jack knife. When the liquor went to his head he would lie down on his bed and stare out of the window until he went to sleep. He drank alone and in solitude not for pleasure or good cheer, but to forget the awful loneliness and level of the Divide. Milton made a sad blunder when he put mountains in hell. Mountains postulate faith and aspiration. All mountain peoples are religious. It was the cities of the plains that, because of their utter lack of spirituality and the mad caprice of their vice, were cursed of God.

Alcohol is perfectly consistent in its effects upon man. Drunkenness is merely an exaggeration. A foolish man drunk becomes maudlin; a bloody man, vicious; a coarse man, vulgar. Canute was none of these, but he was morose and gloomy, and liquor took him through all the hells of Dante. As he lay on his giant's bed all the horrors of this world and every other were laid bare to his chilled senses. He was a man who knew no joy, a man who toiled in silence and bitterness. The skull and the serpent were always before him, the symbols of eternal futileness and of eternal hate.

When the first Norwegians near enough to be called neighbors came, Canute rejoiced, and planned to escape from his bosom vice. But he was not a social man by nature and had not the power of drawing out the social side of other people. His new neighbors rather feared him because of his great strength and size, his silence and his lowering brows. Perhaps, too, they knew that he was mad, mad from the eternal treachery of the plains, which every spring stretch green and rustle with the promises of Eden, showing long grassy lagoons full of clear water and cattle whose hoofs are stained with wild roses. Before autumn the lagoons are dried up, and the ground is burnt dry and hard until it blisters and cracks open.

So instead of becoming a friend and neighbor to the men that settled about him, Canute became a mystery and a terror. They told awful stories of his size and strength and of the alcohol he drank. They said that one night, when he went out to see to his horses just before he went to bed, his steps were unsteady and the rotten planks of the floor gave way and threw him behind the feet of a fiery young stallion. His foot was caught fast in the floor, and the nervous horse began kicking frantically. When Canute felt the blood trickling down in his eyes from a scalp wound in his head, he roused himself from his kingly indifference, and with the quiet stoical courage of a drunken man leaned forward and wound his arms about the horse's hind legs and held them against his breast with crushing embrace. All through the darkness and cold of the night he lay there, matching strength against strength. When little Jim Peterson went over the next morning at four o'clock to go with him to the Blue to cut wood, he found him so, and the horse was on its fore knees, trembling and whinnying with fear. This is the story the Norwegians tell of him, and if it is true it is no wonder that they feared and hated this Holder of the Heels of Horses.

One spring there moved to the next "eighty" a family that made a great change in Canute's life. Ole Yensen was too drunk most of the time to be afraid of any one, and his wife Mary was too garrulous to be afraid of any one who listened to her talk, and Lena, their pretty daughter, was not afraid of man nor devil. So it came about that Canute went over to take his alcohol with Ole oftener than he took it alone. After a while the report spread that he was going to marry Yensen's daughter, and the Norwegian girls began to tease Lena about the great bear she was going to keep house for. No one could quite see how the affair had come about, for Canute's tactics of courtship were somewhat peculiar. He apparently never spoke to her at all: he would sit for hours with Mary chattering on one side of him and Ole drinking on the other and watch Lena at her work. She teased him, and threw flour in his face and put vinegar in his coffee, but he took her rough jokes with silent wonder, never even smiling. He took her to church occasionally, but the most watchful and curious people never saw him speak to her. He would sit staring at her while she giggled and flirted with the other men.

Next spring Mary Lee went to town to work in a steam laundry. She came home every Sunday, and always ran across to Yensens to startle Lena with stories of ten cent theaters, firemen's dances, and all the other esthetic delights of metropolitan life. In a few weeks Lena's head was completely turned, and she gave her father no rest until he let her go to town to seek her fortune at the ironing board. From the time she came home on her first visit she began to treat Canute with contempt. She had bought a plush cloak and kid gloves, had her clothes made by the dress-maker, and assumed airs and graces that made the other women of the neighborhood cordially detest her. She generally brought with her a young man from town who waxed his mustache and wore a red necktie, and she did not even introduce him to Canute.

The neighbors teased Canute a good deal until he knocked one of them down. He gave no sign of suffering from her neglect except that he drank more and avoided the other Norwegians more carefully than ever. He lay around in his den and no one knew what he felt or thought, but little Jim Peterson, who had seen him glowering at Lena in church one Sunday when she was there with the town man, said that he would not give an acre of his wheat for Lena's life or the town chap's either; and Jim's wheat was so wondrously worthless that the statement was an exceedingly strong one.

Canute had bought a new suit of clothes that looked as nearly like the town man's as possible. They had cost him half a millet crop; for tailors are not accustomed to fitting giants and they charge for it. He had hung those clothes in his shanty two months ago and had never put them on, partly from fear of ridicule, partly from discouragement, and partly because there was something in his own soul that revolted at the littleness of the device.

Lena was at home just at this time. Work was slack in the laundry and Mary had not been well, so Lena stayed at home, glad enough to get an opportunity to torment Canute once more.

She was washing in the side kitchen, singing loudly as she worked. Mary was on her knees, blacking the stove and scolding violently about the young man who was coming out from town that night. The young man had committed the fatal error of laughing at Mary's ceaseless babble and had never been forgiven.

"He is no good, and you will come to a bad end by running with him! I do not see why a daughter of mine should act so. I do not see why the Lord should visit such a punishment upon me as to give me such a daughter. There are plenty of good men you can marry."

Lena tossed her head and answered curtly, "I don't happen to want to marry any man right away, and so long as Dick dresses nice and has plenty of money to spend, there is no harm in my going with him."

"Money to spend? Yes, and that is all he does with it I'll be bound. You think it very fine now, but you will change your tune when you have been married five years and see your children running naked and your cupboard empty. Did Anne Hermanson come to any good end by marrying a town man?"

"I don't know anything about Anne Hermanson, but I know any of the laundry girls would have Dick quick enough if they could get him."

"Yes, and a nice lot of store clothes huzzies you are too. Now there is Canuteson who has an 'eighty' proved up and fifty head of cattle and——"

"And hair that ain't been cut since he was a baby, and a big dirty beard, and he wears overalls on Sundays, and drinks like a pig. Besides he will keep. I can have all the fun I want, and when I am old and ugly like you he can have me and take care of me. The Lord knows there ain't nobody else going to marry him."

Canute drew his hand back from the latch as though it were red hot. He was not the kind of a man to make a good eavesdropper, and he wished he had knocked sooner. He pulled himself together and struck the door like a battering ram. Mary jumped and opened it with a screech.

"God! Canute, how you scared us! I thought it was crazy Lou,—he has been tearing around the neighborhood trying to convert folks. I am afraid as death of him. He ought to sent off, I think. He is just as liable as not to kill us all, or burn the barn, or poison the dogs. He has been worrying even the poor minister to death, and he laid up with the rheumatism, too! Did you notice that he was too sick to preach last Sunday? But don't stand there in the cold,—come in. Yensen isn't here, but he just went over to Sorenson's for the mail; he won't be gone long. Walk right in the other room and sit down."

Canute followed her, looking steadily in front of him and not noticing Lena as he passed her. But Lena's vanity would not allow him to pass unmolested. She took the wet sheet she was wringing out and cracked him across the face with it, and ran giggling to the other side of the room. The blow stung his cheeks and the soapy water flew in his eyes, and he involuntarily began rubbing them with his hands. Lena giggled with delight at his discomfiture, and the wrath in Canute's face grew blacker than ever. A big man humiliated is vastly more undignified than a little one. He forgot the sting of his face in the bitter consciousness that he had made a fool of himself. He stumbled blindly into the living room, knocking his head against the door jamb because he forgot to stoop. He dropped into a chair behind the stove, thrusting his big feet back helplessly on either side of him.

Ole was a long time in coming, and Canute sat there, still and silent, with his hands clenched on his knees, and the skin of his face seemed to have shriveled up into little wrinkles that trembled when he lowered his brows. His life had been one long lethargy of solitude and alcohol, but now he was awakening, and it was as when the dumb stagnant heat of summer breaks out into thunder.

When Ole came staggering in, heavy with liquor, Canute rose at once.

"Yensen," he said quietly, "I have come to see if you will let me marry your daughter today."

"Today!" gasped Ole.

"Yes, I will not wait until tomorrow. I am tired of living alone."

Ole braced his staggering knees against the bedstead, and stammered eloquently: "Do you think I will marry my daughter to a drunkard? a man who drinks raw alcohol? a man who sleeps with rattle snakes? Get out of my house or I will kick you out for your impudence." And Ole began looking anxiously for his feet.

Canute answered not a word, but he put on his hat and went out into the kitchen. He went up to Lena and said without looking at her, "Get your things on and come with me!"

The tones of his voice startled her, and she said angrily, dropping the soap, "Are you drunk?"

"If you do not come with me, I will take you,—you had better come," said Canute quietly.

She lifted a sheet to strike him, but he caught her arm roughly and wrenched the sheet from her. He turned to the wall and took down a hood and shawl that hung there, and began wrapping her up. Lena scratched and fought like a wild thing. Ole stood in the door, cursing, and Mary howled and screeched at the top of her voice. As for Canute, he lifted the girl in his arms and went out of the house. She kicked and struggled, but the helpless wailing of Mary and Ole soon died away in the distance, and her face was held down tightly on Canute's shoulder so that she could not see whither he was taking her. She was conscious only of the north wind whistling in her ears, and of rapid steady motion and of a great breast that heaved beneath her in quick, irregular breaths. The harder she struggled the tighter those iron arms that had held the heels of horses crushed about her, until she felt as if they would crush the breath from her, and lay still with fear. Canute was striding across the level fields at a pace at which man never went before, drawing the stinging north wind into his lungs in great gulps. He walked with his eyes half closed and looking straight in front of him, only lowering them when he bent his head to blow away the snow flakes that settled on her hair. So it was that Canute took her to his home, even as his bearded barbarian ancestors took the fair frivolous women of the South in their hairy arms and bore them down to their war ships. For ever and anon the soul becomes weary of the conventions that are not of it, and with a single stroke shatters the civilized lies with which it is unable to cope, and the strong arm reaches out and takes by force what it cannot win by cunning.

When Canute reached his shanty he placed the girl upon a chair, where she sat sobbing. He stayed only a few minutes. He filled the stove with wood and lit the lamp, drank a huge swallow of alcohol and put the bottle in his pocket. He paused a moment, staring heavily at the weeping girl, then he went off and locked the door and disappeared in the gathering gloom of the night.

Wrapped in flannels and soaked with turpentine, the little Norwegian preacher sat reading his Bible, when he heard a thundering knock at his door, and Canute entered, covered with snow and with his beard frozen fast to his coat.

"Come in, Canute, you must be frozen," said the little man, shoving a chair towards his visitor.

Canute remained standing with his hat on and said quietly, "I want you to come over to my house tonight to marry me to Lena Yensen."

"Have you got a license, Canute?"

"No, I don't want a license. I want to be married."

"But I can't marry you without a license, man. It would not be legal."

A dangerous light came in the big Norwegian's eye. "I want you to come over to my house to marry me to Lena Yensen."

"No, I can't, it would kill an ox to go out in a storm like this, and my rheumatism is bad tonight."

"Then if you will not go I must take you," said Canute with a sigh.

He took down the preacher's bearskin coat and bade him put it on while he hitched up his buggy. He went out and closed the door softly after him. Presently he returned and found the frightened minister crouching before the fire with his coat lying beside him. Canute helped him put it on and gently wrapped his head in his big muffler. Then he picked him up and carried him out and placed him in his buggy. As he tucked the buffalo robes around him he said: "Your horse is old, he might flounder or lose his way in this storm. I will lead him."

The minister took the reins feebly in his hands and sat shivering with the cold. Sometimes when there was a lull in the wind, he could see the horse struggling through the snow with the man plodding steadily beside him. Again the blowing snow would hide them from him altogether. He had no idea where they were or what direction they were going. He felt as though he were being whirled away in the heart of the storm, and he said all the prayers he knew. But at last the long four miles were over, and Canute set him down in the snow while he unlocked the door. He saw the bride sitting by the fire with her eyes red and swollen as though she had been weeping. Canute placed a huge chair for him, and said roughly,—

"Warm yourself."

Lena began to cry and moan afresh, begging the minister to take her home. He looked helplessly at Canute. Canute said simply,—

"If you are warm now, you can marry us."

"My daughter, do you take this step of your own free will?" asked the minister in a trembling voice.

"No sir, I don't, and it is disgraceful he should force me into it! I won't marry him."

"Then, Canute, I cannot marry you," said the minister, standing as straight as his rheumatic limbs would let him.

"Are you ready to marry us now, sir?" said Canute, laying one iron hand on his stooped shoulder. The little preacher was a good man, but like most men of weak body he was a coward and had a horror of physical suffering, although he had known so much of it. So with many qualms of conscience he began to repeat the marriage service. Lena sat sullenly in her chair, staring at the fire. Canute stood beside her, listening with his head bent reverently and his hands folded on his breast. When the little man had prayed and said amen, Canute began bundling him up again.

"I will take you home, now," he said as he carried him out and placed him in his buggy, and started off with him through the fury of the storm, floundering among the snow drifts that brought even the giant himself to his knees.

After she was left alone, Lena soon ceased weeping. She was not of a particularly sensitive temperament, and had little pride beyond that of vanity. After the first bitter anger wore itself out, she felt nothing more than a healthy sense of humiliation and defeat. She had no inclination to run away, for she was married now, and in her eyes that was final and all rebellion was useless. She knew nothing about a license, but she knew that a preacher married folks. She consoled herself by thinking that she had always intended to marry Canute some day, any way.

She grew tired of crying and looking into the fire, so she got up and began to look about her. She had heard queer tales about the inside of Canute's shanty, and her curiosity soon got the better of her rage. One of the first things she noticed was the new black suit of clothes hanging on the wall. She was dull, but it did not take a vain woman long to interpret anything so decidedly flattering, and she was pleased in spite of herself. As she looked through the cupboard, the general air of neglect and discomfort made her pity the man who lived there.

"Poor fellow, no wonder he wants to get married to get somebody to wash up his dishes. Batchin's pretty hard on a man."

It is easy to pity when once one's vanity has been tickled. She looked at the window sill and gave a little shudder and wondered if the man were crazy. Then she sat down again and sat a long time wondering what her Dick and Ole would do.

"It is queer Dick didn't come right over after me. He surely came, for he would have left town before the storm began and he might just as well come right on as go back. If he'd hurried he would have gotten here before the preacher came. I suppose he was afraid to come, for he knew Canuteson could pound him to jelly, the coward!" Her eyes flashed angrily.

The weary hours wore on and Lena began to grow horribly lonesome. It was an uncanny night and this was an uncanny place to be in. She could hear the coyotes howling hungrily a little way from the cabin, and more terrible still were all the unknown noises of the storm. She remembered the tales they told of the big log overhead and she was afraid of those snaky things on the window sills. She remembered the man who had been killed in the draw, and she wondered what she would do if she saw crazy Lou's white face glaring into the window. The rattling of the door became unbearable, she thought the latch must be loose and took the lamp to look at it. Then for the first time she saw the ugly brown snake skins whose death rattle sounded every time the wind jarred the door.

"Canute, Canute!" she screamed in terror.

Outside the door she heard a heavy sound as of a big dog getting up and shaking himself. The door opened and Canute stood before her, white as a snow drift.

"What is it?" he asked kindly.

"I am cold," she faltered.

He went out and got an armful of wood and a basket of cobs and filled the stove. Then he went out and lay in the snow before the door. Presently he heard her calling again.

"What is it?" he said, sitting up.

"I'm so lonesome, I'm afraid to stay in here all alone."

"I will go over and get your mother." And he got up.

"She won't come."

"I'll bring her," said Canute grimly.

"No, no. I don't want her, she will scold all the time."

"Well, I will bring your father."

She spoke again and it seemed as though her mouth was close up to the key-hole. She spoke lower than he had ever heard her speak before, so low that he had to put his ear up to the lock to hear her.

"I don't want him either, Canute,—I'd rather have you."

For a moment she heard no noise at all, then something like a groan. With a cry of fear she opened the door, and saw Canute stretched in the snow at her feet, his face in his hands, sobbing on the door step.

Overland Monthly, January 1896

Eric Hermannson's Soul

I

It was a great night at the Lone Star schoolhouse—a night when the Spirit was present with power and when God was very near to man. So it seemed to Asa Skinner, servant of God and Free Gospeller. The schoolhouse was crowded with the saved and sanctified, robust men and women, trembling and quailing before the power of some mysterious psychic force. Here and there among this cowering, sweating multitude crouched some poor wretch who had felt the pangs of an awakened conscience, but had not yet experienced that complete divestment of reason, that frenzy born of a convulsion of the mind, which, in the parlance of the Free Gospellers, is termed "the Light." On the floor, before the mourners' bench, lay the unconscious figure of a man in whom outraged nature had sought her last resort. This "trance" state is the highest evidence of grace among the Free Gospellers, and indicates a close walking with God.

Before the desk stood Asa Skinner, shouting of the mercy and vengeance of God, and in his eyes shone a terrible earnestness, an almost prophetic flame. Asa was a converted train gambler who used to run between Omaha and Denver. He was a man made for the extremes of life; from the most debauched of men he had become the most ascetic. His was a bestial face, a face that bore the stamp of Nature's eternal injustice. The forehead was low, projecting over the eyes, and the sandy hair was plastered down over it and then brushed back at an abrupt right angle. The chin was heavy, the nostrils were low and wide, and the lower lip hung loosely except in his moments of spasmodic earnestness, when it shut like a steel trap. Yet about those coarse features there were deep, rugged furrows, the scars of many a hand-to-hand struggle with the weakness of the flesh, and about that drooping lip were sharp, strenuous lines that had conquered it and taught it to pray. Over those seamed cheeks there was a certain pallor, a grayness caught from many a vigil. It was as though, after Nature had done her worst with that face, some fine chisel had gone over it, chastening and almost transfiguring it. To-night, as his muscles twitched with emotion, and the perspiration dropped from his hair and chin, there was a certain convincing power in the man. For Asa Skinner was a man possessed of a belief, of that sentiment of the sublime before which all inequalities are leveled, that transport of conviction which seems superior to all laws of condition, under which debauchees have become martyrs; which made a tinker an artist and a camel-driver the founder of an empire. This was with Asa Skinner to-night, as he stood proclaiming the vengeance of God.

It might have occurred to an impartial observer that Asa Skinner's God was indeed a vengeful God if he could reserve vengeance for those of his creatures who were packed into the Lone Star schoolhouse that night. Poor exiles of all nations; men from the south and the north, peasants from almost every country of Europe, most of them from the mountainous, night-bound coast of Norway. Honest men for the most part, but men with whom the world had dealt hardly; the failures of all countries, men sobered by toil and saddened by exile, who had been driven to fight for the dominion of an untoward soil, to sow where others should gather, the advance-guard of a mighty civilization to be.

Never had Asa Skinner spoken more earnestly than now. He felt that the Lord had this night a special work for him to do. To-night Eric Hermannson, the wildest lad on all the Divide, sat in his audience with a fiddle on his knee, just as he had dropped in on his way to play for some dance. The violin is an object of particular abhorrence to the Free Gospellers. Their antagonism to the church organ is bitter enough, but the fiddle they regard as a very incarnation of evil desires, singing forever of worldly pleasures and inseparably associated with all forbidden things.

Eric Hermannson had long been the object of the prayers of the revivalists. His mother had felt the power of the Spirit weeks ago, and special prayer-meetings had been held at her house for her son. But Eric had only gone his ways laughing, the ways of youth, which are short enough at best, and none too flowery on the Divide. He slipped away from the prayer-meetings to meet the Campbell boys in Genereau's saloon, or hug the plump little French girls at Chevalier's dances, and sometimes, of a summer night, he even went across the dewy cornfields and through the wild-plum thicket to play the fiddle for Lena Hanson, whose name was a reproach through all the Divide country, where the women are usually too plain and too busy and too tired to depart from the ways of virtue. On such occasions Lena, attired in a pink wrapper and silk stockings and tiny pink slippers, would sing to him, accompanying herself on a battered guitar. It gave him a delicious sense of freedom and experience to be with a woman who, no matter how, had lived in big cities and knew the ways of town-folk, who had never worked in the fields and had kept her hands white and soft, her throat fair and tender, who had heard great singers in Denver and Salt Lake, and who knew the strange language of flattery and idleness and mirth.

Yet, careless as he seemed, the frantic prayers of his mother were not altogether without their effect upon Eric. For days he had been fleeing before them as a criminal from his pursuers, and over his pleasures had fallen the shadow of something dark and terrible that dogged his steps. The harder he danced, the louder he sang, the more was he conscious that this phantom was gaining upon him, that in time it would track him down. One Sunday afternoon, late in the fall, when he had been drinking beer with Lena Hanson and listening to a song which made his cheeks burn, a rattlesnake had crawled out of the side of the sod house and thrust its ugly head in under the screen door. He was not afraid of snakes, but he knew enough of Gospellism to feel the significance of the reptile lying coiled there upon her doorstep. His lips were cold when he kissed Lena good-by, and he went there no more.

The final barrier between Eric and his mother's faith was his violin, and to that he clung as a man sometimes will cling to his dearest sin, to the weakness more precious to him than all his strength. In the great world beauty comes to men in many guises, and art in a hundred forms, but for Eric there was only his violin. It stood, to him, for all the manifestations of art; it was his only bridge into the kingdom of the soul.

It was to Eric Hermannson that the evangelist directed his impassioned pleading that night.

"*Saul, Saul, why persecutest thou me?* Is there a Saul here to-night who has stopped his ears to that gentle pleading, who has thrust a spear into that bleeding side? Think of it, my brother; you are offered this wonderful love and you prefer the worm that dieth not and the fire which will not be quenched. What right have you to lose one of God's precious souls? *Saul, Saul, why persecutest thou me?*"

A great joy dawned in Asa Skinner's pale face, for he saw that Eric Hermannson was swaying to and fro in his seat. The minister fell upon his knees and threw his long arms up over his head.

"O my brothers! I feel it coming, the blessing we have prayed for. I tell you the Spirit is coming! Just a little more prayer, brothers, a little more zeal, and he will be here. I can feel his cooling wing upon my brow. Glory be to God forever and ever, amen!"

The whole congregation groaned under the pressure of this spiritual panic. Shouts and hallelujahs went up from every lip. Another figure fell prostrate upon the floor. From the mourners' bench rose a chant of terror and rapture:

"Eating honey and drinking wine,

Glory to the bleeding Lamb!
I am my Lord's and he is mine,
Glory to the bleeding Lamb!"

The hymn was sung in a dozen dialects and voiced all the vague yearning of these hungry lives, of these people who had starved all the passions so long, only to fall victims to the basest of them all, fear.

A groan of ultimate anguish rose from Eric Hermannson's bowed head, and the sound was like the groan of a great tree when it falls in the forest.

The minister rose suddenly to his feet and threw back his head, crying in a loud voice:

"*Lazarus, come forth!* Eric Hermannson, you are lost, going down at sea. In the name of God, and Jesus Christ his Son, I throw you the life-line. Take hold! Almighty God, my soul for his!" The minister threw his arms out and lifted his quivering face.

Eric Hermannson rose to his feet; his lips were set and the lightning was in his eyes. He took his violin by the neck and crushed it to splinters across his knee, and to Asa Skinner the sound was like the shackles of sin broken audibly asunder.

II

For more than two years Eric Hermannson kept the austere faith to which he had sworn himself, kept it until a girl from the East came to spend a week on the Nebraska Divide. She was a girl of other manners and conditions, and there were greater distances between her life and Eric's than all the miles which separated Rattlesnake Creek from New York city. Indeed, she had no business to be in the West at all; but ah! across what leagues of land and sea, by what improbable chances, do the unrelenting gods bring to us our fate!

It was in a year of financial depression that Wyllis Elliot came to Nebraska to buy cheap land and revisit the country where he had spent a year of his youth. When he had graduated from Harvard it was still customary for moneyed gentlemen to send their scapegrace sons to rough it on ranches in the wilds of Nebraska or Dakota, or to consign them to a living death in the sage-brush of the Black Hills. These young men did not always return to the ways of civilized life. But Wyllis Elliot had not married a half-breed, nor been shot in a cow-punchers' brawl, nor wrecked by bad whisky, nor appropriated by a smirched adventuress. He had been saved from these things by a girl, his sister, who had been very near to his life ever since the days when they read fairy tales together and dreamed the dreams that never come true. On this, his first visit to his father's ranch since he left it six years before, he brought her with him. She had been laid up half the winter from a sprain received while skating, and had had too much time for reflection during those months. She was restless and filled with a desire to see something of the wild country of which her brother had told her so much. She was to be married the next winter, and Wyllis understood her when she begged him to take her with him on this long, aimless jaunt across the continent, to taste the last of their freedom together. It comes to all women of her type—that desire to taste the unknown which allures and terrifies, to run one's whole soul's length out to the wind—just once.

It had been an eventful journey. Wyllis somehow understood that strain of gypsy blood in his sister, and he knew where to take her. They had slept in sod houses on the Platte River, made the acquaintance of the personnel of a third-rate opera company on the train to Deadwood, dined in a camp of railroad constructors at the world's end beyond New Castle, gone through the Black Hills on horseback, fished for trout in Dome Lake, watched a dance at Cripple Creek, where the lost souls who hide in the hills gathered for their besotted revelry. And now, last of all, before the return to thraldom, there was this little shack, anchored on the windy crest of the Divide, a little black dot against the flaming sunsets, a scented sea of cornland bathed in opalescent air and blinding sunlight.

Margaret Elliot was one of those women of whom there are so many in this day, when old order, passing, giveth place to new; beautiful, talented, critical, unsatisfied, tired of the world at twenty-four. For the moment the life and people of the Divide interested her. She was there but a week; perhaps had she stayed longer, that inexorable ennui which travels faster even than the Vestibule Limited would have overtaken her. The week she tarried there was the week that Eric Hermannson was helping Jerry Lockhart thresh; a week earlier or a week later, and there would have been no story to write.

It was on Thursday and they were to leave on Saturday. Wyllis and his sister were sitting on the wide piazza of the ranchhouse, staring out into the afternoon sunlight and protesting against the gusts of hot wind that blew up from the sandy river-bottom twenty miles to the southward.

The young man pulled his cap lower over his eyes and remarked:

"This wind is the real thing; you don't strike it anywhere else. You remember we had a touch of it in Algiers and I told you it came from Kansas. It's the key-note of this country."

Wyllis touched her hand that lay on the hammock and continued gently:

"I hope it's paid you, Sis. Roughing it's dangerous business; it takes the taste out of things."

She shut her fingers firmly over the brown hand that was so like her own.

"Paid? Why, Wyllis, I haven't been so happy since we were children and were going to discover the ruins of Troy together some day. Do you know, I believe I could just stay on here forever and let the world go on its own gait. It seems as though the tension and strain we used to talk of last winter were gone for good, as though one could never give one's strength out to such petty things any more."

Wyllis brushed the ashes of his pipe away from the silk handkerchief that was knotted about his neck and stared moodily off at the sky-line.

"No, you're mistaken. This would bore you after a while. You can't shake the fever of the other life. I've tried it. There was a time when the gay fellows of Rome could trot down into the Thebaid and burrow into the sandhills and get rid of it. But it's all too complex now. You see we've made our dissipations so dainty and respectable that they've gone further in than the flesh, and taken hold of the ego proper. You couldn't rest, even here. The war-cry would follow you."

"You don't waste words, Wyllis, but you never miss fire. I talk more than you do, without saying half so much. You must have learned the art of silence from these taciturn Norwegians. I think I like silent men."

"Naturally," said Wyllis, "since you have decided to marry the most brilliant talker you know."

Both were silent for a time, listening to the sighing of the hot wind hrough the parched morning-glory vines. Margaret spoke first.

"Tell me, Wyllis, were many of the Norwegians you used to know as interesting as Eric Hermannson?"

"Who, Siegfried? Well, no. He used to be the flower of the Norwegian youth in my day, and he's rather an exception, even now. He has retrograded, though. The bonds of the soil have tightened on him, I fancy."

"Siegfried? Come, that's rather good, Wyllis. He looks like a dragon-slayer. What is it that makes him so different from the others? I can talk to him; he seems quite like a human being."

"Well," said Wyllis, meditatively, "I don't read Bourget as much as my cultured sister, and I'm not so well up in analysis, but I fancy it's because one keeps cherishing a perfectly unwarranted suspicion that under that big, hulking anatomy of his, he may conceal a soul somewhere. Nicht wahr?"

"Something like that," said Margaret, thoughtfully, "except that it's more than a suspicion, and it isn't groundless. He has one, and he makes it known, somehow, without speaking."

"I always have my doubts about loquacious souls," Wyllis remarked, with the unbelieving smile that had grown habitual with him.

Margaret went on, not heeding the interruption. "I knew it from the first, when he told me about the suicide of his cousin, the Bernstein boy. That kind of blunt pathos can't be summoned at will in anybody. The earlier novelists rose to it, sometimes, unconsciously. But last night when I sang for him I was doubly sure. Oh, I haven't told you about that yet! Better light your pipe again. You see, he stumbled in on me in the dark when I was pumping away at that old parlor organ to please Mrs. Lockhart. It's her household fetish and I've forgotten how many pounds of butter she made and sold to buy it. Well, Eric stumbled in, and in some inarticulate manner made me understand that he wanted me to sing for him. I sang just the old things, of course. It's queer to sing familiar things here at the world's end. It makes one think how the hearts of men have carried them around the world, into the wastes of Iceland and the jungles of Africa and the islands of the Pacific. I think if one lived here long enough one would quite forget how to be trivial, and would read only the great books that we never get time to read in the world, and would remember only the great music, and the things that are really worth while would stand out clearly against that horizon over there. And of course I played the intermezzo from 'Cavalleria Rusticana' for him; it goes rather better on an organ than most things do. He shuffled his feet and twisted his big hands up into knots and blurted out that he didn't know there was any music like that in the world. Why, there were tears in his voice, Wyllis! Yes, like Rossetti, I *heard* his tears. Then it dawned upon me that it was probably the first good music he had ever heard in all his life. Think of it, to care for music as he does and never to hear it, never to know that it exists on earth! To long for it as we long for other perfect experiences that never come. I can't tell you what music means to that man. I never saw any one so susceptible to it. It gave him speech, he became alive. When I had finished the intermezzo, he began telling me about a little crippled brother who died and whom he loved and used to carry everywhere in his arms. He did not wait for encouragement. He took up the story and told it slowly, as if to himself, just sort of rose up and told his own woe to answer Mascagni's. It overcame me."

"Poor devil," said Wyllis, looking at her with mysterious eyes, "and so you've given him a new woe. Now he'll go on wanting Grieg and Schubert the rest of his days and never getting them. That's a girl's philanthropy for you!"

Jerry Lockhart came out of the house screwing his chin over the unusual luxury of a stiff white collar, which his wife insisted upon as a necessary article of toilet while Miss Elliot was at the house. Jerry sat down on the step and smiled his broad, red smile at Margaret.

"Well, I've got the music for your dance, Miss Elliot. Olaf Oleson will bring his accordion and Mollie will play the organ, when she isn't lookin' after the grub, and a little chap from Frenchtown will bring his fiddle— though the French don't mix with the Norwegians much."

"Delightful! Mr. Lockhart, that dance will be the feature of our trip, and it's so nice of you to get it up for us. We'll see the Norwegians in character at last," cried Margaret, cordially.

"See here, Lockhart, I'll settle with you for backing her in this scheme," said Wyllis, sitting up and knocking the ashes out of his pipe. "She's done crazy things enough on this trip, but to talk of dancing all night with a gang of half-mad Norwegians and taking the carriage at four to catch the six o'clock train out of Riverton—well, it's tommy-rot, that's what it is!"

"Wyllis, I leave it to your sovereign power of reason to decide whether it isn't easier to stay up all night than to get up at three in the morning. To get up at three, think what that means! No, sir, I prefer to keep my vigil and then get into a sleeper."

"But what do you want with the Norwegians? I thought you were tired of dancing."

"So I am, with some people. But I want to see a Norwegian dance, and I intend to. Come, Wyllis, you know how seldom it is that one really wants to do anything nowadays. I wonder when I have really wanted to go to a party before. It will be something to remember next month at Newport, when we have to and don't want to. Remember your own theory that contrast is about the only thing that makes life endurable. This is my party and Mr. Lockhart's; your whole duty to-morrow night will consist in being nice to the Norwegian girls. I'll warrant you were adept enough at it once. And you'd better be very nice indeed, for if there are many such young valkyrs as Eric's sister among them, they would simply tie you up in a knot if they suspected you were guying them."

Wyllis groaned and sank back into the hammock to consider his fate, while his sister went on.

"And the guests, Mr. Lockhart, did they accept?"

Lockhart took out his knife and began sharpening it on the sole of his plowshoe.

"Well, I guess we'll have a couple dozen. You see it's pretty hard to get a crowd together here any more. Most of 'em have gone over to the Free Gospellers, and they'd rather put their feet in the fire than shake 'em to a fiddle."

Margaret made a gesture of impatience.

"Those Free Gospellers have just cast an evil spell over this country, haven't they?"

"Well," said Lockhart, cautiously, "I don't just like to pass judgment on any Christian sect, but if you're to know the chosen by their works, the Gospellers can't make a very proud showin', an' that's a fact. They're responsible for a few suicides, and they've sent a good-sized delegation to the state insane asylum, an' I don't see as they've made the rest of us much better than we were before. I had a little herdboy last spring, as square a little Dane as I want to work for me, but after the Gospellers got hold of him and sanctified him, the little beggar used to get down on his knees out on the prairie and pray by the hour and let the cattle get into the corn, an' I had to fire him. That's about the way it goes. Now there's Eric; that chap used to be a hustler and the spryest dancer in all this section—called all the dances. Now he's got no ambition and he's glum as a preacher. I don't suppose we can even get him to come in to-morrow night."

"Eric? Why, he must dance, we can't let him off," said Margaret, quickly. "Why, I intend to dance with him myself!"

"I'm afraid he won't dance. I asked him this morning if he'd help us out and he said, 'I don't dance now, any more,'" said Lockhart, imitating the labored English of the Norwegian.

"'The Miller of Hoffbau, the Miller of Hoffbau, O my Princess!'" chirped Wyllis, cheerfully, from his hammock.

The red on his sister's cheek deepened a little, and she laughed mischievously. "We'll see about that, sir. I'll not admit that I am beaten until I have asked him myself."

Every night Eric rode over to St. Anne, a little village in the heart of the French settlement, for the mail. As the road lay through the most attractive part of the Divide country, on several occasions Margaret Elliot and her brother had accompanied him. To-night Wyllis had business with Lockhart, and Margaret rode with Eric, mounted on a frisky little mustang that Mrs. Lockhart had broken to the side-saddle. Margaret regarded her escort very much as she did the servant who always accompanied her on long rides at home, and the ride to the village was a silent one. She was occupied with thoughts of another world, and Eric was wrestling with more thoughts than had ever been crowded into his head before. He rode with his eyes riveted on that slight figure before him, as though he wished to absorb it through the optic nerves and hold it in his brain forever. He understood the situation perfectly. His brain worked slowly, but he had a keen sense of the values of things. This girl represented an entirely new species of humanity to him, but he knew where to place her. The prophets of old, when an angel first appeared unto them, never doubted its high origin.

Eric was patient under the adverse conditions of his life, but he was not servile. The Norse blood in him had not entirely lost its self-reliance. He came of a proud fisher line, men who were not afraid of anything but the ice and the devil, and he had prospects before him when his father went down off the North Cape in the long Arctic night, and his mother, seized by a violent horror of seafaring life, had followed her brother to America. Eric was eighteen then, handsome as young Siegfried, a giant in stature, with a skin singularly pure and delicate, like a Swede's; hair as yellow as the locks of Tennyson's amorous Prince, and eyes of a fierce, burning blue, whose flash was most dangerous to women. He had in those days a certain pride of bearing, a certain confidence of approach, that usually accompanies physical perfection. It was even said of him then that he was in love with life, and inclined to levity, a vice most unusual on the Divide. But the sad history of those Norwegian exiles, transplanted in an arid soil and under a scorching sun, had repeated itself in his case. Toil and isolation had sobered him, and he grew more and more like the clods among which he labored. It was as though some red-hot instrument had touched for a moment those delicate fibers of the brain which respond to acute pain or pleasure, in which lies the power of exquisite sensation, and had seared them quite away. It is a painful thing to watch the light die out of the eyes of those Norsemen, leaving an expression of impenetrable sadness, quite passive, quite hopeless, a shadow that is never lifted. With some this change comes almost at once, in the first bitterness of homesickness, with others it comes more slowly, according to the time it takes each man's heart to die.

Oh, those poor Northmen of the Divide! They are dead many a year before they are put to rest in the little graveyard on the windy hill where exiles of all nations grow akin.

The peculiar species of hypochondria to which the exiles of his people sooner or later succumb had not developed in Eric until that night at the Lone Star schoolhouse, when he had broken his violin across his knee. After that, the gloom of his people settled down upon him, and the gospel of maceration began its work. *"If thine eye offend thee, pluck it out,"* et cetera. The pagan smile that once hovered about his lips was gone, and he was one with sorrow. Religion heals a hundred hearts for one that it embitters, but when it destroys, its work is quick and deadly, and where the agony of the cross has been, joy will not come again. This man understood things literally: one must live without pleasure to die without fear; to save the soul it was necessary to starve the soul.

The sun hung low above the cornfields when Margaret and her cavalier left St. Anne. South of the town there is a stretch of road that runs for some three miles through the French settlement, where the prairie is as level as the surface of a lake. There the fields of flax and wheat and rye are bordered by precise rows of slender, tapering Lombard poplars. It was a yellow world that Margaret Elliot saw under the wide light of the setting sun.

The girl gathered up her reins and called back to Eric, "It will be safe to run the horses here, won't it?"

"Yes, I think so, now," he answered, touching his spur to his pony's flank. They were off like the wind. It is an old saying in the West that newcomers always ride a horse or two to death before they get broken in to the country. They are tempted by the great open spaces and try to outride the horizon, to get to the end of something. Margaret galloped over the level road, and Eric, from behind, saw her long veil fluttering in the wind. It had fluttered just so in his dreams last night and the night before. With a sudden inspiration of courage he overtook her and rode beside her, looking intently at her half-averted face. Before, he had only stolen occasional glances at it, seen it in blinding flashes, always with more or less embarrassment, but now he determined to let every line of it sink into his memory. Men of the world would have said that it was an unusual face, nervous, finely cut, with clear, elegant lines that betokened ancestry. Men of letters would have called it a historic face, and would have conjectured at what old passions, long asleep, what old sorrows forgotten time out of mind, doing battle together in ages gone, had curved those delicate nostrils, left their unconscious memory in those eyes. But Eric read no meaning in these details. To him this beauty was something more than color and line; it was as a flash of white light, in which one cannot distinguish color because all colors are there. To him it was a complete revelation, an embodiment of those dreams of impossible loveliness that linger by a young man's pillow on midsummer nights; yet, because it held something more than the attraction of health and youth and shapeliness, it troubled him, and in its presence he felt as the Goths before the white marbles in the Roman Capitol, not knowing whether they were men or gods. At times he felt like uncovering his head before it, again the fury seized him to break and despoil, to find the clay in this spirit-thing and stamp upon it. Away from her, he longed to strike out with his arms, and take and hold; it maddened him that this woman whom he could break in his hands should be so much stronger than he. But near her, he never questioned this strength; he admitted its potentiality as he admitted the miracles of the Bible; it enervated and conquered him. To-night, when he rode so close to her that he could have touched her, he knew that he might as well reach out his hand to take a star.

Margaret stirred uneasily under his gaze and turned questioningly in her saddle.

"This wind puts me a little out of breath when we ride fast," she said.

Eric turned his eyes away.

"I want to ask you if I go to New York to work, if I maybe hear music like you sang last night? I been a purty good hand to work," he asked, timidly.

Margaret looked at him with surprise, and then, as she studied the outline of his face, pityingly.

"Well, you might—but you'd lose a good deal else. I shouldn't like you to go to New York—and be poor, you'd be out of atmosphere, some way," she said, slowly. Inwardly she was thinking: "There he would be altogether sordid, impossible—a machine who would carry one's trunks upstairs, perhaps. Here he is every inch a man, rather picturesque; why is it?" "No," she added aloud, "I shouldn't like that."

"Then I not go," said Eric, decidedly.

Margaret turned her face to hide a smile. She was a trifle amused and a trifle annoyed. Suddenly she spoke again.

"But I'll tell you what I do want you to do, Eric. I want you to dance with us to-morrow night and teach me some of the Norwegian dances; they say you know them all. Won't you?"

Eric straightened himself in his saddle and his eyes flashed as they had done in the Lone Star schoolhouse when he broke his violin across his knee.

"Yes, I will," he said, quietly, and he believed that he delivered his soul to hell as he said it.

They had reached the rougher country now, where the road wound through a narrow cut in one of the bluffs along the creek, when a beat of hoofs ahead and the sharp neighing of horses made the ponies start and Eric rose in his stirrups. Then down the gulch in front of them and over the steep clay banks thundered a herd of wild ponies, nimble as monkeys and wild as rabbits, such as horse-traders drive east from the plains of Montana to sell in the farming country. Margaret's pony made a shrill sound, a neigh that was almost a scream, and started up the clay bank to meet them, all the wild blood of the range breaking out in an instant. Margaret called to Eric just as he threw himself out of the saddle and caught her pony's bit. But the wiry little animal had gone mad and was kicking and biting like a devil. Her wild brothers of the range were all about her, neighing, and pawing the earth, and striking her with their fore feet and snapping at her flanks. It was the old liberty of the range that the little beast fought for.

"Drop the reins and hold tight, tight!" Eric called, throwing all his weight upon the bit, struggling under those frantic fore feet that now beat at his breast, and now kicked at the wild mustangs that surged and tossed about him. He succeeded in wrenching the pony's head toward him and crowding her withers against the clay bank, so that she could not roll.

"Hold tight, tight!" he shouted again, launching a kick at a snorting animal that reared back against Margaret's saddle. If she should lose her courage and fall now, under those hoofs— —He struck out again and again, kicking right and left with all his might. Already the negligent drivers had galloped into the cut, and their long quirts were whistling over the heads of the herd. As suddenly as it had come, the struggling, frantic wave of wild life swept up out of the gulch and on across the open prairie, and with a long despairing whinny of farewell the pony dropped her head and stood trembling in her sweat, shaking the foam and blood from her bit.

Eric stepped close to Margaret's side and laid his hand on her saddle. "You are not hurt?" he asked, hoarsely. As he raised his face in the soft starlight she saw that it was white and drawn and that his lips were working nervously.

"No, no, not at all. But you, you are suffering; they struck you!" she cried in sharp alarm.

He stepped back and drew his hand across his brow.

"No, it is not that," he spoke rapidly now, with his hands clenched at his side. "But if they had hurt you, I would beat their brains out with my hands, I would kill them all. I was never afraid before. You are the only beautiful thing that has ever come close to me. You came like an angel out of the sky. You are like the music you sing, you are like the stars and the snow on the mountains where I played when I was a little boy. You are like all that I wanted once and never had, you are all that they have killed in me. I die for you to-night, to-morrow, for all eternity. I am not a coward; I was afraid because I love you more than Christ who died for me, more than I am afraid of hell, or hope for heaven. I was never afraid before. If you had fallen—oh, my God!" he threw his arms out blindly and dropped his head upon the pony's mane, leaning limply against the animal like a man struck by some sickness. His shoulders rose and fell perceptibly with his labored breathing.

The horse stood cowed with exhaustion and fear. Presently Margaret laid her hand on Eric's head and said gently:

"You are better now, shall we go on? Can you get your horse?"

"No, he has gone with the herd. I will lead yours, she is not safe. I will not frighten you again." His voice was still husky, but it was steady now. He took hold of the bit and tramped home in silence.

When they reached the house, Eric stood stolidly by the pony's head until Wyllis came to lift his sister from the saddle.

"The horses were badly frightened, Wyllis. I think I was pretty thoroughly scared myself," she said as she took her brother's arm and went slowly up the hill toward the house. "No, I'm not hurt, thanks to Eric. You must thank him for taking such good care of me. He's a mighty fine fellow. I'll tell you all about it in the morning, dear. I was pretty well shaken up and I'm going right to bed now. Good-night."

When she reached the low room in which she slept, she sank upon the bed in her riding-dress face downward.

"Oh, I pity him! I pity him!" she murmured, with a long sigh of exhaustion. She must have slept a little. When she rose again, she took from her dress a letter that had been waiting for her at the village post-office. It was closely written in a long, angular hand, covering a dozen pages of foreign note-paper, and began:—

"My Dearest Margaret: If I should attempt to say *how like a winter hath thine absence been*, I should incur the risk of being tedious. Really, it takes the sparkle out of everything. Having nothing better to do, and not caring to go anywhere in particular without you, I remained in the city until Jack Courtwell noted my general despondency and brought me down here to his place on the sound to manage some open-air theatricals he is getting up. 'As You Like It' is of course the piece selected. Miss Harrison plays Rosalind. I wish you had been here to take the part. Miss Harrison reads her lines well, but she is either a maiden-all-forlorn or a tomboy; insists on reading into the part all sorts of deeper meanings and highly colored suggestions wholly out of harmony with the pastoral setting. Like most of the professionals, she exaggerates the emotional element and quite fails to do justice to Rosalind's facile wit and really brilliant mental qualities. Gerard will do Orlando, but rumor says he is épris of your sometime friend, Miss Meredith, and his memory is treacherous and his interest fitful.

"My new pictures arrived last week on the 'Gascogne.' The Puvis de Chavannes is even more beautiful than I thought it in Paris. A pale dream-maiden sits by a pale dream-cow, and a stream of anemic water flows at her feet. The Constant, you will remember, I got because you admired it. It is here in all its florid splendor, the whole dominated by a glowing sensuosity. The drapery of the female figure is as wonderful as you said; the fabric all barbaric pearl and gold, painted with an easy, effortless voluptuousness, and that white, gleaming line of African coast in the background recalls memories of you very precious to me. But it is useless to deny that Constant irritates me. Though I cannot prove the charge against him, his brilliancy always makes me suspect him of cheapness."

Here Margaret stopped and glanced at the remaining pages of this strange love-letter. They seemed to be filled chiefly with discussions of pictures and books, and with a slow smile she laid them by.

She rose and began undressing. Before she lay down she went to open the window. With her hand on the sill, she hesitated, feeling suddenly as though some danger were lurking outside, some inordinate desire waiting to spring upon her in the darkness. She stood there for a long time, gazing at the infinite sweep of the sky.

"Oh, it is all so little, so little there," she murmured. "When everything else is so dwarfed, why should one expect love to be great? Why should one try to read highly colored suggestions into a life like that? If only I could find one thing in it all that mattered greatly, one thing that would warm me when I am alone! Will life never give me that one great moment?"

As she raised the window, she heard a sound in the plum-bushes outside. It was only the house-dog roused from his sleep, but Margaret started violently and trembled so that she caught the foot of the bed for support. Again she felt herself pursued by some overwhelming longing, some desperate necessity for herself, like the outstretching of helpless, unseen arms in the darkness, and the air seemed heavy with sighs of yearning. She fled to her bed with the words, "I love you more than Christ, who died for me!" ringing in her ears.

III

About midnight the dance at Lockhart's was at its height. Even the old men who had come to "look on" caught the spirit of revelry and stamped the floor with the vigor of old Silenus. Eric took the violin from the Frenchman, and Minna Oleson sat at the organ, and the music grew more and more characteristic—rude, half-mournful music, made up of the folk-songs of the North, that the villagers sing through the long night in hamlets by the sea, when they are thinking of the sun, and the spring, and the fishermen so long away. To Margaret some of it sounded like Grieg's Peer Gynt music. She found something irresistibly infectious in the mirth of these people who were so seldom merry, and she felt almost one of them. Something seemed struggling for freedom in them to-night, something of the joyous childhood of the nations which exile had not killed. The girls were all boisterous with delight. Pleasure came to them but rarely, and when it came, they caught at it wildly and crushed its fluttering wings in their strong brown fingers. They had a hard life enough, most of them. Torrid summers and freezing winters, labor and drudgery and ignorance, were the portion of their girlhood; a short wooing, a hasty, loveless marriage, unlimited maternity, thankless sons, premature age and ugliness, were the dower of their womanhood. But what matter? To-night there was hot liquor in the glass and hot blood in the heart; to-night they danced.

To-night Eric Hermannson had renewed his youth. He was no longer the big, silent Norwegian who had sat at Margaret's feet and looked hopelessly into her eyes. To-night he was a man, with a man's rights and a man's power. To-night he was Siegfried indeed. His hair was yellow as the heavy wheat in the ripe of summer, and his eyes flashed like the blue water between the ice-packs in the North Seas. He was not afraid of Margaret to-night, and when he danced with her he held her firmly. She was tired and dragged on his arm a little, but the strength of the man was like an all-pervading fluid, stealing through her veins, awakening under her heart some nameless, unsuspected existence that had slumbered there all these years and that went out through her throbbing fingertips to his that answered. She wondered if the hoydenish blood of some lawless ancestor, long asleep, were calling out in her to-night, some drop of a hotter fluid that the centuries had failed to cool, and why, if this curse were in her, it had not spoken before. But was it a curse, this awakening, this wealth before undiscovered, this music set free? For the first time in her life her heart held something stronger than herself, was not this worth while? Then she ceased to wonder. She lost sight of the lights and the faces, and the music was drowned by the beating of her own arteries. She saw only the blue eyes that flashed above her, felt only the warmth of that throbbing hand which held hers and which the blood of his heart fed. Dimly, as in a dream, she saw the drooping shoulders, high white forehead and tight, cynical mouth of the man she was to marry in December. For an hour she had been crowding back the memory of that face with all her strength.

"Let us stop, this is enough," she whispered. His only answer was to tighten the arm behind her. She sighed and let that masterful strength bear her where it would. She forgot that this man was little more than a savage, that they would part at dawn. The blood has no memories, no reflections, no regrets for the past, no consideration of the future.

"Let us go out where it is cooler," she said when the music stopped; thinking, "I am growing faint here, I shall be all right in the open air." They stepped out into the cool, blue air of the night.

Since the older folk had begun dancing, the young Norwegians had been slipping out in couples to climb the windmill tower into the cooler atmosphere, as is their custom.

"You like to go up?" asked Eric, close to her ear.

She turned and looked at him with suppressed amusement. "How high is it?"

"Forty feet, about. I not let you fall." There was a note of irresistible pleading in his voice, and she felt that he tremendously wished her to go. Well, why not? This was a night of the unusual, when she was not herself at all, but was living an unreality. To-morrow, yes, in a few hours, there would be the Vestibule Limited and the world.

"Well, if you'll take good care of me. I used to be able to climb, when I was a little girl."

Once at the top and seated on the platform, they were silent. Margaret wondered if she would not hunger for that scene all her life, through all the routine of the days to come. Above them stretched the great Western sky, serenely blue, even in the night, with its big, burning stars, never so cold and dead and far away as in denser atmospheres. The moon would not be up for twenty minutes yet, and all about the horizon, that wide horizon, which seemed to reach around the world, lingered a pale, white light, as of a universal dawn. The weary wind brought up to them the heavy odors of the cornfields. The music of the dance sounded faintly from below. Eric leaned on his elbow beside her, his legs swinging down on the ladder. His great shoulders looked more than ever like those of the stone Doryphorus, who stands in his perfect, reposeful strength in the Louvre, and had often made her wonder if such men died forever with the youth of Greece.

"How sweet the corn smells at night," said Margaret nervously.

"Yes, like the flowers that grow in paradise, I think."

She was somewhat startled by this reply, and more startled when this taciturn man spoke again.

"You go away to-morrow?"

"Yes, we have stayed longer than we thought to now."

"You not come back any more?"

"No, I expect not. You see, it is a long trip; half-way across the continent."

"You soon forget about this country, I guess." It seemed to him now a little thing to lose his soul for this woman, but that she should utterly forget this night into which he threw all his life and all his eternity, that was a bitter thought.

"No, Eric, I will not forget. You have all been too kind to me for that. And you won't be sorry you danced this one night, will you?"

"I never be sorry. I have not been so happy before. I not be so happy again, ever. You will be happy many nights yet, I only this one. I will dream sometimes, maybe."

The mighty resignation of his tone alarmed and touched her. It was as when some great animal composes itself for death, as when a great ship goes down at sea.

She sighed, but did not answer him. He drew a little closer and looked into her eyes.

"You are not always happy, too?" he asked.

"No, not always, Eric; not very often, I think."

"You have a trouble?"

"Yes, but I cannot put it into words. Perhaps if I could do that, I could cure it."

He clasped his hands together over his heart, as children do when they pray, and said falteringly, "If I own all the world, I give him you."

Margaret felt a sudden moisture in her eyes, and laid her hand on his.

"Thank you, Eric; I believe you would. But perhaps even then I should not be happy. Perhaps I have too much of it already."

She did not take her hand away from him; she did not dare. She sat still and waited for the traditions in which she had always believed to speak and save her. But they were dumb. She belonged to an ultra-refined civilization which tries to cheat nature with elegant sophistries. Cheat nature? Bah! One generation may do it, perhaps two, but the third — — Can we ever rise above nature or sink below her? Did she not turn on Jerusalem as upon Sodom, upon St. Anthony in his desert as upon Nero in his seraglio? Does she not always cry in brutal triumph: "I am here still, at the bottom of things, warming the roots of life; you cannot starve me nor tame me nor thwart me; I made the world, I rule it, and I am its destiny."

This woman, on a windmill tower at the world's end with a giant barbarian, heard that cry to-night, and she was afraid! Ah! the terror and the delight of that moment when first we fear ourselves! Until then we have not lived.

"Come, Eric, let us go down; the moon is up and the music has begun again," she said.

He rose silently and stepped down upon the ladder, putting his arm about her to help her. That arm could have thrown Thor's hammer out in the cornfields yonder, yet it scarcely touched her, and his hand trembled as it had done in the dance. His face was level with hers now and the moonlight fell sharply upon it. All her life she had searched the faces of men for the look that lay in his eyes. She knew that that look had never shone for her before, would never shine for her on earth again, that such love comes to one only in dreams or in impossible places like this, unattainable always. This was Love's self, in a moment it would die. Stung by the agonized appeal that emanated from the man's whole being, she leaned forward and laid her lips on his. Once, twice and again she heard the deep respirations rattle in his throat while she held them there, and the riotous force under her heart became an engulfing weakness. He drew her up to him until he felt all the resistance go out of her body, until every nerve relaxed and yielded. When she drew her face back from his, it was white with fear.

"Let us go down, oh, my God! let us go down!" she muttered. And the drunken stars up yonder seemed reeling to some appointed doom as she clung to the rounds of the ladder. All that she was to know of love she had left upon his lips.

"The devil is loose again," whispered Olaf Oleson, as he saw Eric dancing a moment later, his eyes blazing.

But Eric was thinking with an almost savage exultation of the time when he should pay for this. Ah, there would be no quailing then! If ever a soul went fearlessly, proudly down to the gates infernal, his should go. For a moment he fancied he was there already, treading down the tempest of flame, hugging the fiery hurricane to his breast. He wondered whether in ages gone, all the countless years of sinning in which men had sold and lost and flung their souls away, any man had ever so cheated Satan, had ever bartered his soul for so great a price.

It seemed but a little while till dawn.

The carriage was brought to the door and Wyllis Elliot and his sister said good-by. She could not meet Eric's eyes as she gave him her hand, but as he stood by the horse's head, just as the carriage moved off, she gave him one swift glance that said, "I will not forget." In a moment the carriage was gone.

Eric changed his coat and plunged his head into the watertank and went to the barn to hook up his team. As he led his horses to the door, a shadow fell across his path, and he saw Skinner rising in his stirrups. His rugged face was pale and worn with looking after his wayward flock, with dragging men into the way of salvation.

"Good-morning, Eric. There was a dance here last night?" he asked, sternly.

"A dance? Oh, yes, a dance," replied Eric, cheerfully.

"Certainly you did not dance, Eric?"

"Yes, I danced. I danced all the time."

The minister's shoulders drooped, and an expression of profound discouragement settled over his haggard face. There was almost anguish in the yearning he felt for this soul.

"Eric, I didn't look for this from you. I thought God had set his mark on you if he ever had on any man. And it is for things like this that you set your soul back a thousand years from God. O foolish and perverse generation!"

Eric drew himself up to his full height and looked off to where the new day was gilding the corn-tassels and flooding the uplands with light. As his nostrils drew in the breath of the dew and the morning, something from the only poetry he had ever read flashed across his mind, and he murmured, half to himself, with dreamy exultation:

"'And a day shall be as a thousand years, and a thousand years as a day.'"

Cosmopolitan, April 1900

The Sentimentality of William Tavener

It takes a strong woman to make any sort of success of living in the West, and Hester undoubtedly was that. When people spoke of William Tavener as the most prosperous farmer in McPherson County, they usually added that his wife was a "good manager." She was an executive woman, quick of tongue and something of an imperatrix. The only reason her husband did not consult her about his business was that she did not wait to be consulted.

It would have been quite impossible for one man, within the limited sphere of human action, to follow all Hester's advice, but in the end William usually acted upon some of her suggestions. When she incessantly denounced the "shiftlessness" of letting a new threshing machine stand unprotected in the open, he eventually built a shed for it. When she sniffed contemptuously at his notion of fencing a hog corral with sod walls, he made a spiritless beginning on the structure—merely to "show his temper," as she put it—but in the end he went off quietly to town and bought enough barbed wire to complete the fence. When the first heavy rains came on, and the pigs rooted down the sod wall and made little paths all over it to facilitate their ascent, he heard his wife relate with relish the story of the little pig that built a mud house, to the minister at the dinner table, and William's gravity never relaxed for an instant. Silence, indeed, was William's refuge and his strength.

William set his boys a wholesome example to respect their mother. People who knew him very well suspected that he even admired her. He was a hard man towards his neighbors, and even towards his sons; grasping, determined and ambitious.

There was an occasional blue day about the house when William went over the store bills, but he never objected to items relating to his wife's gowns or bonnets. So it came about that many of the foolish, unnecessary little things that Hester bought for boys, she had charged to her personal account.

One spring night Hester sat in a rocking chair by the sitting room window, darning socks. She rocked violently and sent her long needle vigorously back and forth over her gourd, and it took only a very casual glance to see that she was wrought up over something. William sat on the other side of the table reading his farm paper. If he had noticed his wife's agitation, his calm, clean-shaven face betrayed no sign of concern. He must have noticed the sarcastic turn of her remarks at the supper table, and he must have noticed the moody silence of the older boys as they ate. When supper was but half over little Billy, the youngest, had suddenly pushed back his plate and slipped away from the table, manfully trying to swallow a sob. But William Tavener never heeded ominous forecasts in the domestic horizon, and he never looked for a storm until it broke.

After supper the boys had gone to the pond under the willows in the big cattle corral, to get rid of the dust of plowing. Hester could hear an occasional splash and a laugh ringing clear through the stillness of the night, as she sat by the open window. She sat silent for almost an hour reviewing in her mind many plans of attack. But she was too vigorous a woman to be much of a strategist, and she usually came to her point with directness. At last she cut her thread and suddenly put her darning down, saying emphatically:

"William, I don't think it would hurt you to let the boys go to that circus in town to-morrow."

William continued to read his farm paper, but it was not Hester's custom to wait for an answer. She usually divined his arguments and assailed them one by one before he uttered them.

"You've been short of hands all summer, and you've worked the boys hard, and a man ought use his own flesh and blood as well as he does his hired hands. We're plenty able to afford it, and it's little enough our boys ever spend. I don't see how you can expect 'em to be steady and hard workin', unless you encourage 'em a little. I never could see much harm in circuses, and our boys have never been to one. Oh, I know Jim Howley's boys get drunk an' carry on when they go, but our boys ain't that sort, an' you know it, William. The animals are real instructive, an' our boys don't get to see much out here on the prairie. It was different where we were raised, but the boys have got no advantages here, an' if you don't take care, they'll grow up to be greenhorns."

Hester paused a moment, and William folded up his paper, but vouchsafed no remark. His sisters in Virginia had often said that only a quiet man like William could ever have lived with Hester Perkins. Secretly, William was rather proud of his wife's "gift of speech," and of the fact that she could talk in prayer meeting as fluently as a man. He confined his own efforts in that line to a brief prayer at Covenant meetings.

Hester shook out another sock and went on.

"Nobody was ever hurt by goin' to a circus. Why, law me! I remember I went to one myself once, when I was little. I had most forgot about it. It was over at Pewtown, an' I remember how I had set my heart on going. I don't think I'd ever forgiven my father if he hadn't taken me, though that red clay road was in a frightful way after the rain. I mind they had an elephant and six poll parrots, an' a Rocky Mountain lion, an' a cage of monkeys, an' two camels. My! but they were a sight to me then!"

Hester dropped the black sock and shook her head and smiled at the recollection. She was not expecting anything from William yet, and she was fairly startled when he said gravely, in much the same tone in which he announced the hymns in prayer meeting:

"No, there was only one camel. The other was a dromedary."

She peered around the lamp and looked at him keenly.

"Why, William, how come you to know?"

William folded his paper and answered with some hesitation, "I was there, too."

Hester's interest flashed up.—"Well, I never, William! To think of my finding it out after all these years! Why, you couldn't have been much bigger'n our Billy then. It seems queer I never saw you when you was little, to remember about you. But then you Back Creek folks never have anything to do with us Gap people. But how come you to go? Your father was stricter with you than you are with your boys."

"I reckon I shouldn't 'a gone," he said slowly, "but boys will do foolish things. I had done a good deal of fox hunting the winter before, and father let me keep the bounty money. I hired Tom Smith's Tap to weed the corn for me, an' I slipped off unbeknownst to father an' went to the show."

Hester spoke up warmly: "Nonsense, William! It didn't do you no harm, I guess. You was always worked hard enough. It must have been a big sight for a little fellow. That clown must have just tickled you to death."

William crossed his knees and leaned back in his chair.

"I reckon I could tell all that fool's jokes now. Sometimes I can't help thinkin' about 'em in meetin' when the sermon's long. I mind I had on a pair of new boots that hurt me like the mischief, but I forgot all about 'em when that fellow rode the donkey. I recall I had to take them boots off as soon as I got out of sight o' town, and walked home in the mud barefoot."

"O poor little fellow!" Hester ejaculated, drawing her chair nearer and leaning her elbows on the table. "What cruel shoes they did use to make for children. I remember I went up to Back Creek to see the circus wagons go by. They came down from Romney, you know. The circus men stopped at the creek to water the animals, an' the elephant got stubborn an' broke a big limb off the yellow willow tree that grew there by the toll house porch, an' the Scribners were 'fraid as death he'd pull the house down. But this much I saw him do; he waded in the creek an' filled his trunk with water, and squirted it in at the window and nearly ruined Ellen Scribner's pink lawn dress that she had just ironed an' laid out on the bed ready to wear to the circus."

"I reckon that must have been a trial to Ellen," chuckled William, "for she was mighty prim in them days."

Hester drew her chair still nearer William's. Since the children had begun growing up, her conversation with her husband had been almost wholly confined to questions of economy and expense. Their relationship had become purely a business one, like that between landlord and tenant. In her desire to indulge her boys she had unconsciously assumed a defensive and almost hostile attitude towards her husband. No debtor ever haggled with his usurer more doggedly than did Hester with her husband in behalf of her sons. The strategic contest had gone on so long that it had almost crowded out the memory of a closer relationship. This exchange of confidences to-night, when common recollections took them unawares and opened their hearts, had all the miracle of romance. They talked on and on; of old neighbors, of old familiar faces in the valley where they had grown up, of long forgotten incidents of their youth—weddings, picnics, sleighing parties and baptizings. For years they had talked of nothing else but butter and eggs and the prices of things, and now they had as much to say to each other as people who meet after a long separation.

When the clock struck ten, William rose and went over to his walnut secretary and unlocked it. From his red leather wallet he took out a ten dollar bill and laid it on the table beside Hester.

"Tell the boys not to stay late, an' not to drive the horses hard," he said quietly, and went off to bed.

Hester blew out the lamp and sat still in the dark a long time. She left the bill lying on the table where William had placed it. She had a painful sense of having missed something, or lost something; she felt that somehow the years had cheated her.

The little locust trees that grew by the fence were white with blossoms. Their heavy odor floated in to her on the night wind and recalled a night long ago, when the first whip-poor-Will of the Spring was heard, and the rough, buxom girls of Hawkins Gap had held her laughing and struggling under the locust trees, and searched in her bosom for a lock of her sweetheart's hair, which is supposed to be on every girl's breast when the first whip-poor-Will sings. Two of those same girls had been her bridesmaids. Hester had been a very happy bride. She rose and went softly into the room where William lay. He was sleeping heavily, but occasionally moved his hand before his face to ward off the flies. Hester went into the parlor and took the piece of mosquito net from the basket of wax apples and pears that her sister had made before she died. One of the boys had brought it all the way from Virginia, packed in a tin pail, since Hester would not risk shipping so precious an ornament by freight. She went back to the bed room and spread the net over William's head.

Then she sat down by the bed and listened to his deep, regular breathing until she heard the boys returning. She went out to meet them and warn them not to waken their father.

"I'll be up early to get your breakfast, boys. Your father says you can go to the show." As she handed the money to the eldest, she felt a sudden throb of allegiance to her husband and said sharply, "And you be careful of that, an' don't waste it. Your father works hard for his money."

The boys looked at each other in astonishment and felt that they had lost a powerful ally.

Library, May 12, 1900

The Namesake

Seven of us, students, sat one evening in Hartwell's studio on the Boulevard St. Michel. We were all fellow-countrymen; one from New Hampshire, one from Colorado, another from Nevada, several from the farm lands of the Middle West, and I myself from California. Lyon Hartwell, though born abroad, was simply, as every one knew, "from America." He seemed, almost more than any other one living man, to mean all of it—from ocean to ocean. When he was in Paris, his studio was always open to the seven of us who were there that evening, and we intruded upon his leisure as often as we thought permissible.

Although we were within the terms of the easiest of all intimacies, and although the great sculptor, even when he was more than usually silent, was at all times the most gravely cordial of hosts, yet, on that long remembered evening, as the sunlight died on the burnished brown of the horse-chestnuts below the windows, a perceptible dullness yawned through our conversation.

We were, indeed, somewhat low in spirit, for one of our number, Charley Bentley, was leaving us indefinitely, in response to an imperative summons from home. To-morrow his studio, just across the hall from Hartwell's, was to pass into other hands, and Bentley's luggage was even now piled in discouraged resignation before his door. The various bales and boxes seemed literally to weigh upon us as we sat in his neighbor's hospitable rooms, drearily putting in the time until he should leave us to catch the ten o'clock express for Dieppe.

The day we had got through very comfortably, for Bentley made it the occasion of a somewhat pretentious luncheon at Maxim's. There had been twelve of us at table, and the two young Poles were thirsty, the Gascon so fabulously entertaining, that it was near upon five o'clock when we put down our liqueur glasses for the last time, and the red, perspiring waiter, having pocketed the reward of his arduous and protracted services, bowed us affably to the door, flourishing his napkin and brushing back the streaks of wet, black hair from his rosy forehead. Our guests having betaken themselves belated to their respective engagements, the rest of us returned with Bentley—only to be confronted by the depressing array before his door. A glance about his denuded rooms had sufficed to chill the glow of the afternoon, and we fled across the hall in a body and begged Lyon Hartwell to take us in.

Bentley had said very little about it, but we all knew what it meant to him to be called home. Each of us knew what it would mean to himself, and each had felt something of that quickened sense of opportunity which comes at seeing another man in any way counted out of the race. Never had the game seemed so enchanting, the chance to play it such a piece of unmerited, unbelievable good fortune.

It must have been, I think, about the middle of October, for I remember that the sycamores were almost bare in the Luxembourg Gardens that morning, and the terrace about the queens of France were strewn with crackling brown leaves. The fat red roses, out the summer long on the stand of the old flower woman at the corner, had given place to dahlias and purple asters. First glimpses of autumn toilettes flashed from the carriages; wonderful little bonnets nodded at one along the Champs-Elysées; and in the Quarter an occasional feather boa, red or black or white, brushed one's coat sleeve in the gay twilight of the early evening. The crisp, sunny autumn air was all day full of the stir of people and carriages and of the cheer of salutations; greetings of the students, returned brown and bearded from their holiday, gossip of people come back from Trouville, from St. Valery, from Dieppe, from all over Brittany and the Norman coast. Everywhere was the joyousness of return, the taking up again of life and work and play.

I had felt ever since early morning that this was the saddest of all possible seasons for saying good-by to that old, old city of youth, and to that little corner of it on the south shore which since the Dark Ages themselves — yes, and before — has been so peculiarly the land of the young.

I can recall our very postures as we lounged about Hartwell's rooms that evening, with Bentley making occasional hurried trips to his desolated workrooms across the hall — as if haunted by a feeling of having forgotten something — or stopping to poke nervously at his *perroquets*, which he had bequeathed to Hartwell, gilt cage and all. Our host himself sat on the couch, his big, bronze-like shoulders backed up against the window, his shaggy head, beaked nose, and long chin cut clean against the gray light.

Our drowsing interest, in so far as it could be said to be fixed upon anything, was centered upon Hartwell's new figure, which stood on the block ready to be cast in bronze, intended as a monument for some American battlefield. He called it "The Color Sergeant." It was the figure of a young soldier running, clutching the folds of a flag, the staff of which had been shot away. We had known it in all the stages of its growth, and the splendid action and feeling of the thing had come to have a kind of special significance for the half dozen of us who often gathered at Hartwell's rooms—though, in truth, there was as much to dishearten one as to inflame, in the case of a man who had done so much in a field so amazingly difficult; who had thrown up in bronze all the restless, teeming force of that adventurous wave still climbing westward in our own land across the waters. We recalled his "Scout," his "Pioneer," his "Gold Seekers," and those monuments in which he had invested one and another of the heroes of the Civil War with such convincing dignity and power.

"Where in the world does he get the heat to make an idea like that carry?" Bentley remarked morosely, scowling at the clay figure. "Hang me, Hartwell, if I don't think it's just because you're not really an American at all, that you can look at it like that."

The big man shifted uneasily against the window. "Yes," he replied smiling, "perhaps there is something in that. My citizenship was somewhat belated and emotional in its flowering. I've half a mind to tell you about it, Bentley." He rose uncertainly, and, after hesitating a moment, went back into his workroom, where he began fumbling among the litter in the corners.

At the prospect of any sort of personal expression from Hartwell, we glanced questioningly at one another; for although he made us feel that he liked to have us about, we were always held at a distance by a certain diffidence of his. There were rare occasions—when he was in the heat of work or of ideas—when he forgot to be shy, but they were so exceptional that no flattery was quite so seductive as being taken for a moment into Hartwell's confidence. Even in the matter of opinions—the commonest of currency in our circle—he was niggardly and prone to qualify. No man ever guarded his mystery more effectually. There was a singular, intense spell, therefore, about those few evenings when he had broken through this excessive modesty, or shyness, or melancholy, and had, as it were, committed himself.

When Hartwell returned from the back room, he brought with him an unframed canvas which he put on an easel near his clay figure. We drew close about it, for the darkness was rapidly coming on. Despite the dullness of the light, we instantly recognized the boy of Hartwell's "Color Sergeant." It was the portrait of a very handsome lad in uniform, standing beside a charger impossibly rearing. Not only in his radiant countenance and flashing eyes, but in every line of his young body there was an energy, a gallantry, a joy of life, that arrested and challenged one.

"Yes, that's where I got the notion," Hartwell remarked, wandering back to his seat in the window. "I've wanted to do it for years, but I've never felt quite sure of myself. I was afraid of missing it. He was an uncle of mine, my father's half-brother, and I was named for him. He was killed in one of the big battles of Sixty-four, when I was a child. I never saw him—never knew him until he had been dead for twenty years. And then, one night, I came to know him as we sometimes do living persons—intimately, in a single moment."

He paused to knock the ashes out of his short pipe, refilled it, and puffed at it thoughtfully for a few moments with his hands on his knees. Then, settling back heavily among the cushions and looking absently out of the window, he began his story. As he proceeded further and further into the experience which he was trying to convey to us, his voice sank so low and was sometimes so charged with feeling, that I almost thought he had forgotten our presence and was remembering aloud. Even Bentley forgot his nervousness in astonishment and sat breathless under the spell of the man's thus breathing his memories out into the dusk.

"It was just fifteen years ago this last spring that I first went home, and Bentley's having to cut away like this brings it all back to me.

"I was born, you know, in Italy. My father was a sculptor, though I dare say you've not heard of him. He was one of those first fellows who went over after Story and Powers,—went to Italy for 'Art,' quite simply; to lift from its native bough the willing, iridescent bird. Their story is told, informingly enough, by some of those ingenuous marble things at the Metropolitan. My father came over some time before the outbreak of the Civil War, and was regarded as a renegade by his family because he did not go home to enter the army. His half-brother, the only child of my grandfather's second marriage, enlisted at fifteen and was killed the next year. I was ten years old when the news of his death reached us. My mother died the following winter, and I was sent away to a Jesuit school, while my father, already ill himself, stayed on at Rome, chipping away at his Indian maidens and marble goddesses, still gloomily seeking the thing for which he had made himself the most unhappy of exiles.

"He died when I was fourteen, but even before that I had been put to work under an Italian sculptor. He had an almost morbid desire that I should carry on his work, under, as he often pointed out to me, conditions so much more auspicious. He left me in the charge of his one intimate friend, an American gentleman in the consulate at Rome, and his instructions were that I was to be educated there and to live there until I was twenty-one. After I was of age, I came to Paris and studied under one master after another until I was nearly thirty. Then, almost for the first time, I was confronted by a duty which was not my pleasure.

"My grandfather's death, at an advanced age, left an invalid maiden sister of my father's quite alone in the world. She had suffered for years from a cerebral disease, a slow decay of the faculties which rendered her almost helpless. I decided to go to America and, if possible, bring her back to Paris, where I seemed on my way toward what my poor father had wished for me.

"On my arrival at my father's birthplace, however, I found that this was not to be thought of. To tear this timid, feeble, shrinking creature, doubly aged by years and illness, from the spot where she had been rooted for a lifetime, would have been little short of brutality. To leave her to the care of strangers seemed equally heartless. There was clearly nothing for me to do but to remain and wait for that slow and painless malady to run its course. I was there something over two years.

"My grandfather's home, his father's homestead before him, lay on the high banks of a river in Western Pennsylvania. The little town twelve miles down the stream, whither my great-grandfather used to drive his ox-wagon on market days, had become, in two generations, one of the largest manufacturing cities in the world. For hundreds of miles about us the gentle hill slopes were honeycombed with gas wells and coal shafts; oil derricks creaked in every valley and meadow; the brooks were sluggish and discolored with crude petroleum, and the air was impregnated by its searching odor. The great glass and iron manufactories had come up and up the river almost to our very door; their smoky exhalations brooded over us, and their crashing was always in our ears. I was plunged into the very incandescence of human energy. But, though my nerves tingled with the feverish, passionate endeavor which snapped in the very air about me, none of these great arteries seemed to feed me; this tumultuous life did not warm me. On every side were the great muddy rivers, the ragged mountains from which the timber was being ruthlessly torn away, the vast tracts of wild country, and the gulches that were like wounds in the earth; everywhere the glare of that relentless energy which followed me like a searchlight and seemed to scorch and consume me. I could only hide myself in the tangled garden, where the dropping of a leaf or the whistle of a bird was the only incident.

"The Hartwell homestead had been sold away little by little, until all that remained of it was garden and orchard. The house, a square brick structure, stood in the midst of a great garden which sloped toward the river, ending in a grassy bank which fell some forty feet to the water's edge. The garden was now little more than a tangle of neglected shrubbery; damp, rank, and of that intense blue-green peculiar to vegetation in smoky places where the sun shines but rarely, and the mists form early in the evening and hang late in the morning.

"I shall never forget it as I saw it first, when I arrived there in the chill of a backward June. The long, rank grass, thick and soft and falling in billows, was always wet until midday. The gravel walks were bordered with great lilac-bushes, mock-orange, and bridal-wreath. Back of the house was a neglected rose garden, surrounded by a low stone wall over which the long suckers trailed and matted. They had wound their pink, thorny tentacles, layer upon layer, about the lock and the hinges of the rusty iron gate. Even the porches of the house, and the very windows, were damp and heavy with growth: wistaria, clematis, honeysuckle, and trumpet vine. The garden was grown up with trees, especially that part of it which lay above the river. The bark of the old locusts was blackened by the smoke that crept continually up the valley, and their feathery foliage, so merry in its movement and so yellow and joyous in its color, seemed peculiarly precious under that somber sky. There were sycamores and copper beeches; gnarled apple-trees, too old to bear; and fall pear-trees, hung with a sharp, hard fruit in October; all with a leafage singularly rich and luxuriant, and peculiarly vivid in color. The oaks about the house had been old trees when my great-grandfather built his cabin there, more than a century before, and this garden was almost the only spot for miles along the river where any of the original forest growth still survived. The smoke from the mills was fatal to trees of the larger sort, and even these had the look of doomed things—bent a little toward the town and seemed to wait with head inclined before that on-coming, shrieking force.

"About the river, too, there was a strange hush, a tragic submission—it was so leaden and sullen in its color, and it flowed so soundlessly forever past our door.

"I sat there every evening, on the high veranda overlooking it, watching the dim outlines of the steep hills on the other shore, the flicker of the lights on the island, where there was a boat-house, and listening to the call of the boatmen through the mist. The mist came as certainly as night, whitened by moonshine or starshine. The tin water-pipes went splash, splash, with it all evening, and the wind, when it rose at all, was little more than a sighing of the old boughs and a troubled breath in the heavy grasses.

"At first it was to think of my distant friends and my old life that I used to sit there; but after awhile it was simply to watch the days and weeks go by, like the river which seemed to carry them away.

"Within the house I was never at home. Month followed month, and yet I could feel no sense of kinship with anything there. Under the roof where my father and grandfather were born, I remained utterly detached. The somber rooms never spoke to me, the old furniture never seemed tinctured with race. This portrait of my boy uncle was the only thing to which I could draw near, the only link with anything I had ever known before.

"There is a good deal of my father in the face, but it is my father transformed and glorified; his hesitating discontent drowned in a kind of triumph. From my first day in that house, I continually turned to this handsome kinsman of mine, wondering in what terms he had lived and had his hope; what he had found there to look like that, to bound at one, after all those years, so joyously out of the canvas.

"From the timid, clouded old woman over whose life I had come to watch, I learned that in the backyard, near the old rose garden, there was a locust-tree which my uncle had planted. After his death, while it was still a slender sapling, his mother had a seat built round it, and she used to sit there on summer evenings. His grave was under the apple-trees in the old orchard.

"My aunt could tell me little more than this. There were days when she seemed not to remember him at all.

"It was from an old soldier in the village that I learned the boy's story. Lyon was, the old man told me, but fourteen when the first enlistment occurred, but was even then eager to go. He was in the court-house square every evening to watch the recruits at their drill, and when the home company was ordered off he rode into the city on his pony to see the men board the train and to wave them good-by. The next year he spent at home with a tutor, but when he was fifteen he held his parents to their promise and went into the army. He was color sergeant of his regiment and fell in a charge upon the breastworks of a fort about a year after his enlistment.

"The veteran showed me an account of this charge which had been written for the village paper by one of my uncle's comrades who had seen his part in the engagement. It seems that as his company were running at full speed across the bottom lands toward the fortified hill, a shell burst over them. This comrade, running beside my uncle, saw the colors waver and sink as if falling, and looked to see that the boy's hand and forearm had been torn away by the exploding shrapnel. The boy, he thought, did not realize the extent of his injury, for he laughed, shouted something which his comrade did not catch, caught the flag in his left hand, and ran on up the hill. They went splendidly up over the breastworks, but just as my uncle, his colors flying, reached the top of the embankment, a second shell carried away his left arm at the arm-pit, and he fell over the wall with the flag settling about him.

"It was because this story was ever present with me, because I was unable to shake it off, that I began to read such books as my grandfather had collected upon the Civil War. I found that this war was fought largely by boys, that more men enlisted at eighteen than at any other age. When I thought of those battlefields—and I thought of them much in those days—there was always that glory of youth above them, that impetuous, generous passion stirring the long lines on the march, the blue battalions in the plain. The bugle, whenever I have heard it since, has always seemed to me the very golden throat of that boyhood which spent itself so gaily, so incredibly.

"I used often to wonder how it was that this uncle of mine, who seemed to have possessed all the charm and brilliancy allotted to his family and to have lived up its vitality in one splendid hour, had left so little trace in the house where he was born and where he had awaited his destiny. Look as I would, I could find no letters from him, no clothing or books that might have been his. He had been dead but twenty years, and yet nothing seemed to have survived except the tree he had planted. It seemed incredible and cruel that no physical memory of him should linger to be cherished among his kindred,—nothing but the dull image in the brain of that aged sister. I used to pace the garden walks in the evening, wondering that no breath of his, no echo of his laugh, of his call to his pony or his whistle to his dogs, should linger about those shaded paths where the pale roses exhaled their dewy, country smell. Sometimes, in the dim starlight, I have thought that I heard on the grasses beside me the stir of a footfall lighter than my own, and under the black arch of the lilacs I have fancied that he bore me company.

"There was, I found, one day in the year for which my old aunt waited, and which stood out from the months that were all of a sameness to her. On the thirtieth of May she insisted that I should bring down the big flag from the attic and run it up upon the tall flagstaff beside Lyon's tree in the garden. Later in the morning she went with me to carry some of the garden flowers to the grave in the orchard,—a grave scarcely larger than a child's.

"I had noticed, when I was hunting for the flag in the attic, a leather trunk with my own name stamped upon it, but was unable to find the key. My aunt was all day less apathetic than usual; she seemed to realize more clearly who I was, and to wish me to be with her. I did not have an opportunity to return to the attic until after dinner that evening, when I carried a lamp up-stairs and easily forced the lock of the trunk. I found all the things that I had looked for; put away, doubtless, by his mother, and still smelling faintly of lavender and rose leaves; his clothes, his exercise books, his letters from the army, his first boots, his riding-whip, some of his toys, even. I took them out and replaced them gently. As I was about to shut the lid, I picked up a copy of the Æneid, on the fly-leaf of which was written in a slanting, boyish hand,

Lyon Hartwell, January, 1862.

He had gone to the wars in Sixty-three, I remembered.

"My uncle, I gathered, was none too apt at his Latin, for the pages were dog-eared and rubbed and interlined, the margins mottled with pencil sketches—bugles, stacked bayonets, and artillery carriages. In the act of putting the book down, I happened to run over the pages to the end, and on the fly-leaf at the back I saw his name again, and a drawing—with his initials and a date—of the Federal flag; above it, written in a kind of arch and in the same unformed hand:

'Oh, say, can you see by the dawn's early light

What so proudly we hailed at the twilight's last gleaming?'

It was a stiff, wooden sketch, not unlike a detail from some Egyptian inscription, but, the moment I saw it, wind and color seemed to touch it. I caught up the book, blew out the lamp, and rushed down into the garden.

"I seemed, somehow, at last to have known him; to have been with him in that careless, unconscious moment and to have known him as he was then.

"As I sat there in the rush of this realization, the wind began to rise, stirring the light foliage of the locust over my head and bringing, fresher than before, the woody odor of the pale roses that overran the little neglected garden. Then, as it grew stronger, it brought the sound of something sighing and stirring over my head in the perfumed darkness.

"I thought of that sad one of the Destinies who, as the Greeks believed, watched from birth over those marked for a violent or untimely death. Oh, I could see him, there in the shine of the morning, his book idly on his knee, his flashing eyes looking straight before him, and at his side that grave figure, hidden in her draperies, her eyes following his, but seeing so much farther—seeing what he never saw, that great moment at the end, when he swayed above his comrades on the earthen wall.

"All the while, the bunting I had run up in the morning flapped fold against fold, heaving and tossing softly in the dark—against a sky so black with rain clouds that I could see above me only the blur of something in soft, troubled motion.

"The experience of that night, coming so overwhelmingly to a man so dead, almost rent me in pieces. It was the same feeling that artists know when we, rarely, achieve truth in our work; the feeling of union with some great force, of purpose and security, of being glad that we have lived. For the first time I felt the pull of race and blood and kindred, and felt beating within me things that had not begun with me. It was as if the earth under my feet had grasped and rooted me, and were pouring its essence into me. I sat there until the dawn of morning, and all night long my life seemed to be pouring out of me and running into the ground."

Hartwell drew a long breath that lifted his heavy shoulders, and then let them fall again. He shifted a little and faced more squarely the scattered, silent company before him. The darkness had made us almost invisible to each other, and, except for the occasional red circuit of a cigarette end traveling upward from the arm of a chair, he might have supposed us all asleep.

"And so," Hartwell added thoughtfully, "I naturally feel an interest in fellows who are going home. It's always an experience."

No one said anything, and in a moment there was a loud rap at the door, — the concierge, come to take down Bentley's luggage and to announce that the cab was below. Bentley got his hat and coat, enjoined Hartwell to take good care of his *perroquets*, gave each of us a grip of the hand, and went briskly down the long flights of stairs. We followed him into the street, calling our good wishes, and saw him start on his drive across the lighted city to the Gare St. Lazare.

McClure's, March 1907

The Enchanted Bluff

Harper's, April 1909

We had our swim before sundown, and while we were cooking our supper the oblique rays of light made a dazzling glare on the white sand about us. The translucent red ball itself sank behind the brown stretches of corn field as we sat down to eat, and the warm layer of air that had rested over the water and our clean sand-bar grew fresher and smelled of the rank ironweed and sunflowers growing on the flatter shore. The river was brown and sluggish, like any other of the half-dozen streams that water the Nebraska corn lands. On one shore was an irregular line of bald clay bluffs where a few scrub-oaks with thick trunks and flat, twisted tops threw light shadows on the long grass. The western shore was low and level, with corn fields that stretched to the sky-line, and all along the water's edge were little sandy coves and beaches where slim cottonwoods and willow saplings flickered.

The turbulence of the river in spring-time discouraged milling, and, beyond keeping the old red bridge in repair, the busy farmers did not concern themselves with the stream; so the Sandtown boys were left in undisputed possession. In the autumn we hunted quail through the miles of stubble and fodder land along the flat shore, and, after the winter skating season was over and the ice had gone out, the spring freshets and flooded bottoms gave us our great excitement of the year. The channel was never the same for two successive seasons. Every spring the swollen stream undermined a bluff to the east, or bit out a few acres of corn field to the west and whirled the soil away to deposit it in spumy mud banks somewhere else. When the water fell low in midsummer, new sand-bars were thus exposed to dry and whiten in the August sun. Sometimes these were banked so firmly that the fury of the next freshet failed to unseat them; the little willow seedlings emerged triumphantly from the yellow froth, broke into spring leaf, shot up into summer growth, and with their mesh of roots bound together the moist sand beneath them against the batterings of another April. Here and there a cottonwood soon glittered among them, quivering in the low current of air that, even on breathless days when the dust hung like smoke above the wagon road, trembled along the face of the water.

It was on such an island, in the third summer of its yellow green, that we built our watch-fire; not in the thicket of dancing willow wands, but on the level terrace of fine sand which had been added that spring; a little new bit of world, beautifully ridged with ripple marks, and strewn with the tiny skeletons of turtles and fish, all as white and dry as if they had been expertly cured. We had been careful not to mar the freshness of the place, although we often swam out to it on summer evenings and lay on the sand to rest.

This was our last watch-fire of the year, and there were reasons why I should remember it better than any of the others. Next week the other boys were to file back to their old places in the Sandtown High School, but I was to go up to the Divide to teach my first country school in the Norwegian district. I was already homesick at the thought of quitting the boys with whom I had always played; of leaving the river, and going up into a windy plain that was all windmills and corn fields and big pastures; where there was nothing wilful or unmanageable in the landscape, no new islands, and no chance of unfamiliar birds—such as often followed the watercourses.

Other boys came and went and used the river for fishing or skating, but we six were sworn to the spirit of the stream, and we were friends mainly because of the river. There were the two Hassler boys, Fritz and Otto, sons of the little German tailor. They were the youngest of us; ragged boys of ten and twelve, with sunburned hair, weather-stained faces, and pale blue eyes. Otto, the elder, was the best mathematician in school, and clever at his books, but he always dropped out in the spring term as if the river could not get on without him. He and Fritz caught the fat, horned catfish and sold them about the town, and they lived so much in the water that they were as brown and sandy as the river itself.

There was Percy Pound, a fat, freckled boy with chubby cheeks, who took half a dozen boys' story-papers and was always being kept in for reading detective stories behind his desk. There was Tip Smith, destined by his freckles and red hair to be the buffoon in all our games, though he walked like a timid little old man and had a funny, cracked laugh. Tip worked hard in his father's grocery store every afternoon, and swept it out before school in the morning. Even his recreations were laborious. He collected cigarette cards and tin tobacco-tags indefatigably, and would sit for hours humped up over a snarling little scroll-saw which he kept in his attic. His dearest possessions were some little pill-bottles that purported to contain grains of wheat from the Holy Land, water from the Jordan and the Dead Sea, and earth from the Mount of Olives. His father had bought these dull things from a Baptist missionary who peddled them, and Tip seemed to derive great satisfaction from their remote origin.

The tall boy was Arthur Adams. He had fine hazel eyes that were almost too reflective and sympathetic for a boy, and such a pleasant voice that we all loved to hear him read aloud. Even when he had to read poetry aloud at school, no one ever thought of laughing. To be sure, he was not at school very much of the time. He was seventeen and should have finished the High School the year before, but he was always off somewhere with his gun. Arthur's mother was dead, and his father, who was feverishly absorbed in promoting schemes, wanted to send the boy away to school and get him off his hands; but Arthur always begged off for another year and promised to study. I remember him as a tall, brown boy with an intelligent face, always lounging among a lot of us little fellows, laughing at us oftener than with us, but such a soft, satisfied laugh that we felt rather flattered when we provoked it. In after-years people said that Arthur had been given to evil ways even as a lad, and it is true that we often saw him with the gambler's sons and with old Spanish Fanny's boy, but if he learned anything ugly in their company he never betrayed it to us. We would have followed Arthur anywhere, and I am bound to say that he led us into no worse places than the cattail marshes and the stubble fields. These, then, were the boys who camped with me that summer night upon the sand-bar.

After we finished our supper we beat the willow thicket for driftwood. By the time we had collected enough, night had fallen, and the pungent, weedy smell from the shore increased with the coolness. We threw ourselves down about the fire and made another futile effort to show Percy Pound the Little Dipper. We had tried it often before, but he could never be got past the big one.

"You see those three big stars just below the handle, with the bright one in the middle?" said Otto Hassler; "that's Orion's belt, and the bright one is the clasp." I crawled behind Otto's shoulder and sighted up his arm to the star that seemed perched upon the tip of his steady forefinger. The Hassler boys did seine-fishing at night, and they knew a good many stars.

Percy gave up the Little Dipper and lay back on the sand, his hands clasped under his head. "I can see the North Star," he announced, contentedly, pointing toward it with his big toe. "Any one might get lost and need to know that."

We all looked up at it.

"How do you suppose Columbus felt when his compass didn't point north any more?" Tip asked.

Otto shook his head. "My father says that there was another North Star once, and that maybe this one won't last always. I wonder what would happen to us down here if anything went wrong with it?"

Arthur chuckled. "I wouldn't worry, Ott. Nothing's apt to happen to it in your time. Look at the Milky Way! There must be lots of good dead Indians."

We lay back and looked, meditating, at the dark cover of the world. The gurgle of the water had become heavier. We had often noticed a mutinous, complaining note in it at night, quite different from its cheerful daytime chuckle, and seeming like the voice of a much deeper and more powerful stream. Our water had always these two moods: the one of sunny complaisance, the other of inconsolable, passionate regret.

"Queer how the stars are all in sort of diagrams," remarked Otto. "You could do most any proposition in geometry with 'em. They always look as if they meant something. Some folks say everybody's fortune is all written out in the stars, don't they?"

"They believe so in the old country," Fritz affirmed.

But Arthur only laughed at him. "You're thinking of Napoleon, Fritzey. He had a star that went out when he began to lose battles. I guess the stars don't keep any close tally on Sandtown folks."

We were speculating on how many times we could count a hundred before the evening star went down behind the corn fields, when some one cried, "There comes the moon, and it's as big as a cart wheel!"

We all jumped up to greet it as it swam over the bluffs behind us. It came up like a galleon in full sail; an enormous, barbaric thing, red as an angry heathen god.

"When the moon came up red like that, the Aztecs used to sacrifice their prisoners on the temple top," Percy announced.

"Go on, Perce. You got that out of *Golden Days*. Do you believe that, Arthur?" I appealed.

Arthur answered, quite seriously: "Like as not. The moon was one of their gods. When my father was in Mexico City he saw the stone where they used to sacrifice their prisoners."

As we dropped down by the fire again some one asked whether the Mound-Builders were older than the Aztecs. When we once got upon the Mound-Builders we never willingly got away from them, and we were still conjecturing when we heard a loud splash in the water.

"Must have been a big cat jumping," said Fritz. "They do sometimes. They must see bugs in the dark. Look what a track the moon makes!"

There was a long, silvery streak on the water, and where the current fretted over a big log it boiled up like gold pieces.

"Suppose there ever *was* any gold hid away in this old river?" Fritz asked. He lay like a little brown Indian, close to the fire, his chin on his hand and his bare feet in the air. His brother laughed at him, but Arthur took his suggestion seriously.

"Some of the Spaniards thought there was gold up here somewhere. Seven cities chuck full of gold, they had it, and Coronado and his men came up to hunt it. The Spaniards were all over this country once."

Percy looked interested. "Was that before the Mormons went through?"

We all laughed at this.

"Long enough before. Before the Pilgrim Fathers, Perce. Maybe they came along this very river. They always followed the watercourses."

"I wonder where this river really does begin?" Tip mused. That was an old and a favorite mystery which the map did not clearly explain. On the map the little black line stopped somewhere in western Kansas; but since rivers generally rose in mountains, it was only reasonable to suppose that ours came from the Rockies. Its destination, we knew, was the Missouri, and the Hassler boys always maintained that we could embark at Sandtown in flood-time, follow our noses, and eventually arrive at New Orleans. Now they took up their old argument. "If us boys had grit enough to try it, it wouldn't take no time to get to Kansas City and St. Joe."

We began to talk about the places we wanted to go to. The Hassler boys wanted to see the stock-yards in Kansas City, and Percy wanted to see a big store in Chicago. Arthur was interlocutor and did not betray himself.

"Now it's your turn, Tip."

Tip rolled over on his elbow and poked the fire, and his eyes looked shyly out of his queer, tight little face. "My place is awful far away. My uncle Bill told me about it."

Tip's Uncle Bill was a wanderer, bitten with mining fever, who had drifted into Sandtown with a broken arm, and when it was well had drifted out again.

"Where is it?"

"Aw, it's down in New Mexico somewheres. There aren't no railroads or anything. You have to go on mules, and you run out of water before you get there and have to drink canned tomatoes."

"Well, go on, kid. What's it like when you do get there?"

Tip sat up and excitedly began his story.

"There's a big red rock there that goes right up out of the sand for about nine hundred feet. The country's flat all around it, and this here rock goes up all by itself, like a monument. They call it the Enchanted Bluff down there, because no white man has ever been on top of it. The sides are smooth rock, and straight up, like a wall. The Indians say that hundreds of years ago, before the Spaniards came, there was a village away up there in the air. The tribe that lived there had some sort of steps, made out of wood and bark, hung down over the face of the bluff, and the braves went down to hunt and carried water up in big jars swung on their backs. They kept a big supply of water and dried meat up there, and never went down except to hunt. They were a peaceful tribe that made cloth and pottery, and they went up there to get out of the wars. You see, they could pick off any war party that tried to get up their little steps. The Indians say they were a handsome people, and they had some sort of a queer religion. Uncle Bill thinks they were Cliff-Dwellers who had got into trouble and left home. They weren't fighters, anyhow.

"One time the braves were down hunting and an awful storm came up—a kind of waterspout—and when they got back to their rock they found their little staircase had been all broken to pieces, and only a few steps were left hanging away up in the air. While they were camped at the foot of the rock, wondering what to do, a war party from the north came along and massacred 'em to a man, with all the old folks and women looking on from the rock. Then the war party went on south and left the village to get down the best way they could. Of course they never got down. They starved to death up there, and when the war party came back on their way north, they could hear the children crying from the edge of the bluff where they had crawled out, but they didn't see a sign of a grown Indian, and nobody has ever been up there since."

We exclaimed at this dolorous legend and sat up.

"There couldn't have been many people up there," Percy demurred. "How big is the top, Tip?"

"Oh, pretty big. Big enough so that the rock doesn't look nearly as tall as it is. The top's bigger than the base. The bluff is sort of worn away for several hundred feet up. That's one reason it's so hard to climb."

I asked how the Indians got up, in the first place.

"Nobody knows how they got up or when. A hunting party came along once and saw that there was a town up there, and that was all."

Otto rubbed his chin and looked thoughtful. "Of course there must be some way to get up there. Couldn't people get a rope over someway and pull a ladder up?"

Tip's little eyes were shining with excitement. "I know a way. Me and Uncle Bill talked it all over. There's a kind of rocket that would take a rope over—life-savers use 'em—and then you could hoist a rope-ladder and peg it down at the bottom and make it tight with guy-ropes on the other side. I'm going to climb that there bluff, and I've got it all planned out."

Fritz asked what he expected to find when he got up there.

"Bones, maybe, or the ruins of their town, or pottery, or some of their idols. There might be 'most anything up there. Anyhow, I want to see."

"Sure nobody else has been up there, Tip?" Arthur asked.

"Dead sure. Hardly anybody ever goes down there. Some hunters tried to cut steps in the rock once, but they didn't get higher than a man can reach. The Bluff's all red granite, and Uncle Bill thinks it's a boulder the glaciers left. It's a queer place, anyhow. Nothing but cactus and desert for hundreds of miles, and yet right under the bluff there's good water and plenty of grass. That's why the bison used to go down there."

Suddenly we heard a scream above our fire, and jumped up to see a dark, slim bird floating southward far above us—a whooping-crane, we knew by her cry and her long neck. We ran to the edge of the island, hoping we might see her alight, but she wavered southward along the rivercourse until we lost her. The Hassler boys declared that by the look of the heavens it must be after midnight, so we threw more wood on our fire, put on our jackets, and curled down in the warm sand. Several of us pretended to doze, but I fancy we were really thinking about Tip's Bluff and the extinct people. Over in the wood the ring-doves were calling mournfully to one another, and once we heard a dog bark, far away. "Somebody getting into old Tommy's melon patch," Fritz murmured, sleepily, but nobody answered him. By and by Percy spoke out of the shadow.

"Say, Tip, when you go down there will you take me with you?"

"Maybe."

"Suppose one of us beats you down there, Tip?"

"Whoever gets to the Bluff first has got to promise to tell the rest of us exactly what he finds," remarked one of the Hassler boys, and to this we all readily assented.

Somewhat reassured, I dropped off to sleep. I must have dreamed about a race for the Bluff, for I awoke in a kind of fear that other people were getting ahead of me and that I was losing my chance. I sat up in my damp clothes and looked at the other boys, who lay tumbled in uneasy attitudes about the dead fire. It was still dark, but the sky was blue with the last wonderful azure of night. The stars glistened like crystal globes, and trembled as if they shone through a depth of clear water. Even as I watched, they began to pale and the sky brightened. Day came suddenly, almost instantaneously. I turned for another look at the blue night, and it was gone. Everywhere the birds began to call, and all manner of little insects began to chirp and hop about in the willows. A breeze sprang up from the west and brought the heavy smell of ripened corn. The boys rolled over and shook themselves. We stripped and plunged into the river just as the sun came up over the windy bluffs.

When I came home to Sandtown at Christmas time, we skated out to our island and talked over the whole project of the Enchanted Bluff, renewing our resolution to find it.

Although that was twenty years ago, none of us have ever climbed the Enchanted Bluff. Percy Pound is a stockbroker in Kansas City and will go nowhere that his red touring-car cannot carry him. Otto Hassler went on the railroad and lost his foot braking; after which he and Fritz succeeded their father as the town tailors.

Arthur sat about the sleepy little town all his life—he died before he was twenty-five. The last time I saw him, when I was home on one of my college vacations, he was sitting in a steamer-chair under a cottonwood tree in the little yard behind one of the two Sandtown saloons. He was very untidy and his hand was not steady, but when he rose, unabashed, to greet me, his eyes were as clear and warm as ever. When I had talked with him for an hour and heard him laugh again, I wondered how it was that when Nature had taken such pains with a man, from his hands to the arch of his long foot, she had ever lost him in Sandtown. He joked about Tip Smith's Bluff, and declared he was going down there just as soon as the weather got cooler; he thought the Grand Cañon might be worth while, too.

I was perfectly sure when I left him that he would never get beyond the high plank fence and the comfortable shade of the cottonwood. And, indeed, it was under that very tree that he died one summer morning.

Tip Smith still talks about going to New Mexico. He married a slatternly, unthrifty country girl, has been much tied to a perambulator, and has grown stooped and gray from irregular meals and broken sleep. But the worst of his difficulties are now over, and he has, as he says, come into easy water. When I was last in Sandtown I walked home with him late one moonlight night, after he had balanced his cash and shut up his store. We took the long way around and sat down on the schoolhouse steps, and between us we quite revived the romance of the lone red rock and the extinct people. Tip insists that he still means to go down there, but he thinks now he will wait until his boy, Bert, is old enough to go with him. Bert has been let into the story, and thinks of nothing but the Enchanted Bluff.

The Joy of Nelly Deane

Nell and I were almost ready to go on for the last act of "Queen Esther," and we had for the moment got rid of our three patient dressers, Mrs. Dow, Mrs. Freeze, and Mrs. Spinny. Nell was peering over my shoulder into the little cracked looking-glass that Mrs. Dow had taken from its nail on her kitchen wall and brought down to the church under her shawl that morning. When she realized that we were alone, Nell whispered to me in the quick, fierce way she had:

"Say, Peggy, won't you go up and stay with me to-night? Scott Spinny's asked to take me home, and I don't want to walk up with him alone."

"I guess so, if you'll ask my mother."

"Oh, I'll fix her!" Nell laughed, with a toss of her head which meant that she usually got what she wanted, even from people much less tractable than my mother.

In a moment our tiring-women were back again. The three old ladies—at least they seemed old to us—fluttered about us, more agitated than we were ourselves. It seemed as though they would never leave off patting Nell and touching her up. They kept trying things this way and that, never able in the end to decide which way was best. They wouldn't hear to her using rouge, and as they powdered her neck and arms, Mrs. Freeze murmured that she hoped we wouldn't get into the habit of using such things. Mrs. Spinny divided her time between pulling up and tucking down the "illusion" that filled in the square neck of Nelly's dress. She didn't like things much low, she said; but after she had pulled it up, she stood back and looked at Nell thoughtfully through her glasses. While the excited girl was reaching for this and that, buttoning a slipper, pinning down a curl, Mrs. Spinny's smile softened more and more until, just before *Esther* made her entrance, the old lady tiptoed up to her and softly tucked the illusion down as far as it would go.

"She's so pink; it seems a pity not," she whispered apologetically to Mrs. Dow.

Every one admitted that Nelly was the prettiest girl in Riverbend, and the gayest—oh, the gayest! When she was not singing, she was laughing.

When she was not laid up with a broken arm, the outcome of a foolhardy coasting feat, or suspended from school because she ran away at recess to go buggy-riding with Guy Franklin, she was sure to be up to mischief of some sort. Twice she broke through the ice and got soused in the river because she never looked where she skated or cared what happened so long as she went fast enough. After the second of these duckings our three dressers declared that she was trying to be a Baptist despite herself.

Mrs. Spinny and Mrs. Freeze and Mrs. Dow, who were always hovering about Nelly, often whispered to me their hope that she would eventually come into our church and not "go with the Methodists"; her family were Wesleyans. But to me these artless plans of theirs never wholly explained their watchful affection. They had good daughters themselves,—except Mrs. Spinny, who had only the sullen Scott,—and they loved their plain girls and thanked God for them. But they loved Nelly differently. They were proud of her pretty figure and yellow-brown eyes, which dilated so easily and sparkled with a kind of golden effervescence. They were always making pretty things for her, always coaxing her to come to the sewing-circle, where she knotted her thread, and put in the wrong sleeve, and laughed and chattered and said a great many things that she should not have said, and somehow always warmed their hearts. I think they loved her for her unquenchable joy.

All the Baptist ladies liked Nell, even those who criticized her most severely, but the three who were first in fighting the battles of our little church, who held it together by their prayers and the labor of their hands, watched over her as they did over Mrs. Dow's century-plant before it blossomed. They looked for her on Sunday morning and smiled at her as she hurried, always a little late, up to the choir. When she rose and stood behind the organ and sang "There Is a Green Hill," one could see Mrs. Dow and Mrs. Freeze settle back in their accustomed seats and look up at her as if she had just come from that hill and had brought them glad tidings.

It was because I sang contralto, or, as we said, alto, in the Baptist choir that Nell and I became friends. She was so gay and grown up, so busy with parties and dances and picnics, that I would scarcely have seen much of her had we not sung together. She liked me better than she did any of the older girls, who tried clumsily to be like her, and I felt almost as solicitous and admiring as did Mrs. Dow and Mrs. Spinny. I think even then I must have loved to see her bloom and glow, and I loved to hear her sing, in "The Ninety and Nine,"

But one was out on the hills away

in her sweet, strong voice. Nell had never had a singing lesson, but she had sung from the time she could talk, and Mrs. Dow used fondly to say that it was singing so much that made her figure so pretty.

After I went into the choir it was found to be easier to get Nelly to choir practice. If I stopped outside her gate on my way to church and coaxed her, she usually laughed, ran in for her hat and jacket, and went along with me. The three old ladies fostered our friendship, and because I was "quiet," they esteemed me a good influence for Nelly. This view was propounded in a sewing-circle discussion and, leaking down to us through our mothers, greatly amused us. Dear old ladies! It was so manifestly for what Nell was that they loved her, and yet they were always looking for "influences" to change her.

The "Queen Esther" performance had cost us three months of hard practice, and it was not easy to keep Nell up to attending the tedious rehearsals. Some of the boys we knew were in the chorus of Assyrian youths, but the solo cast was made up of older people, and Nell found them very poky. We gave the cantata in the Baptist church on Christmas eve, "to a crowded house," as the Riverbend "Messenger" truly chronicled. The country folk for miles about had come in through a deep snow, and their teams and wagons stood in a long row at the hitch-bars on each side of the church door. It was certainly Nelly's night, for however much the tenor—he was her schoolmaster, and naturally thought poorly of her—might try to eclipse her in his dolorous solos about the rivers of Babylon, there could be no doubt as to whom the people had come to hear—and to see.

After the performance was over, our fathers and mothers came back to the dressing-rooms—the little rooms behind the baptistry where the candidates for baptism were robed—to congratulate us, and Nell persuaded my mother to let me go home with her. This arrangement may not have been wholly agreeable to Scott Spinny, who stood glumly waiting at the baptistry door; though I used to think he dogged Nell's steps not so much for any pleasure he got from being with her as for the pleasure of keeping other people away. Dear little Mrs. Spinny was perpetually in a state of humiliation on account of his bad manners, and she tried by a very special tenderness to make up to Nelly for the remissness of her ungracious son.

Scott was a spare, muscular fellow, good-looking, but with a face so set and dark that I used to think it very like the castings he sold. He was taciturn and domineering, and Nell rather liked to provoke him. Her father was so easy with her that she seemed to enjoy being ordered about now and then. That night, when every one was praising her and telling her how well she sang and how pretty she looked, Scott only said, as we came out of the dressing-room:

"Have you got your high shoes on?"

"No; but I've got rubbers on over my low ones. Mother doesn't care."

"Well, you just go back and put 'em on as fast as you can."

Nell made a face at him and ran back, laughing. Her mother, fat, comfortable Mrs. Deane, was immensely amused at this.

"That's right, Scott," she chuckled. "You can do enough more with her than I can. She walks right over me an' Jud."

Scott grinned. If he was proud of Nelly, the last thing he wished to do was to show it. When she came back he began to nag again. "What are you going to do with all those flowers? They'll freeze stiff as pokers."

"Well, there won't none of *your* flowers freeze, Scott Spinny, so there!" Nell snapped. She had the best of him that time, and the Assyrian youths rejoiced. They were most of them high-school boys, and the poorest of them had "chipped in" and sent all the way to Denver for *Queen Esther's* flowers. There were bouquets from half a dozen townspeople, too, but none from Scott. Scott was a prosperous hardware merchant and notoriously penurious, though he saved his face, as the boys said, by giving liberally to the church.

"There's no use freezing the fool things, anyhow. You get me some newspapers, and I'll wrap 'em up." Scott took from his pocket a folded copy of the Riverbend "Messenger" and began laboriously to wrap up one of the bouquets. When we left the church door he bore three large newspaper bundles, carrying them as carefully as if they had been so many newly frosted wedding-cakes, and left Nell and me to shift for ourselves as we floundered along the snow-burdened sidewalk.

Although it was after midnight, lights were shining from many of the little wooden houses, and the roofs and shrubbery were so deep in snow that Riverbend looked as if it had been tucked down into a warm bed. The companies of people, all coming from church, tramping this way and that toward their homes and calling "Good night" and "Merry Christmas" as they parted company, all seemed to us very unusual and exciting.

When we got home, Mrs. Deane had a cold supper ready, and Jud Deane had already taken off his shoes and fallen to on his fried chicken and pie. He was so proud of his pretty daughter that he must give her her Christmas presents then and there, and he went into the sleeping-chamber behind the dining-room and from the depths of his wife's closet brought out a short sealskin jacket and a round cap and made Nelly put them on.

Mrs. Deane, who sat busy between a plate of spice cake and a tray piled with her famous whipped-cream tarts, laughed inordinately at his behavior.

"Ain't he worse than any kid you ever see? He's been running to that closet like a cat shut away from her kittens. I wonder Nell ain't caught on before this. I did think he'd make out now to keep 'em till Christmas morning; but he's never made out to keep anything yet."

That was true enough, and fortunately Jud's inability to keep anything seemed always to present a highly humorous aspect to his wife. Mrs. Deane put her heart into her cooking, and said that so long as a man was a good provider she had no cause to complain. Other people were not so charitable toward Jud's failing. I remember how many strictures were passed upon that little sealskin and how he was censured for his extravagance. But what a public-spirited thing, after all, it was for him to do! How, the winter through, we all enjoyed seeing Nell skating on the river or running about the town with the brown collar turned up about her bright cheeks and her hair blowing out from under the round cap! "No seal," Mrs. Dow said, "would have begrudged it to her. Why should we?" This was at the sewing-circle, when the new coat was under grave discussion.

At last Nelly and I got up-stairs and undressed, and the pad of Jud's slippered feet about the kitchen premises—where he was carrying up from the cellar things that might freeze—ceased. He called "Good night, daughter," from the foot of the stairs, and the house grew quiet. But one is not a prima donna the first time for nothing, and it seemed as if we could not go to bed. Our light must have burned long after every other in Riverbend was out. The muslin curtains of Nell's bed were drawn back; Mrs. Deane had turned down the white counterpane and taken off the shams and smoothed the pillows for us. But their fair plumpness offered no temptation to two such hot young heads. We could not let go of life even for a little while. We sat and talked in Nell's cozy room, where there was a tiny, white fur rug—the only one in Riverbend—before the bed; and there were white sash curtains, and the prettiest little desk and dressing-table I had ever seen. It was a warm, gay little room, flooded all day long with sunlight from east and south windows that had climbing-roses all about them in summer. About the dresser were photographs of adoring high-school boys; and one of Guy Franklin, much groomed and barbered, in a dress-coat and a boutonnière. I never liked to see that photograph there. The home boys looked properly modest and bashful on the dresser, but he seemed to be staring impudently all the time.

I knew nothing definite against Guy, but in Riverbend all "traveling-men" were considered worldly and wicked. He traveled for a Chicago dry-goods firm, and our fathers didn't like him because he put extravagant ideas into our mothers' heads. He had very smooth and nattering ways, and he introduced into our simple community a great variety of perfumes and scented soaps, and he always reminded me of the merchants in Cæsar, who brought into Gaul "those things which effeminate the mind," as we translated that delightfully easy passage.

Nell was silting before the dressing-table in her nightgown, holding the new fur coat and rubbing her cheek against it, when I saw a sudden gleam of tears in her eyes. "You know, Peggy," she said in her quick, impetuous way, "this makes me feel bad. I've got a secret from my daddy."

I can see her now, so pink and eager, her brown hair in two springy braids down her back, and her eyes shining with tears and with something even softer and more tremulous.

"I'm engaged, Peggy," she whispered, "really and truly."

She leaned forward, unbuttoning her nightgown, and there on her breast, hung by a little gold chain about her neck, was a diamond ring—Guy Franklin's solitaire; every one in Riverbend knew it well.

"I'm going to live in Chicago, and take singing lessons, and go to operas, and do all those nice things—oh, everything! I know you don't like him, Peggy, but you know you *are* a kid. You'll see how it is yourself when you grow up. He's so *different* from our boys, and he's just terribly in love with me. And then, Peggy," —flushing all down over her soft shoulders,— "I'm awfully fond of him, too. Awfully."

"Are you, Nell, truly?" I whispered. She seemed so changed to me by the warm light in her eyes and that delicate suffusion of color. I felt as I did when I got up early on picnic mornings in summer, and saw the dawn come up in the breathless sky above the river meadows and make all the cornfields golden.

"Sure I do, Peggy; don't look so solemn. It's nothing to look that way about, kid. It's nice." She threw her arms about me suddenly and hugged me.

"I hate to think about your going so far away from us all, Nell."

"Oh, you'll love to come and visit me. Just you wait."

She began breathlessly to go over things Guy Franklin had told her about Chicago, until I seemed to see it all looming up out there under the stars that kept watch over our little sleeping town. We had neither of us ever been to a city, but we knew what it would be like. We heard it throbbing like great engines, and calling to us, that far-away world. Even after we had opened the windows and scurried into bed, we seemed to feel a pulsation across all the miles of snow. The winter silence trembled with it, and the air was full of something new that seemed to break over us in soft waves. In that snug, warm little bed I had a sense of imminent change and danger. I was somehow afraid for Nelly when I heard her breathing so quickly beside me, and I put my arm about her protectingly as we drifted toward sleep.

In the following spring we were both graduated from the Riverbend high school, and I went away to college. My family moved to Denver, and during the next four years I heard very little of Nelly Deane. My life was crowded with new people and new experiences, and I am afraid I held her little in mind. I heard indirectly that Jud Deane had lost what little property he owned in a luckless venture in Cripple Creek, and that he had been able to keep his house in Riverbend only through the clemency of his creditors. Guy Franklin had his route changed and did not go to Riverbend any more. He married the daughter of a rich cattle-man out near Long Pine, and ran a dry-goods store of his own. Mrs. Dow wrote me a long letter about once a year, and in one of these she told me that Nelly was teaching in the sixth grade in the Riverbend school.

"Dear Nelly does not like teaching very well. The children try her, and she is so pretty it seems a pity for her to be tied down to uncongenial employment. Scott is still very attentive, and I have noticed him look up at the window of Nelly's room in a very determined way as he goes home to dinner. Scott continues prosperous; he has made money during these hard times and now owns both our hardware stores. He is close, but a very honorable fellow. Nelly seems to hold off, but I think Mrs. Spinny has hopes. Nothing would please her more. If Scott were more careful about his appearance, it would help. He of course gets black about his business, and Nelly, you know, is very dainty. People do say his mother does his courting for him, she is so eager. If only Scott does not turn out hard and penurious like his father! We must all have our schooling in this life, but I don't want Nelly's to be too severe. She is a dear girl, and keeps her color."

Mrs. Dow's own schooling had been none too easy. Her husband had long been crippled with rheumatism, and was bitter and faultfinding. Her daughters had married poorly, and one of her sons had fallen into evil ways. But her letters were always cheerful, and in one of them she gently remonstrated with me because I "seemed inclined to take a sad view of life."

In the winter vacation of my senior year I stopped on my way home to visit Mrs. Dow. The first thing she told me when I got into her old buckboard at the station was that "Scott had at last prevailed," and that Nelly was to marry him in the spring. As a preliminary step, Nelly was about to join the Baptist church. "Just think, you will be here for her baptizing! How that will please Nelly! She is to be immersed to-morrow night."

I met Scott Spinny in the post-office that morning, and he gave me a hard grip with one black hand. There was something grim and saturnine about his powerful body and bearded face and his strong, cold hands. I wondered what perverse fate had driven him for eight years to dog the footsteps of a girl whose charm was due to qualities naturally distasteful to him. It still seems strange to me that in easy-going Riverbend, where there were so many boys who could have lived contentedly enough with my little grasshopper, it was the pushing ant who must have her and all her careless ways.

By a kind of unformulated etiquette one did not call upon candidates for baptism on the day of the ceremony, so I had my first glimpse of Nelly that evening. The baptistry was a cemented pit directly under the pulpit rostrum, over which we had our stage when we sang "Queen Esther." I sat through the sermon somewhat nervously. After the minister, in his long, black gown, had gone down into the water and the choir had finished singing, the door from the dressing-room opened, and, led by one of the deacons, Nelly came down the steps into the pool. Oh, she looked so little and meek and chastened! Her white cashmere robe clung about her, and her brown hair was brushed straight back and hung in two soft braids from a little head bent humbly. As she stepped down into the water I shivered with the cold of it, and I remembered sharply how much I had loved her. She went down until the water was well above her waist, and stood white and small, with her hands crossed on her breast, while the minister said the words about being buried with Christ in baptism. Then, lying in his arm, she disappeared under the dark water. "It will be like that when she dies," I thought, and a quick pain caught my heart. The choir began to sing "Washed in the Blood of the Lamb" as she rose again, the door behind the baptistry opened, revealing those three dear guardians, Mrs. Dow, Mrs. Freeze, and Mrs. Spinny, and she went up into their arms.

I went to see Nell next day, up in the little room of many memories. Such a sad, sad visit! She seemed changed—a little embarrassed and quietly despairing. We talked of many of the old Riverbend girls and boys, but she did not mention Guy Franklin or Scott Spinny, except to say that her father had got work in Scott's hardware store. She begged me, putting her hands on my shoulders with something of her old impulsiveness, to come and stay a few days with her. But I was afraid—afraid of what she might tell me and of what I might say. When I sat in that room with all her trinkets, the foolish harvest of her girlhood, lying about, and the white curtains and the little white rug, I thought of Scott Spinny with positive terror and could feel his hard grip on my hand again. I made the best excuse I could about having to hurry on to Denver; but she gave me one quick look, and her eyes ceased to plead. I saw that she understood me perfectly. We had known each other so well. Just once, when I got up to go and had trouble with my veil, she laughed her old merry laugh and told me there were some things I would never learn, for all my schooling.

The next day, when Mrs. Dow drove me down to the station to catch the morning train for Denver, I saw Nelly hurrying to school with several books under her arm. She had been working up her lessons at home, I thought. She was never quick at her books, dear Nell.

It was ten years before I again visited Riverbend. I had been in Rome for a long time, and had fallen into bitter homesickness. One morning, sitting among the dahlias and asters that bloom so bravely upon those gigantic heaps of earth-red ruins that were once the palaces of the Cæsars, I broke the seal of one of Mrs. Dow's long yearly letters. It brought so much sad news that I resolved then and there to go home to Riverbend, the only place that had ever really been home to me. Mrs. Dow wrote me that her husband, after years of illness, had died in the cold spell last March. "So good and patient toward the last," she wrote, "and so afraid of giving extra trouble." There was another thing she saved until the last. She wrote on and on, dear woman, about new babies and village improvements, as if she could not bear to tell me; and then it came:

"You will be sad to hear that two months ago our dear Nelly left us. It was a terrible blow to us all. I cannot write about it yet, I fear. I wake up every morning feeling that I ought to go to her. She went three days after her little boy was born. The baby is a fine child and will live, I think, in spite of everything. He and her little girl, now eight years old, whom she named Margaret, after you, have gone to Mrs. Spinny's. She loves them more than if they were her own. It seems as if already they had made her quite young again. I wish you could see Nelly's children."

Ah, that was what I wanted, to see Nelly's children! The wish came aching from my heart along with the bitter homesick tears; along with a quick, torturing recollection that flashed upon me, as I looked about and tried to collect myself, of how we two had sat in our sunny seat in the corner of the old bare school-room one September afternoon and learned the names of the seven hills together. In that place, at that moment, after so many years, how it all came back to me—the warm sun on my back, the chattering girl beside me, the curly hair, the laughing yellow eyes, the stubby little finger on the page! I felt as if even then, when we sat in the sun with our heads together, it was all arranged, written out like a story, that at this moment I should be sitting among the crumbling bricks and drying grass, and she should be lying in the place I knew so well, on that green hill far away.

Mrs. Dow sat with her Christmas sewing in the familiar sitting-room, where the carpet and the wall-paper and the table-cover had all faded into soft, dull colors, and even the chromo of Hagar and Ishmael had been toned to the sobriety of age. In the bay-window the tall wire flower-stand still bore its little terraces of potted plants, and the big fuchsia and the Martha Washington geranium had blossomed for Christmas-tide. Mrs. Dow herself did not look greatly changed to me. Her hair, thin ever since I could remember it, was now quite white, but her spare, wiry little person had all its old activity, and her eyes gleamed with the old friendliness behind her silver-bowed glasses. Her gray house-dress seemed just like those she used to wear when I ran in after school to take her angel-food cake down to the church supper.

The house sat on a hill, and from behind the geraniums I could see pretty much all of Riverbend, tucked down in the soft snow, and the air above was full of big, loose flakes, falling from a gray sky which betokened settled weather. Indoors the hard-coal burner made a tropical temperature, and glowed a warm orange from its isinglass sides. We sat and visited, the two of us, with a great sense of comfort and completeness. I had reached Riverbend only that morning, and Mrs. Dow, who had been haunted by thoughts of shipwreck and suffering upon wintry seas, kept urging me to draw nearer to the fire and suggesting incidental refreshment. We had chattered all through the winter morning and most of the afternoon, taking up one after another of the Riverbend girls and boys, and agreeing that we had reason to be well satisfied with most of them. Finally, after a long pause in which I had listened to the contented ticking of the clock and the crackle of the coal, I put the question I had until then held back:

"And now, Mrs. Dow, tell me about the one we loved best of all. Since I got your letter I've thought of her every day. Tell me all about Scott and Nelly."

The tears flashed behind her glasses, and she smoothed the little pink bag on her knee.

"Well, dear, I'm afraid Scott proved to be a hard man, like his father. But we must remember that Nelly always had Mrs. Spinny. I never saw anything like the love there was between those two. After Nelly lost her own father and mother, she looked to Mrs. Spinny for everything. When Scott was too unreasonable, his mother could 'most always prevail upon him. She never lifted a hand to fight her own battles with Scott's father, but she was never afraid to speak up for Nelly. And then Nelly took great comfort of her little girl. Such a lovely child!"

"Had she been very ill before the little baby came?"

"No, Margaret; I'm afraid 't was all because they had the wrong doctor. I feel confident that either Doctor Tom or Doctor Jones could have brought her through. But, you see, Scott had offended them both, and they'd stopped trading at his store, so he would have young Doctor Fox, a boy just out of college and a stranger. He got scared and didn't know what to do. Mrs. Spinny felt he wasn't doing right, so she sent for Mrs. Freeze and me. It seemed like Nelly had got discouraged. Scott would move into their big new house before the plastering was dry, and though 't was summer, she had taken a terrible cold that seemed to have drained her, and she took no interest in fixing the place up. Mrs. Spinny had been down with her back again and wasn't able to help, and things was just anyway. We won't talk about that, Margaret; I think 't would hurt Mrs. Spinny to have you know. She nearly died of mortification when she sent for us, and blamed her poor back. We did get Nelly fixed up nicely before she died. I prevailed upon Doctor Tom to come in at the last, and it 'most broke his heart. 'Why, Mis' Dow,' he said, 'if you'd only have come and told me how 't was, I'd have come and carried her right off in my arms.'"

"Oh, Mrs. Dow," I cried, "then it needn't have been?"

Mrs. Dow dropped her needle and clasped her hands quickly. "We mustn't look at it that way, dear," she said tremulously and a little sternly; "we mustn't let ourselves. We must just feel that our Lord wanted her *then*, and took her to Himself. When it was all over, she did look so like a child of God, young and trusting, like she did on her baptizing night, you remember?"

I felt that Mrs. Dow did not want to talk any more about Nelly then, and, indeed, I had little heart to listen; so I told her I would go for a walk, and suggested that I might stop at Mrs. Spinny's to see the children.

Mrs. Dow looked up thoughtfully at the clock. "I doubt if you'll find little Margaret there now. It's half-past four, and she'll have been out of school an hour and more. She'll be most likely coasting on Lupton's Hill. She usually makes for it with her sled the minute she is out of the school-house door. You know, it's the old hill where you all used to slide. If you stop in at the church about six o'clock, you'll likely find Mrs. Spinny there with the baby. I promised to go down and help Mrs. Freeze finish up the tree, and Mrs. Spinny said she'd run in with the baby, if 't wasn't too bitter.

She won't leave him alone with the Swede girl. She's like a young woman with her first."

Lupton's Hill was at the other end of town, and when I got there the dusk was thickening, drawing blue shadows over the snowy fields. There were perhaps twenty children creeping up the hill or whizzing down the packed sled-track. When I had been watching them for some minutes, I heard a lusty shout, and a little red sled shot past me into the deep snow-drift beyond. The child was quite buried for a moment, then she struggled out and stood dusting the snow from her short coat and red woolen comforter. She wore a brown fur cap, which was too big for her and of an old-fashioned shape, such as girls wore long ago, but I would have known her without the cap. Mrs. Dow had said a beautiful child, and there would not be two like this in Riverbend. She was off before I had time to speak to her, going up the hill at a trot, her sturdy little legs plowing through the trampled snow. When she reached the top she never paused to take breath, but threw herself upon her sled and came down with a whoop that was quenched only by the deep drift at the end.

"Are you Margaret Spinny?" I asked as she struggled out in a cloud of snow.

"Yes, 'm." She approached me with frank curiosity, pulling her little sled behind her. "Are you the strange lady staying at Mrs. Dow's?" I nodded, and she began to look my clothes over with respectful interest.

"Your grandmother is to be at the church at six o'clock, isn't she?"

"Yes, 'm."

"Well, suppose we walk up there now. It's nearly six, and all the other children are going home." She hesitated, and looked up at the faintly gleaming track on the hill-slope. "Do you want another slide? Is that it?" I asked.

"Do you mind?" she asked shyly.

"No. I'll wait for you. Take your time; don't run."

Two little boys were still hanging about the slide, and they cheered her as she came down, her comforter streaming in the wind.

"Now," she announced, getting up out of the drift, "I'll show you where the church is."

"Shall I tie your comforter again?"

"No, 'm, thanks. I'm plenty warm." She put her mittened hand confidingly in mine and trudged along beside me.

Mrs. Dow must have heard us tramping up the snowy steps of the church, for she met us at the door. Every one had gone except the old ladies. A kerosene lamp flickered over the Sunday-school chart, with the lesson-picture of the Wise Men, and the little barrel-stove threw out a deep glow over the three white heads that bent above the baby. There the three friends sat, patting him, and smoothing his dress, and playing with his hands, which made theirs look so brown.

"You ain't seen nothing finer in all your travels," said Mrs. Spinny, and they all laughed.

They showed me his full chest and how strong his back was; had me feel the golden fuzz on his head, and made him look at me with his round, bright eyes. He laughed and reared himself in my arms as I took him up and held him close to me. He was so warm and tingling with life, and he had the flush of new beginnings, of the new morning and the new rose. He seemed to have come so lately from his mother's heart! It was as if I held her youth and all her young joy. As I put my cheek down against his, he spied a pink flower in my hat, and making a gleeful sound, he lunged at it with both fists.

"Don't let him spoil it," murmured Mrs. Spinny. "He loves color so—like Nelly."

Century, October 1911

The Bohemian Girl

I

The Trans-continental Express swung along the windings of the Sand River Valley, and in the rear seat of the observation car a young man sat greatly at his ease, not in the least discomfited by the fierce sunlight which beat in upon his brown face and neck and strong back. There was a look of relaxation and of great passivity about his broad shoulders, which seemed almost too heavy until he stood up and squared them. He wore a pale flannel shirt and a blue silk necktie with loose ends. His trousers were wide and belted at the waist, and his short sack-coat hung open. His heavy shoes had seen good service. His reddish-brown hair, like his clothes, had a foreign cut. He had deep-set, dark blue eyes under heavy reddish eyebrows. His face was kept clean only by close shaving, and even the sharpest razor left a glint of yellow in the smooth brown of his skin. His teeth and the palms of his hands were very white. His head, which looked hard and stubborn, lay indolently in the green cushion of the wicker chair, and as he looked out at the ripe summer country a teasing, not unkindly smile played over his lips. Once, as he basked thus comfortably, a quick light flashed in his eyes, curiously dilating the pupils, and his mouth became a hard, straight line, gradually relaxing into its former smile of rather kindly mockery. He told himself, apparently, that there was no point in getting excited; and he seemed a master hand at taking his ease when he could. Neither the sharp whistle of the locomotive nor the brakeman's call disturbed him. It was not until after the train had stopped that he rose, put on a Panama hat, took from the rack a small valise and a flute-case, and stepped deliberately to the station platform. The baggage was already unloaded, and the stranger presented a check for a battered sole-leather steamer-trunk.

"Can you keep it here for a day or two?" he asked the agent. "I may send for it, and I may not."

"Depends on whether you like the country, I suppose?" demanded the agent in a challenging tone.

"Just so."

The agent shrugged his shoulders, looked scornfully at the small trunk, which was marked "N.E.," and handed out a claim check without further comment. The stranger watched him as he caught one end of the trunk and dragged it into the express room. The agent's manner seemed to remind him of something amusing. "Doesn't seem to be a very big place," he remarked, looking about.

"It's big enough for us," snapped the agent, as he banged the trunk into a corner.

That remark, apparently, was what Nils Ericson had wanted. He chuckled quietly as he took a leather strap from his pocket and swung his valise around his shoulder. Then he settled his Panama securely on his head, turned up his trousers, tucked the flute-case under his arm, and started off across the fields. He gave the town, as he would have said, a wide berth, and cut through a great fenced pasture, emerging, when he rolled under the barbed wire at the farther corner, upon a white dusty road which ran straight up from the river valley to the high prairies, where the ripe wheat stood yellow and the tin roofs and weather-cocks were twinkling in the fierce sunlight. By the time Nils had done three miles, the sun was sinking and the farm-wagons on their way home from town came rattling by, covering him with dust and making him sneeze. When one of the farmers pulled up and offered to give him a lift, he clambered in willingly. The driver was a thin, grizzled old man with a long lean neck and a foolish sort of beard, like a goat's. "How fur ye goin'?" he asked, as he clucked to his horses and started off.

"Do you go by the Ericson place?"

"Which Ericson?" The old man drew in his reins as if he expected to stop again.

"Preacher Ericson's."

"Oh, the Old Lady Ericson's!" He turned and looked at Nils. "La, me! If you're goin' out there you might 'a' rid out in the automobile. That's a pity, now. The Old Lady Ericson was in town with her auto. You might 'a' heard it snortin' anywhere about the post-office er the butcher-shop."

"Has she a motor?" asked the stranger absently.

"'Deed an' she has! She runs into town every night about this time for her mail and meat for supper. Some folks say she's afraid her auto won't get exercise enough, but I say that's jealousy."

"Aren't there any other motors about here?"

"Oh, yes! we have fourteen in all. But nobody else gets around like the Old Lady Ericson. She's out, rain er shine, over the whole county, chargin' into town and out amongst her farms, an' up to her sons' places. Sure you ain't goin' to the wrong place?" He craned his neck and looked at Nils' flute-case with eager curiosity. "The old woman ain't got any piany that I knows on. Olaf, he has a grand. His wife's musical; took lessons in Chicago."

"I'm going up there to-morrow," said Nils imperturbably. He saw that the driver took him for a piano-tuner.

"Oh, I see!" The old man screwed up his eyes mysteriously. He was a little dashed by the stranger's non-communicativeness, but he soon broke out again.

"I'm one o' Mis' Ericson's tenants. Look after one of her places. I did own the place myself oncet, but I lost it a while back, in the bad years just after the World's Fair. Just as well, too, I say. Lets you out o' payin' taxes. The Ericsons do own most of the county now. I remember the old preacher's fav'rite text used to be, 'To them that hath shall be given.' They've spread something wonderful—run over this here country like bindweed. But I ain't one that begretches it to 'em. Folks is entitled to what they kin git; and they're hustlers. Olaf, he's in the Legislature now, and a likely man fur Congress. Listen, if that ain't the old woman comin' now. Want I should stop her?"

Nils shook his head. He heard the deep chug-chug of a motor vibrating steadily in the clear twilight behind them. The pale lights of the car swam over the hill, and the old man slapped his reins and turned clear out of the road, ducking his head at the first of three angry snorts from behind. The motor was running at a hot, even speed, and passed without turning an inch from its course. The driver was a stalwart woman who sat at ease in the front seat and drove her car bareheaded. She left a cloud of dust and a trail of gasoline behind her. Her tenant threw back his head and sneezed.

"Whew! I sometimes say I'd as lief be *before* Mrs. Ericson as behind her. She does beat all! Nearly seventy, and never lets another soul touch that car. Puts it into commission herself every morning, and keeps it tuned up by the hitch-bar all day. I never stop work for a drink o' water that I don't hear her a-churnin' up the road. I reckon her darter-in-laws never sets down easy nowadays. Never know when she'll pop in. Mis' Otto, she says to me: 'We're so afraid that thing'll blow up and do Ma some injury yet, she's so turrible venturesome.' Says I: 'I wouldn't stew, Mis' Otto; the old lady'll drive that car to the funeral of every darter-in-law she's got.' That was after the old woman had jumped a turrible bad culvert."

The stranger heard vaguely what the old man was saying. Just now he was experiencing something very much like homesickness, and he was wondering what had brought it about. The mention of a name or two, perhaps; the rattle of a wagon along a dusty road; the rank, resinous smell of sunflowers and ironweed, which the night damp brought up from the draws and low places; perhaps, more than all, the dancing lights of the motor that had plunged by. He squared his shoulders with a comfortable sense of strength.

The wagon, as it jolted westward, climbed a pretty steady upgrade. The country, receding from the rough river valley, swelled more and more gently, as if it had been smoothed out by the wind. On one of the last of the rugged ridges, at the end of a branch road, stood a grim square house with a tin roof and double porches. Behind the house stretched a row of broken, wind-racked poplars, and down the hill-slope to the left straggled the sheds and stables. The old man stopped his horses where the Ericsons' road branched across a dry sand creek that wound about the foot of the hill.

"That's the old lady's place. Want I should drive in?"

"No, thank you. I'll roll out here. Much obliged to you. Good night."

His passenger stepped down over the front wheel, and the old man drove on reluctantly, looking back as if he would like to see how the stranger would be received.

As Nils was crossing the dry creek he heard the restive tramp of a horse coming toward him down the hill. Instantly he flashed out of the road and stood behind a thicket of wild plum bushes that grew in the sandy bed. Peering through the dusk, he saw a light horse, under tight rein, descending the hill at a sharp walk. The rider was a slender woman—barely visible against the dark hillside—wearing an old-fashioned derby hat and a long riding-skirt. She sat lightly in the saddle, with her chin high, and seemed to be looking into the distance. As she passed the plum thicket her horse snuffed the air and shied. She struck him, pulling him in sharply, with an angry exclamation, "*Blázne!*" in Bohemian. Once in the main road, she let him out into a lope, and they soon emerged upon the crest of high land, where they moved along the skyline, silhouetted against the band of faint color that lingered in the west. This horse and rider, with their free, rhythmical gallop, were the only moving things to be seen on the face of the flat country. They seemed, in the last sad light of evening, not to be there accidentally, but as an inevitable detail of the landscape.

Nils watched them until they had shrunk to a mere moving speck against the sky, then he crossed the sand creek and climbed the hill. When he reached the gate the front of the house was dark, but a light was shining from the side windows. The pigs were squealing in the hog corral, and Nils could see a tall boy, who carried two big wooden buckets, moving about among them. Half way between the barn and the house, the windmill wheezed lazily. Following the path that ran around to the back porch, Nils stopped to look through the screen door into the lamp-lit kitchen. The kitchen was the largest room in the house; Nils remembered that his older brothers used to give dances there when he was a boy. Beside the stove stood a little girl with two light yellow braids and a broad, flushed face, peering anxiously into a frying-pan. In the dining-room beyond, a large, broad-shouldered woman was moving about the table. She walked with an active, springy step. Her face was heavy and florid, almost without wrinkles, and her hair was black at seventy. Nils felt proud of her as he watched her deliberate activity; never a momentary hesitation, or a movement that did not tell. He waited until she came out into the kitchen and, brushing the child aside, took her place at the stove. Then he tapped on the screen door and entered.

"It's nobody but Nils, Mother. I expect you weren't looking for me."

Mrs. Ericson turned away from the stove and stood staring at him. "Bring the lamp, Hilda, and let me look."

Nils laughed and unslung his valise. "What's the matter, Mother? Don't you know me?"

Mrs. Ericson put down the lamp. "You must be Nils. You don't look very different, anyway."

"Nor you, Mother. You hold your own. Don't you wear glasses yet?"

"Only to read by. Where's your trunk, Nils?"

"Oh, I left that in town. I thought it might not be convenient for you to have company so near threshing-time."

"Don't be foolish, Nils." Mrs. Ericson turned back to the stove. "I don't thresh now. I hitched the wheat land onto the next farm and have a tenant. Hilda, take some hot water up to the company room, and go call little Eric."

The tow-haired child, who had been standing in mute amazement, took up the tea-kettle and withdrew, giving Nils a long, admiring look from the door of the kitchen stairs.

"Who's the youngster?" Nils asked, dropping down on the bench behind the kitchen stove.

"One of your Cousin Henrik's."

"How long has Cousin Henrik been dead?"

"Six years. There are two boys. One stays with Peter and one with Anders. Olaf is their guardeen."

There was a clatter of pails on the porch, and a tall, lanky boy peered wonderingly in through the screen door. He had a fair, gentle face and big gray eyes, and wisps of soft yellow hair hung down under his cap. Nils sprang up and pulled him into the kitchen, hugging him and slapping him on the shoulders. "Well, if it isn't my kid! Look at the size of him! Don't you know me, Eric?"

The boy reddened under his sunburn and freckles, and hung his head. "I guess it's Nils," he said shyly.

"You're a good guesser," laughed Nils, giving the lad's hand a swing. To himself he was thinking: "That's why the little girl looked so friendly. He's taught her to like me. He was only six when I went away, and he's remembered for twelve years."

Eric stood fumbling with his cap and smiling. "You look just like I thought you would," he ventured.

"Go wash your hands, Eric," called Mrs. Ericson. "I've got cob corn for supper, Nils. You used to like it. I guess you don't get much of that in the old country. Here's Hilda; she'll take you up to your room. You'll want to get the dust off you before you eat."

Mrs. Ericson went into the dining-room to lay another plate, and the little girl came up and nodded to Nils as if to let him know that his room was ready. He put out his hand and she took it, with a startled glance up at his face. Little Eric dropped his towel, threw an arm about Nils and one about Hilda, gave them a clumsy squeeze, and then stumbled out to the porch.

During supper Nils heard exactly how much land each of his eight grown brothers farmed, how their crops were coming on, and how much live stock they were feeding. His mother watched him narrowly as she talked. "You've got better looking, Nils," she remarked abruptly, whereupon he grinned and the children giggled. Eric, although he was eighteen and as tall as Nils, was always accounted a child, being the last of so many sons. His face seemed childlike, too, Nils thought, and he had the open, wandering eyes of a little boy. All the others had been men at his age.

After supper Nils went out to the front porch and sat down on the step to smoke a pipe. Mrs. Ericson drew a rocking-chair up near him and began to knit busily. It was one of the few old-world customs she had kept up, for she could not bear to sit with idle hands.

"Where's little Eric, Mother?"

"He's helping Hilda with the dishes. He does it of his own will; I don't like a boy to be too handy about the house."

"He seems like a nice kid."

"He's very obedient."

Nils smiled a little in the dark. It was just as well to shift the line of conversation. "What are you knitting there, Mother?"

"Baby stockings. The boys keep me busy." Mrs. Ericson chuckled and clicked her needles.

"How many grandchildren have you?"

"Only thirty-one now. Olaf lost his three. They were sickly, like their mother."

"I supposed he had a second crop by this time!"

"His second wife has no children. She's too proud. She tears about on horseback all the time. But she'll get caught up with, yet. She sets herself very high, though nobody knows what for. They were low enough Bohemians she came of. I never thought much of Bohemians; always drinking."

Nils puffed away at his pipe in silence, and Mrs. Ericson knitted on. In a few moments she added grimly: "She was down here to-night, just before you came. She'd like to quarrel with me and come between me and Olaf, but I don't give her the chance. I suppose you'll be bringing a wife home some day."

"I don't know. I've never thought much about it."

"Well, perhaps it's best as it is," suggested Mrs. Ericson hopefully. "You'd never be contented tied down to the land. There was roving blood in your father's family, and it's come out in you. I expect your own way of life suits you best." Mrs. Ericson had dropped into a blandly agreeable tone which Nils well remembered. It seemed to amuse him a good deal and his white teeth flashed behind his pipe. His mother's strategies had always diverted him, even when he was a boy—they were so flimsy and patent, so illy proportioned to her vigor and force. "They've been waiting to see which way I'd jump," he reflected. He felt that Mrs. Ericson was pondering his case deeply as she sat clicking her needles.

"I don't suppose you've ever got used to steady work," she went on presently. "Men ain't apt to if they roam around too long. It's a pity you didn't come back the year after the World's Fair. Your father picked up a good bit of land cheap then, in the hard times, and I expect maybe he'd have give you a farm. It's too bad you put off comin' back so long, for I always thought he meant to do something by you."

Nils laughed and shook the ashes out of his pipe. "I'd have missed a lot if I had come back then. But I'm sorry I didn't get back to see father."

"Well, I suppose we have to miss things at one end or the other. Perhaps you are as well satisfied with your own doings, now, as you'd have been with a farm," said Mrs. Ericson reassuringly.

"Land's a good thing to have," Nils commented, as he lit another match and sheltered it with his hand.

His mother looked sharply at his face until the match burned out. "Only when you stay on it!" she hastened to say.

Eric came round the house by the path just then, and Nils rose, with a yawn. "Mother, if you don't mind, Eric and I will take a little tramp before bed-time. It will make me sleep."

"Very well; only don't stay long. I'll sit up and wait for you. I like to lock up myself."

Nils put his hand on Eric's shoulder, and the two tramped down the hill and across the sand creek into the dusty highroad beyond. Neither spoke. They swung along at an even gait, Nils puffing at his pipe. There was no moon, and the white road and the wide fields lay faint in the starlight. Over everything was darkness and thick silence, and the smell of dust and sunflowers. The brothers followed the road for a mile or more without finding a place to sit down. Finally Nils perched on a stile over the wire fence, and Eric sat on the lower step.

"I began to think you never would come back, Nils," said the boy softly.

"Didn't I promise you I would?"

"Yes; but people don't bother about promises they make to babies. Did you really know you were going away for good when you went to Chicago with the cattle that time?"

"I thought it very likely, if I could make my way."

"I don't see how you did it, Nils. Not many fellows could." Eric rubbed his shoulder against his brother's knee.

"The hard thing was leaving home—you and father. It was easy enough, once I got beyond Chicago. Of course I got awful homesick; used to cry myself to sleep. But I'd burned my bridges."

"You had always wanted to go, hadn't you?"

"Always. Do you still sleep in our little room? Is that cottonwood still by the window?"

Eric nodded eagerly and smiled up at his brother in the gray darkness.

"You remember how we always said the leaves were whispering when they rustled at night? Well, they always whispered to me about the sea. Sometimes they said names out of the geography books. In a high wind they had a desperate sound, like something trying to tear loose."

"How funny, Nils," said Eric dreamily, resting his chin on his hand. "That tree still talks like that, and 'most always it talks to me about you."

They sat a while longer, watching the stars. At last Eric whispered anxiously: "Hadn't we better go back now? Mother will get tired waiting for us." They rose and took a short cut home, through the pasture.

II

The next morning Nils woke with the first flood of light that came with dawn. The white-plastered walls of his room reflected the glare that shone through the thin window-shades, and he found it impossible to sleep. He dressed hurriedly and slipped down the hall and up the back stairs to the half-story room which he used to share with his little brother. Eric, in a skimpy night-shirt, was sitting on the edge of the bed, rubbing his eyes, his pale yellow hair standing up in tufts all over his head. When he saw Nils, he murmured something confusedly and hustled his long legs into his trousers. "I didn't expect you'd be up so early, Nils," he said, as his head emerged from his blue shirt.

"Oh, you thought I was a dude, did you?" Nils gave him a playful tap which bent the tall boy up like a clasp-knife. "See here; I must teach you to box." Nils thrust his hands into his pockets and walked about. "You haven't changed things much up here. Got most of my old traps, haven't you?"

He took down a bent, withered piece of sapling that hung over the dresser. "If this isn't the stick Lou Sandberg killed himself with!"

The boy looked up from his shoe-lacing.

"Yes; you never used to let me play with that. Just how did he do it, Nils? You were with father when he found Lou, weren't you?"

"Yes. Father was going off to preach somewhere, and, as we drove along, Lou's place looked sort of forlorn, and we thought we'd stop and cheer him up. When we found him father said he'd been dead a couple days. He'd tied a piece of binding twine round his neck, made a noose in each end, fixed the nooses over the ends of a bent stick, and let the stick spring straight; strangled himself."

"What made him kill himself such a silly way?"

The simplicity of the boy's question set Nils laughing. He clapped little Eric on the shoulder. "What made him such a silly as to kill himself at all, I should say!"

"Oh, well! But his hogs had the cholera, and all up and died on him, didn't they?"

"Sure they did; but he didn't have cholera; and there were plenty of hogs left in the world, weren't there?"

"Well, but, if they weren't his, how could they do him any good?" Eric asked, in astonishment.

"Oh, scat! He could have had lots of fun with other people's hogs. He was a chump, Lou Sandberg. To kill yourself for a pig—think of that, now!" Nils laughed all the way downstairs, and quite embarrassed little Eric, who fell to scrubbing his face and hands at the tin basin. While he was patting his wet hair at the kitchen looking-glass, a heavy tread sounded on the stairs. The boy dropped his comb. "Gracious, there's Mother. We must have talked too long." He hurried out to the shed, slipped on his overalls, and disappeared with the milking-pails.

Mrs. Ericson came in, wearing a clean white apron, her black hair shining from the application of a wet brush.

"Good morning, Mother. Can't I make the fire for you?"

"No, thank you, Nils. It's no trouble to make a cob fire, and I like to manage the kitchen stove myself." Mrs. Ericson paused with a shovel full of ashes in her hand. "I expect you will be wanting to see your brothers as soon as possible. I'll take you up to Anders' place this morning. He's threshing, and most of our boys are over there."

"Will Olaf be there?"

Mrs. Ericson went on taking out the ashes, and spoke between shovels. "No; Olaf's wheat is all in, put away in his new barn. He got six thousand bushel this year. He's going to town to-day to get men to finish roofing his barn."

"So Olaf is building a new barn?" Nils asked absently.

"Biggest one in the county, and almost done. You'll likely be here for the barn-raising. He's going to have a supper and a dance as soon as everybody's done threshing. Says it keeps the voters in a good humor. I tell him that's all nonsense; but Olaf has a long head for politics."

"Does Olaf farm all Cousin Henrik's land?"

Mrs. Ericson frowned as she blew into the faint smoke curling up about the cobs. "Yes; he holds it in trust for the children, Hilda and her brothers. He keeps strict account of everything he raises on it, and puts the proceeds out at compound interest for them."

Nils smiled as he watched the little flames shoot up. The door of the back stairs opened, and Hilda emerged, her arms behind her, buttoning up her long gingham apron as she came. He nodded to her gaily, and she twinkled at him out of her little blue eyes, set far apart over her wide cheek-bones.

"There, Hilda, you grind the coffee—and just put in an extra handful; I expect your Cousin Nils likes his strong," said Mrs. Ericson, as she went out to the shed.

Nils turned to look at the little girl, who gripped the coffee-grinder between her knees and ground so hard that her two braids bobbed and her face flushed under its broad spattering of freckles. He noticed on her middle finger something that had not been there last night, and that had evidently been put on for company: a tiny gold ring with a clumsily set garnet stone. As her hand went round and round he touched the ring with the tip of his finger, smiling.

Hilda glanced toward the shed door through which Mrs. Ericson had disappeared. "My Cousin Clara gave me that," she whispered bashfully. "She's Cousin Olaf's wife."

III

Mrs. Olaf Ericson—Clara Vavrika, as many people still called her—was moving restlessly about her big bare house that morning. Her husband had left for the county town before his wife was out of bed—her lateness in rising was one of the many things the Ericson family had against her. Clara seldom came downstairs before eight o'clock, and this morning she was even later, for she had dressed with unusual care. She put on, however, only a tight-fitting black dress, which people thereabouts thought very plain. She was a tall, dark woman of thirty, with a rather sallow complexion and a touch of dull salmon red in her cheeks, where the blood seemed to burn under her brown skin. Her hair, parted evenly above her low forehead, was so black that there were distinctly blue lights in it. Her black eyebrows were delicate half-moons and her lashes were long and heavy. Her eyes slanted a little, as if she had a strain of Tartar or gypsy blood, and were sometimes full of fiery determination and sometimes dull and opaque. Her expression was never altogether amiable; was often, indeed, distinctly sullen, or, when she was animated, sarcastic. She was most attractive in profile, for then one saw to advantage her small, well-shaped head and delicate ears, and felt at once that here was a very positive, if not an altogether pleasing, personality.

The entire management of Mrs. Olaf's household devolved upon her aunt, Johanna Vavrika, a superstitious, doting woman of fifty. When Clara was a little girl her mother died, and Johanna's life had been spent in ungrudging service to her niece. Clara, like many self-willed and discontented persons, was really very apt, without knowing it, to do as other people told her, and to let her destiny be decided for her by intelligences much below her own. It was her Aunt Johanna who had humored and spoiled her in her girlhood, who had got her off to Chicago to study piano, and who had finally persuaded her to marry Olaf Ericson as the best match she would be likely to make in that part of the country. Johanna Vavrika had been deeply scarred by smallpox in the old country. She was short and fat, homely and jolly and sentimental. She was so broad, and took such short steps when she walked, that her brother, Joe Vavrika, always called her his duck. She adored her niece because of her talent, because of her good looks and masterful ways, but most of all because of her selfishness.

Clara's marriage with Olaf Ericson was Johanna's particular triumph. She was inordinately proud of Olaf's position, and she found a sufficiently exciting career in managing Clara's house, in keeping it above the criticism of the Ericsons, in pampering Olaf to keep him from finding fault with his wife, and in concealing from every one Clara's domestic infelicities. While Clara slept of a morning, Johanna Vavrika was bustling about, seeing that Olaf and the men had their breakfast, and that the cleaning or the butter-making or the washing was properly begun by the two girls in the kitchen. Then, at about eight o'clock, she would take Clara's coffee up to her, and chat with her while she drank it, telling her what was going on in the house. Old Mrs. Ericson frequently said that her daughter-in-law would not know what day of the week it was if Johanna did not tell her every morning. Mrs. Ericson despised and pitied Johanna, but did not wholly dislike her. The one thing she hated in her daughter-in-law above everything else was the way in which Clara could come it over people. It enraged her that the affairs of her son's big, barnlike house went on as well as they did, and she used to feel that in this world we have to wait over-long to see the guilty punished. "Suppose Johanna Vavrika died or got sick?" the old lady used to say to Olaf. "Your wife wouldn't know where to look for her own dish-cloth." Olaf only shrugged his shoulders. The fact remained that Johanna did not die, and, although Mrs. Ericson often told her she was looking poorly, she was never ill. She seldom left the house, and she slept in a little room off the kitchen. No Ericson, by night or day, could come prying about there to find fault without her knowing it. Her one weakness was that she was an incurable talker, and she sometimes made trouble without meaning to.

This morning Clara was tying a wine-colored ribbon about her throat when Johanna appeared with her coffee. After putting the tray on a sewing-table, she began to make Clara's bed, chattering the while in Bohemian.

"Well, Olaf got off early, and the girls are baking. I'm going down presently to make some poppy-seed bread for Olaf. He asked for prune preserves at breakfast, and I told him I was out of them, and to bring some prunes and honey and cloves from town."

Clara poured her coffee. "Ugh! I don't see how men can eat so much sweet stuff. In the morning, too!"

Her aunt chuckled knowingly. "Bait a bear with honey, as we say in the old country."

"Was he cross?" her niece asked indifferently.

"Olaf? Oh, no! He was in fine spirits. He's never cross if you know how to take him. I never knew a man to make so little fuss about bills. I gave him a list of things to get a yard long, and he didn't say a word; just folded it up and put it in his pocket."

"I can well believe he didn't say a word," Clara remarked with a shrug. "Some day he'll forget how to talk."

"Oh, but they say he's a grand speaker in the Legislature. He knows when to keep quiet. That's why he's got such influence in politics. The people have confidence in him." Johanna beat up a pillow and held it under her fat chin while she slipped on the case. Her niece laughed.

"Maybe we could make people believe we were wise, Aunty, if we held our tongues. Why did you tell Mrs. Ericson that Norman threw me again last Saturday and turned my foot? She's been talking to Olaf."

Johanna fell into great confusion. "Oh, but, my precious, the old lady asked for you, and she's always so angry if I can't give an excuse. Anyhow, she needn't talk; she's always tearing up something with that motor of hers."

When her aunt clattered down to the kitchen, Clara went to dust the parlor. Since there was not much there to dust, this did not take very long. Olaf had built the house new for her before their marriage, but her interest in furnishing it had been short-lived. It went, indeed, little beyond a bath-tub and her piano. They had disagreed about almost every other article of furniture, and Clara had said she would rather have her house empty than full of things she didn't want. The house was set in a hillside, and the west windows of the parlor looked out above the kitchen yard thirty feet below. The east windows opened directly into the front yard. At one of the latter, Clara, while she was dusting, heard a low whistle. She did not turn at once, but listened intently as she drew her cloth slowly along the round of a chair. Yes, there it was:

"I dreamt that I dwelt in ma-a-arble halls,"

She turned and saw Nils Ericson laughing in the sunlight, his hat in his hand, just outside the window. As she crossed the room he leaned against the wire screen. "Aren't you at all surprised to see me, Clara Vavrika?"

"No; I was expecting to see you. Mother Ericson telephoned Olaf last night that you were here."

Nils squinted and gave a long whistle. "Telephoned? That must have been while Eric and I were out walking. Isn't she enterprising? Lift this screen, won't you?"

Clara lifted the screen, and Nils swung his leg across the window-sill. As he stepped into the room she said: "You didn't think you were going to get ahead of your mother, did you?"

He threw his hat on the piano. "Oh, I do sometimes. You see, I'm ahead of her now. I'm supposed to be in Anders' wheat-field. But, as we were leaving, Mother ran her car into a soft place beside the road and sank up to the hubs. While they were going for horses to pull her out, I cut away behind the stacks and escaped." Nils chuckled. Clara's dull eyes lit up as she looked at him admiringly.

"You've got them guessing already. I don't know what your mother said to Olaf over the telephone, but he came back looking as if he'd seen a ghost, and he didn't go to bed until a dreadful hour—ten o'clock, I should think. He sat out on the porch in the dark like a graven image. It had been one of his talkative days, too." They both laughed, easily and lightly, like people who have laughed a great deal together; but they remained standing.

"Anders and Otto and Peter looked as if they had seen ghosts, too, over in the threshing-field. What's the matter with them all?"

Clara gave him a quick, searching look. "Well, for one thing, they've always been afraid you have the other will."

Nils looked interested. "The other will?"

"Yes. A later one. They knew your father made another, but they never knew what he did with it. They almost tore the old house to pieces looking for it. They always suspected that he carried on a clandestine correspondence with you, for the one thing he would do was to get his own mail himself. So they thought he might have sent the new will to you for safekeeping. The old one, leaving everything to your mother, was made long before you went away, and it's understood among them that it cuts you out—that she will leave all the property to the others. Your father made the second will to prevent that. I've been hoping you had it. It would be such fun to spring it on them." Clara laughed mirthfully, a thing she did not often do now.

Nils shook his head reprovingly. "Come, now, you're malicious."

"No, I'm not. But I'd like something to happen to stir them all up, just for once. There never was such a family for having nothing ever happen to them but dinner and threshing. I'd almost be willing to die, just to have a funeral. *You* wouldn't stand it for three weeks."

Nils bent over the piano and began pecking at the keys with the finger of one hand. "I wouldn't? My dear young lady, how do you know what I can stand? *You* wouldn't wait to find out."

Clara flushed darkly and frowned. "I didn't believe you would ever come back—" she said defiantly.

"Eric believed I would, and he was only a baby when I went away. However, all's well that ends well, and I haven't come back to be a skeleton at the feast. We mustn't quarrel. Mother will be here with a search-warrant pretty soon." He swung round and faced her, thrusting his hands into his coat pockets. "Come, you ought to be glad to see me, if you want something to happen. I'm something, even without a will. We can have a little fun, can't we? I think we can!"

She echoed him, "I think we can!" They both laughed and their eyes sparkled. Clara Vavrika looked ten years younger than when she had put the velvet ribbon about her throat that morning.

"You know, I'm so tickled to see mother," Nils went on. "I didn't know I was so proud of her. A regular pile-driver. How about little pigtails, down at the house? Is Olaf doing the square thing by those children?"

Clara frowned pensively. "Olaf has to do something that looks like the square thing, now that he's a public man!" She glanced drolly at Nils. "But he makes a good commission out of it. On Sundays they all get together here and figure. He lets Peter and Anders put in big bills for the keep of the two boys, and he pays them out of the estate. They are always having what they call accountings. Olaf gets something out of it, too. I don't know just how they do it, but it's entirely a family matter, as they say. And when the Ericsons say that—" Clara lifted her eyebrows.

Just then the angry *honk-honk* of an approaching motor sounded from down the road. Their eyes met and they began to laugh. They laughed as children do when they can not contain themselves, and can not explain the cause of their mirth to grown people, but share it perfectly together. When Clara Vavrika sat down at the piano after he was gone, she felt that she had laughed away a dozen years. She practised as if the house were burning over her head.

When Nils greeted his mother and climbed into the front seat of the motor beside her, Mrs. Ericson looked grim, but she made no comment upon his truancy until she had turned her car and was retracing her revolutions along the road that ran by Olaf's big pasture. Then she remarked dryly:

"If I were you I wouldn't see too much of Olaf's wife while you are here. She's the kind of woman who can't see much of men without getting herself talked about. She was a good deal talked about before he married her."

"Hasn't Olaf tamed her?" Nils asked indifferently.

Mrs. Ericson shrugged her massive shoulders. "Olaf don't seem to have much luck, when it comes to wives. The first one was meek enough, but she was always ailing. And this one has her own way. He says if he quarreled with her she'd go back to her father, and then he'd lose the Bohemian vote. There are a great many Bohunks in this district. But when you find a man under his wife's thumb you can always be sure there's a soft spot in him somewhere."

Nils thought of his own father, and smiled. "She brought him a good deal of money, didn't she, besides the Bohemian vote?"

Mrs. Ericson sniffed. "Well, she has a fair half section in her own name, but I can't see as that does Olaf much good. She will have a good deal of property some day, if old Vavrika don't marry again. But I don't consider a saloonkeeper's money as good as other people's money."

Nils laughed outright. "Come, Mother, don't let your prejudices carry you that far. Money's money. Old Vavrika's a mighty decent sort of saloonkeeper. Nothing rowdy about him."

Mrs. Ericson spoke up angrily: "Oh, I know you always stood up for them! But hanging around there when you were a boy never did you any good, Nils, nor any of the other boys who went there. There weren't so many after her when she married Olaf, let me tell you. She knew enough to grab her chance."

Nils settled back in his seat. "Of course I liked to go there, Mother, and you were always cross about it. You never took the trouble to find out that it was the one jolly house in this country for a boy to go to. All the rest of you were working yourselves to death, and the houses were mostly a mess, full of babies and washing and flies. Oh, it was all right—I understand that; but you are young only once, and I happened to be young then. Now, Vavrika's was always jolly. He played the violin, and I used to take my flute, and Clara played the piano, and Johanna used to sing Bohemian songs. She always had a big supper for us—herrings and pickles and poppyseed bread, and lots of cake and preserves. Old Joe had been in the army in the old country, and he could tell lots of good stories. I can see him cutting bread, at the head of the table, now. I don't know what I'd have done when I was a kid if it hadn't been for the Vavrikas, really."

"And all the time he was taking money that other people had worked hard in the fields for," Mrs. Ericson observed.

"So do the circuses, Mother, and they're a good thing. People ought to get fun for some of their money. Even father liked old Joe."

"Your father," Mrs. Ericson said grimly, "liked everybody."

As they crossed the sand creek and turned into her own place, Mrs. Ericson observed, "There's Olaf's buggy. He's stopped on his way from town." Nils shook himself and prepared to greet his brother, who was waiting on the porch.

Olaf was a big, heavy Norwegian, slow of speech and movement. His head was large and square, like a block of wood. When Nils, at a distance, tried to remember what his brother looked like, he could recall only his heavy head, high forehead, large nostrils, and pale-blue eyes, set far apart. Olaf's features were rudimentary: the thing one noticed was the face itself, wide and flat and pale, devoid of any expression, betraying his fifty years as little as it betrayed anything else, and powerful by reason of its very stolidness. When Olaf shook hands with Nils he looked at him from under his light eyebrows, but Nils felt that no one could ever say what that pale look might mean. The one thing he had always felt in Olaf was a heavy stubbornness, like the unyielding stickiness of wet loam against the plow. He had always found Olaf the most difficult of his brothers.

"How do you do, Nils? Expect to stay with us long?"

"Oh, I may stay forever," Nils answered gaily. "I like this country better than I used to."

"There's been some work put into it since you left," Olaf remarked.

"Exactly. I think it's about ready to live in now—and I'm about ready to settle down." Nils saw his brother lower his big head. ("Exactly like a bull," he thought.) "Mother's been persuading me to slow down now, and go in for farming," he went on lightly.

Olaf made a deep sound in his throat. "Farming ain't learned in a day," he brought out, still looking at the ground.

"Oh, I know! But I pick things up quickly." Nils had not meant to antagonize his brother, and he did not know now why he was doing it. "Of course," he went on, "I shouldn't expect to make a big success, as you fellows have done. But then, I'm not ambitious. I won't want much. A little land, and some cattle, maybe."

Olaf still stared at the ground, his head down. He wanted to ask Nils what he had been doing all these years, that he didn't have a business somewhere he couldn't afford to leave; why he hadn't more pride than to come back with only a little sole-leather trunk to show for himself, and to present himself as the only failure in the family. He did not ask one of these questions, but he made them all felt distinctly.

"Humph!" Nils thought. "No wonder the man never talks, when he can butt his ideas into you like that without ever saying a word. I suppose he uses that kind of smokeless powder on his wife all the time. But I guess she has her innings." He chuckled, and Olaf looked up. "Never mind me, Olaf. I laugh without knowing why, like little Eric. He's another cheerful dog."

"Eric," said Olaf slowly, "is a spoiled kid. He's just let his mother's best cow go dry because he don't milk her right. I was hoping you'd take him away somewhere and put him into business. If he don't do any good among strangers, he never will." This was a long speech for Olaf, and as he finished it he climbed into his buggy.

Nils shrugged his shoulders. "Same old tricks," he thought. "Hits from behind you every time. What a whale of a man!" He turned and went round to the kitchen, where his mother was scolding little Eric for letting the gasoline get low.

IV

Joe Vavrika's saloon was not in the county-seat, where Olaf and Mrs. Ericson did their trading, but in a cheerfuller place, a little Bohemian settlement which lay at the other end of the county, ten level miles north of Olaf's farm. Clara rode up to see her father almost every day. Vavrika's house was, so to speak, in the back yard of his saloon. The garden between the two buildings was inclosed by a high board fence as tight as a partition, and in summer Joe kept beer-tables and wooden benches among the gooseberry bushes under his little cherry tree. At one of these tables Nils

Ericson was seated in the late afternoon, three days after his return home. Joe had gone in to serve a customer, and Nils was lounging on his elbows, looking rather mournfully into his half-emptied pitcher, when he heard a laugh across the little garden. Clara, in her riding-habit, was standing at the back door of the house, under the grapevine trellis that old Joe had grown there long ago. Nils rose.

"Come out and keep your father and me company. We've been gossiping all afternoon. Nobody to bother us but the flies."

She shook her head. "No, I never come out here any more. Olaf doesn't like it. I must live up to my position, you know."

"You mean to tell me you never come out and chat with the boys, as you used to? He *has* tamed you! Who keeps up these flower-beds?"

"I come out on Sundays, when father is alone, and read the Bohemian papers to him. But I am never here when the bar is open. What have you two been doing?"

"Talking, as I told you. I've been telling him about my travels. I find I can't talk much at home, not even to Eric."

Clara reached up and poked with her riding-whip at a white moth that was fluttering in the sunlight among the vine leaves. "I suppose you will never tell me about all those things."

"Where can I tell them? Not in Olaf's house, certainly. What's the matter with our talking here?" He pointed persuasively with his hat to the bushes and the green table, where the flies were singing lazily above the empty beer-glasses.

Clara shook her head weakly. "No, it wouldn't do. Besides, I am going now."

"I'm on Eric's mare. Would you be angry if I overtook you?"

Clara looked back and laughed. "You might try and see. I can leave you if I don't want you. Eric's mare can't keep up with Norman."

Nils went into the bar and attempted to pay his score. Big Joe, six feet four, with curly yellow hair and mustache, clapped him on the shoulder. "Not a God-damn a your money go in my drawer, you hear? Only next time you bring your flute, te-te-te-te-te-ty." Joe wagged his fingers in imitation of the flute-player's position. "My Clara, she come all-a-time Sundays an' play for me. She not like to play at Ericson's place." He shook his yellow curls and laughed. "Not a God-damn a fun at Ericson's. You come a Sunday. You like-a fun. No forget de flute." Joe talked very rapidly and always tumbled over his English. He seldom spoke it to his customers, and had never learned much.

Nils swung himself into the saddle and trotted to the west end of the village, where the houses and gardens scattered into prairie-land and the road turned south. Far ahead of him, in the declining light, he saw Clara Vavrika's slender figure, loitering on horseback. He touched his mare with the whip, and shot along the white, level road, under the reddening sky. When he overtook Olaf's wife he saw that she had been crying. "What's the matter, Clara Vavrika?" he asked kindly.

"Oh, I get blue sometimes. It was awfully jolly living there with father. I wonder why I ever went away."

Nils spoke in a low, kind tone that he sometimes used with women: "That's what I've been wondering these many years. You were the last girl in the country I'd have picked for a wife for Olaf. What made you do it, Clara?"

"I suppose I really did it to oblige the neighbors"—Clara tossed her head. "People were beginning to wonder."

"To wonder?"

"Yes—why I didn't get married. I suppose I didn't like to keep them in suspense. I've discovered that most girls marry out of consideration for the neighborhood."

Nils bent his head toward her and his white teeth flashed. "I'd have gambled that one girl I knew would say, 'Let the neighborhood be damned.'"

Clara shook her head mournfully. "You see, they have it on you, Nils; that is, if you're a woman. They say you're beginning to go off. That's what makes us get married: we can't stand the laugh."

Nils looked sidewise at her. He had never seen her head droop before. Resignation was the last thing he would have expected of her. "In your case, there wasn't something else?"

"Something else?"

"I mean, you didn't do it to spite somebody? Somebody who didn't come back?"

Clara drew herself up. "Oh, I never thought you'd come back. Not after I stopped writing to you, at least. *That* was all over, long before I married Olaf."

"It never occurred to you, then, that the meanest thing you could do to me was to marry Olaf?"

Clara laughed. "No; I didn't know you were so fond of Olaf."

Nils smoothed his horse's mane with his glove. "You know, Clara Vavrika, you are never going to stick it out. You'll cut away some day, and I've been thinking you might as well cut away with me."

Clara threw up her chin. "Oh, you don't know me as well as you think. I won't cut away. Sometimes, when I'm with father, I feel like it. But I can hold out as long as the Ericsons can. They've never got the best of me yet, and one can live, so long as one isn't beaten. If I go back to father, it's all up with Olaf in politics. He knows that, and he never goes much beyond sulking. I've as much wit as the Ericsons. I'll never leave them unless I can show them a thing or two."

"You mean unless you can come it over them?"

"Yes—unless I go away with a man who is cleverer than they are, and who has more money."

Nils whistled. "Dear me, you are demanding a good deal. The Ericsons, take the lot of them, are a bunch to beat. But I should think the excitement of tormenting them would have worn off by this time."

"It has, I'm afraid," Clara admitted mournfully.

"Then why don't you cut away? There are more amusing games than this in the world. When I came home I thought it might amuse me to bully a few quarter sections out of the Ericsons; but I've almost decided I can get more fun for my money somewhere else."

Clara took in her breath sharply. "Ah, you have got the other will! That was why you came home!"

"No, it wasn't. I came home to see how you were getting on with Olaf."

Clara struck her horse with the whip, and in a bound she was far ahead of him. Nils dropped one word, "Damn!" and whipped after her; but she leaned forward in her saddle and fairly cut the wind. Her long riding-skirt rippled in the still air behind her. The sun was just sinking behind the stubble in a vast, clear sky, and the shadows drew across the fields so rapidly that Nils could scarcely keep in sight the dark figure on the road. When he overtook her he caught her horse by the bridle. Norman reared, and Nils was frightened for her; but Clara kept her seat.

"Let me go, Nils Ericson!" she cried. "I hate you more than any of them. You were created to torture me, the whole tribe of you—to make me suffer in every possible way."

She struck her horse again and galloped away from him. Nils set his teeth and looked thoughtful. He rode slowly home along the deserted road, watching the stars come out in the clear violet sky. They flashed softly into the limpid heavens, like jewels let fall into clear water. They were a reproach, he felt, to a sordid world. As he turned across the sand creek, he looked up at the North Star and smiled, as if there were an understanding between them. His mother scolded him for being late for supper.

V

On Sunday afternoon Joe Vavrika, in his shirt-sleeves and carpet-slippers, was sitting in his garden, smoking a long-tasseled porcelain pipe with a hunting scene painted on the bowl. Clara sat under the cherry tree, reading aloud to him from the weekly Bohemian papers. She had worn a white muslin dress under her riding-habit, and the leaves of the cherry tree threw a pattern of sharp shadows over her skirt. The black cat was dozing in the sunlight at her feet, and Joe's dachshund was scratching a hole under the scarlet geraniums and dreaming of badgers. Joe was filling his pipe for the third time since dinner, when he heard a knocking on the fence. He broke into a loud guffaw and unlatched the little door that led into the street. He did not call Nils by name, but caught him by the hand and dragged him in. Clara stiffened and the color deepened under her dark skin. Nils, too, felt a little awkward. He had not seen her since the night when she rode away from him and left him alone on the level road between the fields. Joe dragged him to the wooden bench beside the green table.

"You bring de flute," he cried, tapping the leather case under Nils' arm. "Ah, das-a good! Now we have some liddle fun like old times. I got somet'ing good for you." Joe shook his finger at Nils and winked his blue eyes, a bright clear eye, full of fire, though the tiny blood-vessels on the ball were always a little distended. "I got somet'ing for you from"—he paused and waved his hand—"Hongarie. You know Hongarie? You wait!" He pushed Nils down on the bench, and went through the back door of his saloon.

Nils looked at Clara, who sat frigidly with her white skirts drawn tight about her. "He didn't tell you he had asked me to come, did he? He wanted a party and proceeded to arrange it. Isn't he fun? Don't be cross; let's give him a good time."

Clara smiled and shook out her skirt. "Isn't that like father? And he has sat here so meekly all day. Well, I won't pout. I'm glad you came. He doesn't have very many good times now any more. There are so few of his kind left. The second generation are a tame lot."

Joe came back with a flask in one hand and three wine-glasses caught by the stems between the fingers of the other. These he placed on the table with an air of ceremony, and, going behind Nils, held the flask between him and the sun, squinting into it admiringly. "You know dis, Tokai? A great friend of mine, he bring dis to me, a present out of Hongarie. You know how much it cost, dis wine? Chust so much what it weigh in gold. Nobody but de nobles drink him in Bohemie. Many, many years I save him up, dis Tokai." Joe whipped out his official cork-screw and delicately removed the cork. "De old man die what bring him to me, an' dis wine he lay on his belly in my cellar an' sleep. An' now," carefully pouring out the heavy yellow wine, "an' now he wake up; and maybe he wake us up, too!" He carried one of the glasses to his daughter and presented it with great gallantry.

Clara shook her head, but, seeing her father's disappointment, relented. "You taste it first. I don't want so much."

Joe sampled it with a beatific expression, and turned to Nils. "You drink him slow, dis wine. He very soft, but he go down hot. You see!"

After a second glass Nils declared that he couldn't take any more without getting sleepy. "Now get your fiddle, Vavrika," he said as he opened his flute-case.

But Joe settled back in his wooden rocker and wagged his big carpet-slipper. "No-no-no-no-no-no-no! No play fiddle now any more: too much ache in de finger," waving them, "all-a-time rheumatiz. You play de flute, te-tety-te-tety-te. Bohemie songs."

"I've forgotten all the Bohemian songs I used to play with you and Johanna. But here's one that will make Clara pout. You remember how her eyes used to snap when we called her the Bohemian Girl?" Nils lifted his flute and began "When Other Lips and Other Hearts," and Joe hummed the air in a husky baritone, waving his carpet-slipper. "Oh-h-h, das-a fine music," he cried, clapping his hands as Nils finished. "Now 'Marble Halls, Marble Halls'! Clara, you sing him."

Clara smiled and leaned back in her chair, beginning softly:

> "I dreamt that I dwelt in ma-a-arble halls,
> With vassals and serfs at my knee,"

and Joe hummed like a big bumble-bee.

"There's one more you always played," Clara said quietly; "I remember that best." She locked her hands over her knee and began "The Heart Bowed Down," and sang it through without groping for the words. She was singing with a good deal of warmth when she came to the end of the old song:

"For memory is the only friend
That grief can call its own."

Joe flashed out his red silk handkerchief and blew his nose, shaking his head. "No-no-no-no-no-no-no! Too sad, too sad! I not like-a dat. Play quick somet'ing gay now."

Nils put his lips to the instrument, and Joe lay back in his chair, laughing and singing, "Oh, Evelina, Sweet Evelina!" Clara laughed, too. Long ago, when she and Nils went to high school, the model student of their class was a very homely girl in thick spectacles. Her name was Evelina Oleson; she had a long, swinging walk which somehow suggested the measure of that song, and they used mercilessly to sing it at her.

"Dat ugly Oleson girl, she teach in de school," Joe gasped, "an' she still walk chust like dat, yup-a, yup-a, yup-a, chust like a camel she go! Now, Nils, we have some more li'l drink. Oh, yes-yes-yes-yes-yes-yes-*yes!* Dis time you haf to drink, and Clara she haf to, so she show she not jealous. So, we all drink to your girl. You not tell her name, eh? No-no-no, I no make you tell. She pretty, eh? She make good sweetheart? I bet!" Joe winked and lifted his glass. "How soon you get married?"

Nils screwed up his eyes. "That I don't know. When she says."

Joe threw out his chest. "Das-a way boys talks. No way for mans. Mans say, 'You come to de church, an' get a hurry on you.' Das-a way mans talks."

"Maybe Nils hasn't got enough to keep a wife," put in Clara ironically. "How about that, Nils?" she asked him frankly, as if she wanted to know.

Nils looked at her coolly, raising one eyebrow. "Oh, I can keep her, all right."

"The way she wants to be kept?"

"With my wife, I'll decide that," replied Nils calmly. "I'll give her what's good for her."

Clara made a wry face. "You'll give her the strap, I expect, like old Peter Oleson gave his wife."

"When she needs it," said Nils lazily, locking his hands behind his head and squinting up through the leaves of the cherry tree. "Do you remember the time I squeezed the cherries all over your clean dress, and Aunt Johanna boxed my ears for me? My gracious, weren't you mad! You had both hands full of cherries, and I squeezed 'em and made the juice fly all over you. I liked to have fun with you; you'd get so mad."

"We *did* have fun, didn't we? None of the other kids ever had so much fun. We knew how to play."

Nils dropped his elbows on the table and looked steadily across at her. "I've played with lots of girls since, but I haven't found one who was such good fun."

Clara laughed. The late afternoon sun was shining full in her face, and deep in the back of her eyes there shone something fiery, like the yellow drops of Tokai in the brown glass bottle. "Can you still play, or are you only pretending?"

"I can play better than I used to, and harder."

"Don't you ever work, then?" She had not intended to say it. It slipped out because she was confused enough to say just the wrong thing.

"I work between times." Nils' steady gaze still beat upon her. "Don't you worry about my working, Mrs. Ericson. You're getting like all the rest of them." He reached his brown, warm hand across the table and dropped it on Clara's, which was cold as an icicle. "Last call for play, Mrs. Ericson!" Clara shivered, and suddenly her hands and cheeks grew warm. Her fingers lingered in his a moment, and they looked at each other earnestly. Joe Vavrika had put the mouth of the bottle to his lips and was swallowing the last drops of the Tokai, standing. The sun, just about to sink behind his shop, glistened on the bright glass, on his flushed face and curly yellow hair. "Look," Clara whispered; "that's the way I want to grow old."

VI

On the day of Olaf Ericson's barn-raising, his wife, for once in a way, rose early. Johanna Vavrika had been baking cakes and frying and boiling and spicing meats for a week beforehand, but it was not until the day before the party was to take place that Clara showed any interest in it. Then she was seized with one of her fitful spasms of energy, and took the wagon and little Eric and spent the day on Plum Creek, gathering vines and swamp goldenrod to decorate the barn.

By four o'clock in the afternoon buggies and wagons began to arrive at the big unpainted building in front of Olaf's house. When Nils and his mother came at five, there were more than fifty people in the barn, and a great drove of children. On the ground floor stood six long tables, set with the crockery of seven flourishing Ericson families, lent for the occasion. In the middle of each table was a big yellow pumpkin, hollowed out and filled with woodbine. In one corner of the barn, behind a pile of green-and-white-striped watermelons, was a circle of chairs for the old people; the younger guests sat on bushel measures or barbed-wire spools, and the children tumbled about in the haymow. The box-stalls Clara had converted into booths. The framework was hidden by goldenrod and sheaves of wheat, and the partitions were covered with wild grapevines full of fruit. At one of these Johanna Vavrika watched over her cooked meats, enough to provision an army; and at the next her kitchen girls had ranged the ice-cream freezers, and Clara was already cutting pies and cakes against the hour of serving. At the third stall, little Hilda, in a bright pink lawn dress, dispensed lemonade throughout the afternoon. Olaf, as a public man, had thought it inadvisable to serve beer in his barn; but Joe Vavrika had come over with two demijohns concealed in his buggy, and after his arrival the wagon-shed was much frequented by the men.

"Hasn't Cousin Clara fixed things lovely?" little Hilda whispered, when Nils went up to her stall and asked for lemonade.

Nils leaned against the booth, talking to the excited little girl and watching the people. The barn faced the west, and the sun, pouring in at the big doors, filled the whole interior with a golden light, through which filtered fine particles of dust from the haymow, where the children were romping. There was a great chattering from the stall where Johanna Vavrika exhibited to the admiring women her platters heaped with fried chicken, her roasts of beef, boiled tongues, and baked hams with cloves stuck in the crisp brown fat and garnished with tansy and parsley. The older women, having assured themselves that there were twenty kinds of cake, not counting cookies, and three dozen fat pies, repaired to the corner behind the pile of watermelons, put on their white aprons, and fell to their knitting and fancy-work. They were a fine company of old women, and a Dutch painter would have loved to find them there together, where the sun made bright patches on the floor and sent long, quivering shafts of gold through the dusky shade up among the rafters. There were fat, rosy old women who looked hot in their best black dresses; spare, alert old women with brown, dark-veined hands; and several of almost heroic frame, not less massive than old Mrs. Ericson herself. Few of them wore glasses, and old Mrs. Svendsen, a Danish woman, who was quite bald, wore the only cap among them. Mrs. Oleson, who had twelve big grandchildren, could still show two braids of yellow hair as thick as her own wrists. Among all these grandmothers there were more brown heads than white. They all had a pleased, prosperous air, as if they were more than satisfied with themselves and with life. Nils, leaning against Hilda's lemonade-stand, watched them as they sat chattering in four languages, their fingers never lagging behind their tongues.

"Look at them over there," he whispered, detaining Clara as she passed him. "Aren't they the Old Guard? I've just counted thirty hands. I guess they've wrung many a chicken's neck and warmed many a boy's jacket for him in their time."

In reality he fell into amazement when he thought of the Herculean labors those fifteen pairs of hands had performed: of the cows they had milked, the butter they had made, the gardens they had planted, the children and grandchildren they had tended, the brooms they had worn out, the mountains of food they had cooked. It made him dizzy. Clara Vavrika smiled a hard, enigmatical smile at him and walked rapidly away. Nils' eyes followed her white figure as she went toward the house. He watched her walking alone in the sunlight, looked at her slender, defiant shoulders and her little hard-set head with its coils of blue-black hair. "No," he reflected; "she'd never be like them, not if she lived here a hundred years. She'd only grow more bitter. You can't tame a wild thing; you can only chain it. People aren't all alike. I mustn't lose my nerve." He gave Hilda's pigtail a parting tweak and set out after Clara. "Where to?" he asked, as he came upon her in the kitchen.

"I'm going to the cellar for preserves."

"Let me go with you. I never get a moment alone with you. Why do you keep out of my way?"

Clara laughed. "I don't usually get in anybody's way."

Nils followed her down the stairs and to the far corner of the cellar, where a basement window let in a stream of light. From a swinging shelf Clara selected several glass jars, each labeled in Johanna's careful hand. Nils took up a brown flask. "What's this? It looks good."

"It is. It's some French brandy father gave me when I was married. Would you like some? Have you a corkscrew? I'll get glasses."

When she brought them, Nils took them from her and put them down on the window-sill. "Clara Vavrika, do you remember how crazy I used to be about you?"

Clara shrugged her shoulders. "Boys are always crazy about somebody or other. I dare say some silly has been crazy about Evelina Oleson. You got over it in a hurry."

"Because I didn't come back, you mean? I had to get on, you know, and it was hard sledding at first. Then I heard you'd married Olaf."

"And then you stayed away from a broken heart," Clara laughed.

"And then I began to think about you more than I had since I first went away. I began to wonder if you were really as you had seemed to me when I was a boy. I thought I'd like to see. I've had lots of girls, but no one ever pulled me the same way. The more I thought about you, the more I remembered how it used to be—like hearing a wild tune you can't resist, calling you out at night. It had been a long while since anything had pulled me out of my boots, and I wondered whether anything ever could again." Nils thrust his hands into his coat pockets and squared his shoulders, as his mother sometimes squared hers, as Olaf, in a clumsier manner, squared his. "So I thought I'd come back and see. Of course the family have tried to do me, and I rather thought I'd bring out father's will and make a fuss. But they can have their old land; they've put enough sweat into it." He took the flask and filled the two glasses carefully to the brim. "I've found out what I want from the Ericsons. Drink *skoal*, Clara." He lifted his glass, and Clara took hers with downcast eyes. "Look at me, Clara Vavrika. *Skoal!*"

She raised her burning eyes and answered fiercely: "*Skoal!*"

The barn supper began at six o'clock and lasted for two hilarious hours. Yense Nelson had made a wager that he could eat two whole fried chickens, and he did. Eli Swanson stowed away two whole custard pies, and Nick Hermanson ate a chocolate layer cake to the last crumb. There was even a cooky contest among the children, and one thin, slablike Bohemian boy consumed sixteen and won the prize, a ginger-bread pig which Johanna Vavrika had carefully decorated with red candies and burnt sugar. Fritz Sweiheart, the German carpenter, won in the pickle contest, but he disappeared soon after supper and was not seen for the rest of the evening. Joe Vavrika said that Fritz could have managed the pickles all right, but he had sampled the demijohn in his buggy too often before sitting down to the table.

While the supper was being cleared away the two fiddlers began to tune up for the dance. Clara was to accompany them on her old upright piano, which had been brought down from her father's. By this time Nils had renewed old acquaintances. Since his interview with Clara in the cellar, he had been busy telling all the old women how young they looked, and all the young ones how pretty they were, and assuring the men that they had here the best farm-land in the world. He had made himself so agreeable that old Mrs. Ericson's friends began to come up to her and tell how lucky she was to get her smart son back again, and please to get him to play his flute. Joe Vavrika, who could still play very well when he forgot that he had rheumatism, caught up a fiddle from Johnny Oleson and played a crazy Bohemian dance tune that set the wheels going. When he dropped the bow every one was ready to dance.

Olaf, in a frock-coat and a solemn made-up necktie, led the grand march with his mother. Clara had kept well out of *that* by sticking to the piano. She played the march with a pompous solemnity which greatly amused the prodigal son, who went over and stood behind her.

"Oh, aren't you rubbing it into them, Clara Vavrika? And aren't you lucky to have me here, or all your wit would be thrown away."

"I'm used to being witty for myself. It saves my life."

The fiddles struck up a polka, and Nils convulsed Joe Vavrika by leading out Evelina Oleson, the homely school-teacher. His next partner was a very fat Swedish girl, who, although she was an heiress, had not been asked for the first dance, but had stood against the wall in her tight, high-heeled shoes, nervously fingering a lace handkerchief. She was soon out of breath, so Nils led her, pleased and panting, to her seat, and went over to the piano, from which Clara had been watching his gallantry. "Ask Olena Yenson," she whispered. "She waltzes beautifully."

Olena, too, was rather inconveniently plump, handsome in a smooth, heavy way, with a fine color and good-natured, sleepy eyes. She was redolent of violet sachet powder, and had warm, soft, white hands, but she danced divinely, moving as smoothly as the tide coming in. "There, that's something like," Nils said as he released her. "You'll give me the next waltz, won't you? Now I must go and dance with my little cousin."

Hilda was greatly excited when Nils went up to her stall and held out his arm. Her little eyes sparkled, but she declared that she could not leave her lemonade. Old Mrs. Ericson, who happened along at this moment, said she would attend to that, and Hilda came out, as pink as her pink dress. The dance was a schottische, and in a moment her yellow braids were fairly standing on end. "Bravo!" Nils cried encouragingly. "Where did you learn to dance so nicely?"

"My Cousin Clara taught me," the little girl panted.

Nils found Eric sitting with a group of boys who were too awkward or too shy to dance, and told him that he must dance the next waltz with Hilda.

The boy screwed up his shoulders. "Aw, Nils, I can't dance. My feet are too big; I look silly."

"Don't be thinking about yourself. It doesn't matter how boys look."

Nils had never spoken to him so sharply before, and Eric made haste to scramble out of his corner and brush the straw from his coat.

Clara nodded approvingly. "Good for you, Nils. I've been trying to get hold of him. They dance very nicely together; I sometimes play for them."

"I'm obliged to you for teaching him. There's no reason why he should grow up to be a lout."

"He'll never be that. He's more like you than any of them. Only he hasn't your courage." From her slanting eyes Clara shot forth one of those keen glances, admiring and at the same time challenging, which she seldom bestowed on any one, and which seemed to say, "Yes, I admire you, but I am your equal."

Clara was proving a much better host than Olaf, who, once the supper was over, seemed to feel no interest in anything but the lanterns. He had brought a locomotive headlight from town to light the revels, and he kept skulking about it as if he feared the mere light from it might set his new barn on fire. His wife, on the contrary, was cordial to every one, was animated and even gay. The deep salmon color in her cheeks burned vividly, and her eyes were full of life. She gave the piano over to the fat Swedish heiress, pulled her father away from the corner where he sat gossiping with his cronies, and made him dance a Bohemian dance with her. In his youth Joe had been a famous dancer, and his daughter got him so limbered up that every one sat round and applauded them. The old ladies were particularly delighted, and made them go through the dance again. From their corner where they watched and commented, the old women kept time with their feet and hands, and whenever the fiddles struck up a new air old Mrs. Svendsen's white cap would begin to bob.

Clara was waltzing with little Eric when Nils came up to them, brushed his brother aside, and swung her out among the dancers. "Remember how we used to waltz on rollers at the old skating-rink in town? I suppose people don't do that any more. We used to keep it up for hours. You know, we never did moon around as other boys and girls did. It was dead serious with us from the beginning. When we were most in love with each other, we used to fight. You were always pinching people; your fingers were like little nippers. A regular snapping-turtle, you were. Lord, how you'd like Stockholm! Sit out in the streets in front of cafés and talk all night in summer. Just like a reception—officers and ladies and funny English people. Jolliest people in the world, the Swedes, once you get them going. Always drinking things— champagne and stout mixed, half-and-half; serve it out of big pitchers, and serve plenty. Slow pulse, you know; they can stand a lot. Once they light up, they're glow-worms, I can tell you."

"All the same, you don't really like gay people."

"*I* don't?"

"No; I could see that when you were looking at the old women there this afternoon. They're the kind you really admire, after all; women like your mother. And that's the kind you'll marry."

"Is it, Miss Wisdom? You'll see who I'll marry, and she won't have a domestic virtue to bless herself with. She'll be a snapping-turtle, and she'll be a match for me. All the same, they're a fine bunch of old dames over there. You admire them yourself."

"No, I don't; I detest them."

"You won't, when you look back on them from Stockholm or Budapest. Freedom settles all that. Oh, but you're the real Bohemian Girl, Clara Vavrika!" Nils laughed down at her sullen frown and began mockingly to sing:

> "*Oh, how could a poor gypsy maiden like me*
> *Expect the proud bride of a baron to be?*"

Clara clutched his shoulder. "Hush, Nils; every one is looking at you."

"I don't care. They can't gossip. It's all in the family, as the Ericsons say when they divide up little Hilda's patrimony amongst them. Besides, we'll give them something to talk about when we hit the trail. Lord, it will be a godsend to them! They haven't had anything so interesting to chatter about since the grasshopper year. It'll give them a new lease of life. And Olaf won't lose the Bohemian vote, either. They'll have the laugh on him so that they'll vote two apiece. They'll send him to Congress. They'll never forget his barn party, or us. They'll always remember us as we're dancing together now. We're making a legend. Where's my waltz, boys?" he called as they whirled past the fiddlers.

The musicians grinned, looked at each other, hesitated, and began a new air; and Nils sang with them, as the couples fell from a quick waltz to a long, slow glide:

> "*When other lips and other hearts*
> *Their tale of love shall tell,*
> *In language whose excess imparts*
> *The power they feel so well,*"

The old women applauded vigorously. "What a gay one he is, that Nils!" And old Mrs. Svendsen's cap lurched dreamily from side to side to the flowing measure of the dance.

> "*Of days that have as ha-a-p-py been,*
> *And you'll remember me.*"

VII

The moonlight flooded that great, silent land. The reaped fields lay yellow in it. The straw stacks and poplar windbreaks threw sharp black shadows. The roads were white rivers of dust. The sky was a deep, crystalline blue, and the stars were few and faint. Everything seemed to have succumbed, to have sunk to sleep, under the great, golden, tender, midsummer moon. The splendor of it seemed to transcend human life and human fate. The senses were too feeble to take it in, and every time one looked up at the sky one felt unequal to it, as if one were sitting deaf under the waves of a great river of melody. Near the road, Nils Ericson was lying against a straw stack in Olaf's wheat-field. His own life seemed strange and unfamiliar to him, as if it were something he had read about, or dreamed, and forgotten. He lay very still, watching the white road that ran in front of him, lost itself among the fields, and then, at a distance, reappeared over a little hill. At last, against this white band he saw something moving rapidly, and he got up and walked to the edge of the field. "She is passing the row of poplars now," he thought. He heard the padded beat of hoofs along the dusty road, and as she came into sight he stepped out and waved his arms. Then, for fear of frightening the horse, he drew back and waited. Clara had seen him, and she came up at a walk. Nils took the horse by the bit and stroked his neck.

"What are you doing out so late, Clara Vavrika? I went to the house, but Johanna told me you had gone to your father's."

"Who can stay in the house on a night like this? Aren't you out yourself?"

"Ah, but that's another matter."

Nils turned the horse into the field.

"What are you doing? Where are you taking Norman?"

"Not far, but I want to talk to you to-night; I have something to say to you. I can't talk to you at the house, with Olaf sitting there on the porch, weighing a thousand tons."

Clara laughed. "He won't be sitting there now. He's in bed by this time, and asleep—weighing a thousand tons."

Nils plodded on across the stubble. "Are you really going to spend the rest of your life like this, night after night, summer after summer? Haven't you anything better to do on a night like this than to wear yourself and Norman out tearing across the country to your father's and back? Besides, your father won't live forever, you know. His little place will be shut up or sold, and then you'll have nobody but the Ericsons. You'll have to fasten down the hatches for the winter then."

Clara moved her head restlessly. "Don't talk about that. I try never to think of it. If I lost father I'd lose everything, even my hold over the Ericsons."

"Bah! You'd lose a good deal more than that. You'd lose your race, everything that makes you yourself. You've lost a good deal of it now."

"Of what?"

"Of your love of life, your capacity for delight."

Clara put her hands up to her face. "I haven't, Nils Ericson, I haven't! Say anything to me but that. I won't have it!" she declared vehemently.

Nils led the horse up to a straw stack, and turned to Clara, looking at her intently, as he had looked at her that Sunday afternoon at Vavrika's. "But why do you fight for that so? What good is the power to enjoy, if you never enjoy? Your hands are cold again; what are you afraid of all the time? Ah, you're afraid of losing it; that's what's the matter with you! And you will, Clara Vavrika, you will! When I used to know you—listen; you've caught a wild bird in your hand, haven't you, and felt its heart beat so hard that you were afraid it would shatter its little body to pieces? Well, you used to be just like that, a slender, eager thing with a wild delight inside you. That is how I remembered you. And I come back and find you—a bitter woman. This is a perfect ferret fight here; you live by biting and being bitten. Can't you remember what life used to be? Can't you remember that old delight? I've never forgotten it, or known its like, on land or sea."

He drew the horse under the shadow of the straw stack. Clara felt him take her foot out of the stirrup, and she slid softly down into his arms. He kissed her slowly. He was a deliberate man, but his nerves were steel when he wanted anything. Something flashed out from him like a knife out of a sheath. Clara felt everything slipping away from her; she was flooded by the summer night. He thrust his hand into his pocket, and then held it out at arm's length. "Look," he said. The shadow of the straw stack fell sharp across his wrist, and in the palm of his hand she saw a silver dollar shining. "That's my pile," he muttered; "will you go with me?"

Clara nodded, and dropped her forehead on his shoulder.

Nils took a deep breath. "Will you go with me to-night?"

"Where?" she whispered softly.

"To town, to catch the midnight flyer."

Clara lifted her head and pulled herself together. "Are you crazy, Nils? We couldn't go away like that."

"That's the only way we ever will go. You can't sit on the bank and think about it. You have to plunge. That's the way I've always done, and it's the right way for people like you and me. There's nothing so dangerous as sitting still. You've only got one life, one youth, and you can let it slip through your fingers if you want to; nothing easier. Most people do that. You'd be better off tramping the roads with me than you are here." Nils held back her head and looked into her eyes. "But I'm not that kind of a tramp, Clara. You won't have to take in sewing. I'm with a Norwegian shipping line; came over on business with the New York offices, but now I'm going straight back to Bergen. I expect I've got as much money as the Ericsons. Father sent me a little to get started. They never knew about that. There, I hadn't meant to tell you; I wanted you to come on your own nerve."

Clara looked off across the fields. "It isn't that, Nils, but something seems to hold me. I'm afraid to pull against it. It comes out of the ground, I think."

"I know all about that. One has to tear loose. You're not needed here. Your father will understand; he's made like us. As for Olaf, Johanna will take better care of him than ever you could. It's now or never, Clara Vavrika. My bag's at the station; I smuggled it there yesterday."

Clara clung to him and hid her face against his shoulder. "Not to-night," she whispered. "Sit here and talk to me to-night. I don't want to go anywhere to-night. I may never love you like this again."

Nils laughed through his teeth. "You can't come that on me. That's not my way, Clara Vavrika. Eric's mare is over there behind the stacks, and I'm off on the midnight. It's good-by, or off across the world with me. My carriage won't wait. I've written a letter to Olaf; I'll mail it in town. When he reads it he won't bother us—not if I know him. He'd rather have the land. Besides, I could demand an investigation of his administration of Cousin Henrik's estate, and that would be bad for a public man. You've no clothes, I know; but you can sit up to-night, and we can get everything on the way. Where's your old dash, Clara Vavrika? What's become of your Bohemian blood? I used to think you had courage enough for anything. Where's your nerve—what are you waiting for?"

Clara drew back her head, and he saw the slumberous fire in her eyes. "For you to say one thing, Nils Ericson."

"I never say that thing to any woman, Clara Vavrika." He leaned back, lifted her gently from the ground, and whispered through his teeth: "But I'll never, never let you go, not to any man on earth but me! Do you understand me? Now, wait here."

Clara sank down on a sheaf of wheat and covered her face with her hands. She did not know what she was going to do—whether she would go or stay. The great, silent country seemed to lay a spell upon her. The ground seemed to hold her as if by roots. Her knees were soft under her. She felt as if she could not bear separation from her old sorrows, from her old discontent. They were dear to her, they had kept her alive, they were a part of her. There would be nothing left of her if she were wrenched away from them. Never could she pass beyond that sky-line against which her restlessness had beat so many times. She felt as if her soul had built itself a nest there on that horizon at which she looked every morning and every evening, and it was dear to her, inexpressibly dear. She pressed her fingers against her eyeballs to shut it out. Beside her she heard the tramping of horses in the soft earth. Nils said nothing to her. He put his hands under her arms and lifted her lightly to her saddle. Then he swung himself into his own.

"We shall have to ride fast to catch the midnight train. A last gallop, Clara Vavrika. Forward!"

There was a start, a thud of hoofs along the moonlit road, two dark shadows going over the hill; and then the great, still land stretched untroubled under the azure night. Two shadows had passed.

VIII

A year after the flight of Olaf Ericson's wife, the night train was steaming across the plains of Iowa. The conductor was hurrying through one of the day-coaches, his lantern on his arm, when a lank, fair-haired boy sat up in one of the plush seats and tweaked him by the coat.

"What is the next stop, please, sir?"

"Red Oak, Iowa. But you go through to Chicago, don't you?" He looked down, and noticed that the boy's eyes were red and his face was drawn, as if he were in trouble.

"Yes. But I was wondering whether I could get off at the next place and get a train back to Omaha."

"Well, I suppose you could. Live in Omaha?"

"No. In the western part of the State. How soon do we get to Red Oak?"

"Forty minutes. You'd better make up your mind, so I can tell the baggageman to put your trunk off."

"Oh, never mind about that! I mean, I haven't got any," the boy added, blushing.

"Run away," the conductor thought, as he slammed the coach door behind him.

Eric Ericson crumpled down in his seat and put his brown hand to his forehead. He had been crying, and he had had no supper, and his head was aching violently. "Oh, what shall I do?" he thought, as he looked dully down at his big shoes. "Nils will be ashamed of me; I haven't got any spunk."

Ever since Nils had run away with his brother's wife, life at home had been hard for little Eric. His mother and Olaf both suspected him of complicity. Mrs. Ericson was harsh and fault-finding, constantly wounding the boy's pride; and Olaf was always getting her against him.

Joe Vavrika heard often from his daughter. Clara had always been fond of her father, and happiness made her kinder. She wrote him long accounts of the voyage to Bergen, and of the trip she and Nils took through Bohemia to the little town where her father had grown up and where she herself was born. She visited all her kinsmen there, and sent her father news of his brother, who was a priest; of his sister, who had married a horse-breeder— of their big farm and their many children. These letters Joe always managed to read to little Eric. They contained messages for Eric and Hilda. Clara sent presents, too, which Eric never dared to take home and which poor little Hilda never even saw, though she loved to hear Eric tell about them when they were out getting the eggs together. But Olaf once saw Eric coming out of Vavrika's house,—the old man had never asked the boy to come into his saloon,—and Olaf went straight to his mother and told her. That night Mrs. Ericson came to Eric's room after he was in bed and made a terrible scene. She could be very terrifying when she was really angry. She forbade him ever to speak to Vavrika again, and after that night she would not allow him to go to town alone. So it was a long while before Eric got any more news of his brother. But old Joe suspected what was going on, and he carried Clara's letters about in his pocket. One Sunday he drove out to see a German friend of his, and chanced to catch sight of Eric, sitting by the cattle-pond in the big pasture. They went together into Fritz Oberlies' barn, and read the letters and talked things over. Eric admitted that things were getting hard for him at home. That very night old Joe sat down and laboriously penned a statement of the case to his daughter.

Things got no better for Eric. His mother and Olaf felt that, however closely he was watched, he still, as they said, "heard." Mrs. Ericson could not admit neutrality. She had sent Johanna Vavrika packing back to her brother's, though Olaf would much rather have kept her than Anders' eldest daughter, whom Mrs. Ericson installed in her place. He was not so high-handed as his mother, and he once sulkily told her that she might better have taught her granddaughter to cook before she sent Johanna away. Olaf could have borne a good deal for the sake of prunes spiced in honey, the secret of which Johanna had taken away with her.

At last two letters came to Joe Vavrika: one from Nils, inclosing a postal order for money to pay Eric's passage to Bergen, and one from Clara, saying that Nils had a place for Eric in the offices of his company, that he was to live with them, and that they were only waiting for him to come. He was to leave New York on one of the boats of Nils' own line; the captain was one of their friends, and Eric was to make himself known at once.

Nils' directions were so explicit that a baby could have followed them, Eric felt. And here he was, nearing Red Oak, Iowa, and rocking backward and forward in despair. Never had he loved his brother so much, and never had the big world called to him so hard. But there was a lump in his throat which would not go down. Ever since nightfall he had been tormented by the thought of his mother, alone in that big house that had sent forth so many men. Her unkindness now seemed so little, and her loneliness so great. He remembered everything she had ever done for him: how frightened she had been when he tore his hand in the corn-sheller, and how she wouldn't let Olaf scold him. When Nils went away he didn't leave his mother all alone, or he would never have gone. Eric felt sure of that.

The train whistled. The conductor came in, smiling not unkindly. "Well, young man, what are you going to do? We stop at Red Oak in three minutes."

"Yes, thank you. I'll let you know." The conductor went out, and the boy doubled up with misery. He couldn't let his one chance go like this. He felt for his breast pocket and crackled Nils' kind letter to give him courage. He didn't want Nils to be ashamed of him. The train stopped. Suddenly he remembered his brother's kind, twinkling eyes, that always looked at you as if from far away. The lump in his throat softened. "Ah, but Nils, Nils would *understand*!" he thought. "That's just it about Nils; he always understands."

A lank, pale boy with a canvas telescope stumbled off the train to the Red Oak siding, just as the conductor called, "All aboard!"

The next night Mrs. Ericson was sitting alone in her wooden rocking-chair on the front porch. Little Hilda had been sent to bed and had cried herself to sleep. The old woman's knitting was in her lap, but her hands lay motionless on top of it. For more than an hour she had not moved a muscle. She simply sat, as only the Ericsons and the mountains can sit. The house was dark, and there was no sound but the croaking of the frogs down in the pond of the little pasture.

Eric did not come home by the road, but across the fields, where no one could see him. He set his telescope down softly in the kitchen shed, and slipped noiselessly along the path to the front porch. He sat down on the step without saying anything. Mrs. Ericson made no sign, and the frogs croaked on. At last the boy spoke timidly.

"I've come back, Mother."

"Very well," said Mrs. Ericson.

Eric leaned over and picked up a little stick out of the grass.

"How about the milking?" he faltered.

"That's been done, hours ago."

"Who did you get?"

"Get? I did it myself. I can milk as good as any of you."

Eric slid along the step nearer to her. "Oh, Mother, why did you?" he asked sorrowfully. "Why didn't you get one of Otto's boys?"

"I didn't want anybody to know I was in need of a boy," said Mrs. Ericson bitterly. She looked straight in front of her and her mouth tightened. "I always meant to give you the home farm," she added.

The boy started and slid closer. "Oh, Mother," he faltered, "I don't care about the farm. I came back because I thought you might be needing me, maybe." He hung his head and got no further.

"Very well," said Mrs. Ericson. Her hand went out from her suddenly and rested on his head. Her fingers twined themselves in his soft, pale hair. His tears splashed down on the boards; happiness filled his heart.

McClure's, August 1912

Consequences

Henry Eastman, a lawyer, aged forty, was standing beside the Flatiron building in a driving November rainstorm, signaling frantically for a taxi. It was six-thirty, and everything on wheels was engaged. The streets were in confusion about him, the sky was in turmoil above him, and the Flatiron building, which seemed about to blow down, threw water like a mill-shoot. Suddenly, out of the brutal struggle of men and cars and machines and people tilting at each other with umbrellas, a quiet, well-mannered limousine paused before him, at the curb, and an agreeable, ruddy countenance confronted him through the open window of the car.

"Don't you want me to pick you up, Mr. Eastman? I'm running directly home now."

Eastman recognized Kier Cavenaugh, a young man of pleasure, who lived in the house on Central Park South, where he himself had an apartment.

"Don't I?" he exclaimed, bolting into the car. "I'll risk getting your cushions wet without compunction. I came up in a taxi, but I didn't hold it. Bad economy. I thought I saw your car down on Fourteenth Street about half an hour ago."

The owner of the car smiled. He had a pleasant, round face and round eyes, and a fringe of smooth, yellow hair showed under the rim of his soft felt hat. "With a lot of little broilers fluttering into it? You did. I know some girls who work in the cheap shops down there. I happened to be down-town and I stopped and took a load of them home. I do sometimes. Saves their poor little clothes, you know. Their shoes are never any good."

Eastman looked at his rescuer. "Aren't they notoriously afraid of cars and smooth young men?" he inquired.

Cavenaugh shook his head. "They know which cars are safe and which are chancy. They put each other wise. You have to take a bunch at a time, of course. The Italian girls can never come along; their men shoot. The girls understand, all right; but their fathers don't. One gets to see queer places, sometimes, taking them home."

Eastman laughed drily. "Every time I touch the circle of your acquaintance, Cavenaugh, it's a little wider. You must know New York pretty well by this time."

"Yes, but I'm on my good behavior below Twenty-third Street," the young man replied with simplicity. "My little friends down there would give me a good character. They're wise little girls. They have grand ways with each other, a romantic code of loyalty. You can find a good many of the lost virtues among them."

The car was standing still in a traffic block at Fortieth Street, when Cavenaugh suddenly drew his face away from the window and touched Eastman's arm. "Look, please. You see that hansom with the bony gray horse—driver has a broken hat and red flannel around his throat. Can you see who is inside?"

Eastman peered out. The hansom was just cutting across the line, and the driver was making a great fuss about it, bobbing his head and waving his whip. He jerked his dripping old horse into Fortieth Street and clattered off past the Public Library grounds toward Sixth Avenue. "No, I couldn't see the passenger. Someone you know?"

"Could you see whether there was a passenger?" Cavenaugh asked.

"Why, yes. A man, I think. I saw his elbow on the apron. No driver ever behaves like that unless he has a passenger."

"Yes, I may have been mistaken," Cavenaugh murmured absent-mindedly. Ten minutes or so later, after Cavenaugh's car had turned off Fifth Avenue into Fifty-eighth Street, Eastman exclaimed, "There's your same cabby, and his cart's empty. He's headed for a drink now, I suppose." The driver in the broken hat and the red flannel neck cloth was still brandishing the whip over his old gray. He was coming from the west now, and turned down Sixth Avenue, under the elevated.

Cavenaugh's car stopped at the bachelor apartment house between Sixth and Seventh Avenues where he and Eastman lived, and they went up in the elevator together. They were still talking when the lift stopped at Cavenaugh's floor, and Eastman stepped out with him and walked down the hall, finishing his sentence while Cavenaugh found his latch-key. When he opened the door, a wave of fresh cigarette smoke greeted them. Cavenaugh stopped short and stared into his hallway. "Now how in the devil—!" he exclaimed angrily.

"Someone waiting for you? Oh, no, thanks. I wasn't coming in. I have to work to-night. Thank you, but I couldn't." Eastman nodded and went up the two flights to his own rooms.

Though Eastman did not customarily keep a servant he had this winter a man who had been lent to him by a friend who was abroad. Rollins met him at the door and took his coat and hat.

"Put out my dinner clothes, Rollins, and then get out of here until ten o'clock. I've promised to go to a supper to-night. I shan't be dining. I've had a late tea and I'm going to work until ten. You may put out some kumiss and biscuit for me."

Rollins took himself off, and Eastman settled down at the big table in his sitting-room. He had to read a lot of letters submitted as evidence in a breach of contract case, and before he got very far he found that long paragraphs in some of the letters were written in German. He had a German dictionary at his office, but none here. Rollins had gone, and anyhow, the bookstores would be closed. He remembered having seen a row of dictionaries on the lower shelf of one of Cavenaugh's bookcases. Cavenaugh had a lot of books, though he never read anything but new stuff. Eastman prudently turned down his student's lamp very low—the thing had an evil habit of smoking—and went down two flights to Cavenaugh's door.

The young man himself answered Eastman's ring. He was freshly dressed for the evening, except for a brown smoking jacket, and his yellow hair had been brushed until it shone. He hesitated as he confronted his caller, still holding the door knob, and his round eyes and smooth forehead made their best imitation of a frown. When Eastman began to apologize, Cavenaugh's manner suddenly changed. He caught his arm and jerked him into the narrow hall. "Come in, come in. Right along!" he said excitedly. "Right along," he repeated as he pushed Eastman before him into his sitting-room. "Well I'll—" he stopped short at the door and looked about his own room with an air of complete mystification. The back window was wide open and a strong wind was blowing in. Cavenaugh walked over to the window and stuck out his head, looking up and down the fire escape. When he pulled his head in, he drew down the sash.

"I had a visitor I wanted you to see," he explained with a nervous smile. "At least I thought I had. He must have gone out that way," nodding toward the window.

"Call him back. I only came to borrow a German dictionary, if you have one. Can't stay. Call him back."

Cavenaugh shook his head despondently. "No use. He's beat it. Nowhere in sight."

"He must be active. Has he left something?" Eastman pointed to a very dirty white glove that lay on the floor under the window.

"Yes, that's his." Cavenaugh reached for his tongs, picked up the glove, and tossed it into the grate, where it quickly shriveled on the coals. Eastman felt that he had happened in upon something disagreeable, possibly something shady, and he wanted to get away at once. Cavenaugh stood staring at the fire and seemed stupid and dazed; so he repeated his request rather sternly, "I think I've seen a German dictionary down there among your books. May I have it?"

Cavenaugh blinked at him. "A German dictionary? Oh, possibly! Those were my father's. I scarcely know what there is." He put down the tongs and began to wipe his hands nervously with his handkerchief.

Eastman went over to the bookcase behind the Chesterfield, opened the door, swooped upon the book he wanted and stuck it under his arm. He felt perfectly certain now that something shady had been going on in Cavenaugh's rooms, and he saw no reason why he should come in for any hang-over. "Thanks. I'll send it back to-morrow," he said curtly as he made for the door.

Cavenaugh followed him. "Wait a moment. I wanted you to see him. You did see his glove," glancing at the grate.

Eastman laughed disagreeably. "I saw a glove. That's not evidence. Do your friends often use that means of exit? Somewhat inconvenient."

Cavenaugh gave him a startled glance. "Wouldn't you think so? For an old man, a very rickety old party? The ladders are steep, you know, and rusty." He approached the window again and put it up softly. In a moment he drew his head back with a jerk. He caught Eastman's arm and shoved him toward the window. "Hurry, please. Look! Down there." He pointed to the little patch of paved court four flights down.

The square of pavement was so small and the walls about it were so high, that it was a good deal like looking down a well. Four tall buildings backed upon the same court and made a kind of shaft, with flagstones at the bottom, and at the top a square of dark blue with some stars in it. At the bottom of the shaft Eastman saw a black figure, a man in a caped coat and a tall hat stealing cautiously around, not across the square of pavement, keeping close to the dark wall and avoiding the streak of light that fell on the flagstones from a window in the opposite house. Seen from that height he was of course fore-shortened and probably looked more shambling and decrepit than he was. He picked his way along with exaggerated care and looked like a silly old cat crossing a wet street. When he reached the gate that led into an alley way between two buildings, he felt about for the latch, opened the door a mere crack, and then shot out under the feeble lamp that burned in the brick arch over the gateway. The door closed after him.

"He'll get run in," Eastman remarked curtly, turning away from the window. "That door shouldn't be left unlocked. Any crook could come in. I'll speak to the janitor about it, if you don't mind," he added sarcastically.

"Wish you would." Cavenaugh stood brushing down the front of his jacket, first with his right hand and then with his left. "You saw him, didn't you?"

"Enough of him. Seems eccentric. I have to see a lot of buggy people. They don't take me in any more. But I'm keeping you and I'm in a hurry myself. Good night."

Cavenaugh put out his hand detainingly and started to say something; but Eastman rudely turned his back and went down the hall and out of the door. He had never felt anything shady about Cavenaugh before, and he was sorry he had gone down for the dictionary. In five minutes he was deep in his papers; but in the half hour when he was loafing before he dressed to go out, the young man's curious behavior came into his mind again.

Eastman had merely a neighborly acquaintance with Cavenaugh. He had been to a supper at the young man's rooms once, but he didn't particularly like Cavenaugh's friends; so the next time he was asked, he had another engagement. He liked Cavenaugh himself, if for nothing else than because he was so cheerful and trim and ruddy. A good complexion is always at a premium in New York, especially when it shines reassuringly on a man who does everything in the world to lose it. It encourages fellow mortals as to the inherent vigor of the human organism and the amount of bad treatment it will stand for. "Footprints that perhaps another," etc.

Cavenaugh, he knew, had plenty of money. He was the son of a Pennsylvania preacher, who died soon after he discovered that his ancestral acres were full of petroleum, and Kier had come to New York to burn some of the oil. He was thirty-two and was still at it; spent his life, literally, among the breakers. His motor hit the Park every morning as if it were the first time ever. He took people out to supper every night. He went from restaurant to restaurant, sometimes to half-a-dozen in an evening. The head waiters were his hosts and their cordiality made him happy. They made a life-line for him up Broadway and down Fifth Avenue. Cavenaugh was still fresh and smooth, round and plump, with a lustre to his hair and white teeth and a clear look in his round eyes. He seemed absolutely unwearied and unimpaired; never bored and never carried away.

Eastman always smiled when he met Cavenaugh in the entrance hall, serenely going forth to or returning from gladiatorial combats with joy, or when he saw him rolling smoothly up to the door in his car in the morning after a restful night in one of the remarkable new roadhouses he was always finding. Eastman had seen a good many young men disappear on Cavenaugh's route, and he admired this young man's endurance.

To-night, for the first time, he had got a whiff of something unwholesome about the fellow—bad nerves, bad company, something on hand that he was ashamed of, a visitor old and vicious, who must have had a key to Cavenaugh's apartment, for he was evidently there when Cavenaugh returned at seven o'clock. Probably it was the same man Cavenaugh had seen in the hansom. He must have been able to let himself in, for Cavenaugh kept no man but his chauffeur; or perhaps the janitor had been instructed to let him in. In either case, and whoever he was, it was clear enough that Cavenaugh was ashamed of him and was mixing up in questionable business of some kind.

Eastman sent Cavenaugh's book back by Rollins, and for the next few weeks he had no word with him beyond a casual greeting when they happened to meet in the hall or the elevator. One Sunday morning Cavenaugh telephoned up to him to ask if he could motor out to a roadhouse in Connecticut that afternoon and have supper; but when Eastman found there were to be other guests he declined.

On New Year's eve Eastman dined at the University Club at six o'clock and hurried home before the usual manifestations of insanity had begun in the streets. When Rollins brought his smoking coat, he asked him whether he wouldn't like to get off early.

"Yes, sir. But won't you be dressing, Mr. Eastman?" he inquired.

"Not to-night." Eastman handed him a bill. "Bring some change in the morning. There'll be fees."

Rollins lost no time in putting everything to rights for the night, and Eastman couldn't help wishing that he were in such a hurry to be off somewhere himself. When he heard the hall door close softly, he wondered if there were any place, after all, that he wanted to go. From his window he looked down at the long lines of motors and taxis waiting for a signal to cross Broadway. He thought of some of their probable destinations and decided that none of those places pulled him very hard. The night was warm and wet, the air was drizzly. Vapor hung in clouds about the *Times* Building, half hid the top of it, and made a luminous haze along Broadway. While he was looking down at the army of wet, black carriage-tops and their reflected headlights and tail-lights, Eastman heard a ring at his door. He deliberated. If it were a caller, the hall porter would have telephoned up. It must be the janitor. When he opened the door, there stood a rosy young man in a tuxedo, without a coat or hat.

"Pardon. Should I have telephoned? I half thought you wouldn't be in."

Eastman laughed. "Come in, Cavenaugh. You weren't sure whether you wanted company or not, eh, and you were trying to let chance decide it? That was exactly my state of mind. Let's accept the verdict." When they emerged from the narrow hall into his sitting-room, he pointed out a seat by the fire to his guest. He brought a tray of decanters and soda bottles and placed it on his writing table.

Cavenaugh hesitated, standing by the fire. "Sure you weren't starting for somewhere?"

"Do I look it? No, I was just making up my mind to stick it out alone when you rang. Have one?" he picked up a tall tumbler.

"Yes, thank you. I always do."

Eastman chuckled. "Lucky boy! So will I. I had a very early dinner. New York is the most arid place on holidays," he continued as he rattled the ice in the glasses. "When one gets too old to hit the rapids down there, and tired of gobbling food to heathenish dance music, there is absolutely no place where you can get a chop and some milk toast in peace, unless you have strong ties of blood brotherhood on upper Fifth Avenue. But you, why aren't you starting for somewhere?"

The young man sipped his soda and shook his head as he replied:

"Oh, I couldn't get a chop, either. I know only flashy people, of course." He looked up at his host with such a grave and candid expression that Eastman decided there couldn't be anything very crooked about the fellow. His smooth cheeks were positively cherubic.

"Well, what's the matter with them? Aren't they flashing to-night?"

"Only the very new ones seem to flash on New Year's eve. The older ones fade away. Maybe they are hunting a chop, too."

"Well"—Eastman sat down—"holidays do dash one. I was just about to write a letter to a pair of maiden aunts in my old home town, up-state; old coasting hill, snow-covered pines, lights in the church windows. That's what you've saved me from."

Cavenaugh shook himself. "Oh, I'm sure that wouldn't have been good for you. Pardon me," he rose and took a photograph from the bookcase, a handsome man in shooting clothes. "Dudley, isn't it? Did you know him well?"

"Yes. An old friend. Terrible thing, wasn't it? I haven't got over the jolt yet."

"His suicide? Yes, terrible! Did you know his wife?"

"Slightly. Well enough to admire her very much. She must be terribly broken up. I wonder Dudley didn't think of that."

Cavenaugh replaced the photograph carefully, lit a cigarette, and standing before the fire began to smoke. "Would you mind telling me about him? I never met him, but of course I'd read a lot about him, and I can't help feeling interested. It was a queer thing."

Eastman took out his cigar case and leaned back in his deep chair. "In the days when I knew him best he hadn't any story, like the happy nations. Everything was properly arranged for him before he was born. He came into the world happy, healthy, clever, straight, with the right sort of connections and the right kind of fortune, neither too large nor too small. He helped to make the world an agreeable place to live in until he was twenty-six. Then he married as he should have married. His wife was a Californian, educated abroad. Beautiful. You have seen her picture?"

Cavenaugh nodded. "Oh, many of them."

"She was interesting, too. Though she was distinctly a person of the world, she had retained something, just enough of the large Western manner. She had the habit of authority, of calling out a special train if she needed it, of using all our ingenious mechanical contrivances lightly and easily, without over-rating them. She and Dudley knew how to live better than most people. Their house was the most charming one I have ever known in New York. You felt freedom there, and a zest of life, and safety—absolute sanctuary—from everything sordid or petty. A whole society like that would justify the creation of man and would make our planet shine with a soft, peculiar radiance among the constellations. You think I'm putting it on thick?"

The young man sighed gently. "Oh, no! One has always felt there must be people like that. I've never known any."

"They had two children, beautiful ones. After they had been married for eight years, Rosina met this Spaniard. He must have amounted to something. She wasn't a flighty woman. She came home and told Dudley how matters stood. He persuaded her to stay at home for six months and try to pull up. They were both fair-minded people, and I'm as sure as if I were the Almighty, that she did try. But at the end of the time, Rosina went quietly off to Spain, and Dudley went to hunt in the Canadian Rockies. I met his party out there. I didn't know his wife had left him and talked about her a good deal. I noticed that he never drank anything, and his light used to shine through the log chinks of his room until all hours, even after a hard day's hunting. When I got back to New York, rumors were creeping about. Dudley did not come back. He bought a ranch in Wyoming, built a big log house and kept splendid dogs and horses. One of his sisters went out to keep house for him, and the children were there when they were not in school. He had a great many visitors, and everyone who came back talked about how well Dudley kept things going.

"He put in two years out there. Then, last month, he had to come back on business. A trust fund had to be settled up, and he was administrator. I saw him at the club; same light, quick step, same gracious handshake. He was getting gray, and there was something softer in his manner; but he had a fine red tan on his face and said he found it delightful to be here in the season when everything is going hard. The Madison Avenue house had been closed since Rosina left it. He went there to get some things his sister wanted. That, of course, was the mistake. He went alone, in the afternoon, and didn't go out for dinner—found some sherry and tins of biscuit in the sideboard. He shot himself sometime that night. There were pistols in his smoking-room. They found burnt out candles beside him in the morning. The gas and electricity were shut off. I suppose there, in his own house, among his own things, it was too much for him. He left no letters."

Cavenaugh blinked and brushed the lapel of his coat. "I suppose," he said slowly, "that every suicide is logical and reasonable, if one knew all the facts."

Eastman roused himself. "No, I don't think so. I've known too many fellows who went off like that—more than I deserve, I think—and some of them were absolutely inexplicable. I can understand Dudley; but I can't see why healthy bachelors, with money enough, like ourselves, need such a device. It reminds me of what Dr. Johnson said, that the most discouraging thing about life is the number of fads and hobbies and fake religions it takes to put people through a few years of it."

"Dr. Johnson? The specialist? Oh, the old fellow!" said Cavenaugh imperturbably. "Yes, that's interesting. Still, I fancy if one knew the facts— Did you know about Wyatt?"

"I don't think so."

"You wouldn't, probably. He was just a fellow about town who spent money. He wasn't one of the *forestieri*, though. Had connections here and owned a fine old place over on Staten Island. He went in for botany, and had been all over, hunting things; rusts, I believe. He had a yacht and used to take a gay crowd down about the South Seas, botanizing. He really did botanize, I believe. I never knew such a spender—only not flashy. He helped a lot of fellows and he was awfully good to girls, the kind who come down here to get a little fun, who don't like to work and still aren't really tough, the kind you see talking hard for their dinner. Nobody knows what becomes of them, or what they get out of it, and there are hundreds of new ones every year. He helped dozens of 'em; it was he who got me curious about the little shop girls. Well, one afternoon when his tea was brought, he took prussic acid instead. He didn't leave any letters, either; people of any taste don't. They wouldn't leave any material reminder if they could help it. His lawyers found that he had just $314.72 above his debts when he died. He had planned to spend all his money, and then take his tea; he had worked it out carefully."

Eastman reached for his pipe and pushed his chair away from the fire. "That looks like a considered case, but I don't think philosophical suicides like that are common. I think they usually come from stress of feeling and are really, as the newspapers call them, desperate acts; done without a motive. You remember when Anna Karenina was under the wheels, she kept saying, 'Why am I here?'"

Cavenaugh rubbed his upper lip with his pink finger and made an effort to wrinkle his brows. "May I, please?" reaching for the whiskey. "But have you," he asked, blinking as the soda flew at him, "have you ever known, yourself, cases that were really inexplicable?"

"A few too many. I was in Washington just before Captain Jack Purden was married and I saw a good deal of him. Popular army man, fine record in the Philippines, married a charming girl with lots of money; mutual devotion. It was the gayest wedding of the winter, and they started for Japan. They stopped in San Francisco for a week and missed their boat because, as the bride wrote back to Washington, they were too happy to move. They took the next boat, were both good sailors, had exceptional weather. After they had been out for two weeks, Jack got up from his deck chair one afternoon, yawned, put down his book, and stood before his wife. 'Stop reading for a moment and look at me.' She laughed and asked him why. 'Because you happen to be good to look at.' He nodded to her, went back to the stern and was never seen again. Must have gone down to the lower deck and slipped overboard, behind the machinery. It was the luncheon hour, not many people about; steamer cutting through a soft green sea. That's one of the most baffling cases I know. His friends raked up his past, and it was as trim as a cottage garden. If he'd so much as dropped an ink spot on his fatigue uniform, they'd have found it. He wasn't emotional or moody; wasn't, indeed, very interesting; simply a good soldier, fond of all the pompous little formalities that make up a military man's life. What do you make of that, my boy?"

Cavenaugh stroked his chin. "It's very puzzling, I admit. Still, if one knew everything— —"

"But we do know everything. His friends wanted to find something to help them out, to help the girl out, to help the case of the human creature."

"Oh, I don't mean things that people could unearth," said Cavenaugh uneasily. "But possibly there were things that couldn't be found out."

Eastman shrugged his shoulders. "It's my experience that when there are 'things' as you call them, they're very apt to be found. There is no such thing as a secret. To make any move at all one has to employ human agencies, employ at least one human agent. Even when the pirates killed the men who buried their gold for them, the bones told the story."

Cavenaugh rubbed his hands together and smiled his sunny smile.

"I like that idea. It's reassuring. If we can have no secrets, it means that we can't, after all, go so far afield as we might," he hesitated, "yes, as we might."

Eastman looked at him sourly. "Cavenaugh, when you've practised law in New York for twelve years, you find that people can't go far in any direction, except—" He thrust his forefinger sharply at the floor. "Even in that direction, few people can do anything out of the ordinary. Our range is limited. Skip a few baths, and we become personally objectionable. The slightest carelessness can rot a man's integrity or give him ptomaine poisoning. We keep up only by incessant cleansing operations, of mind and body. What we call character, is held together by all sorts of tacks and strings and glue."

Cavenaugh looked startled. "Come now, it's not so bad as that, is it? I've always thought that a serious man, like you, must know a lot of Launcelots." When Eastman only laughed, the younger man squirmed about in his chair. He spoke again hastily, as if he were embarrassed. "Your military friend may have had personal experiences, however, that his friends couldn't possibly get a line on. He may accidentally have come to a place where he saw himself in too unpleasant a light. I believe people can be chilled by a draft from outside, somewhere."

"Outside?" Eastman echoed. "Ah, you mean the far outside! Ghosts, delusions, eh?"

Cavenaugh winced. "That's putting it strong. Why not say tips from the outside? Delusions belong to a diseased mind, don't they? There are some of us who have no minds to speak of, who yet have had experiences. I've had a little something in that line myself and I don't look it, do I?"

Eastman looked at the bland countenance turned toward him. "Not exactly. What's your delusion?"

"It's not a delusion. It's a haunt."

The lawyer chuckled. "Soul of a lost Casino girl?"

"No; an old gentleman. A most unattractive old gentleman, who follows me about."

"Does he want money?"

Cavenaugh sat up straight. "No. I wish to God he wanted anything— but the pleasure of my society! I'd let him clean me out to be rid of him. He's a real article. You saw him yourself that night when you came to my rooms to borrow a dictionary, and he went down the fire-escape. You saw him down in the court."

"Well, I saw somebody down in the court, but I'm too cautious to take it for granted that I saw what you saw. Why, anyhow, should I see your haunt? If it was your friend I saw, he impressed me disagreeably. How did you pick him up?"

Cavenaugh looked gloomy. "That was queer, too. Charley Burke and I had motored out to Long Beach, about a year ago, sometime in October, I think. We had supper and stayed until late. When we were coming home, my car broke down. We had a lot of girls along who had to get back for morning rehearsals and things; so I sent them all into town in Charley's car, and he was to send a man back to tow me home. I was driving myself, and didn't want to leave my machine. We had not taken a direct road back; so I was stuck in a lonesome, woody place, no houses about. I got chilly and made a fire, and was putting in the time comfortably enough, when this old party steps up. He was in shabby evening clothes and a top hat, and had on his usual white gloves. How he got there, at three o'clock in the morning, miles from any town or railway, I'll leave it to you to figure out. *He* surely had no car. When I saw him coming up to the fire, I disliked him. He had a silly, apologetic walk. His teeth were chattering, and I asked him to sit down. He got down like a clothes-horse folding up. I offered him a cigarette, and when he took off his gloves I couldn't help noticing how knotted and spotty his hands were. He was asthmatic, and took his breath with a wheeze. 'Haven't you got anything—refreshing in there?' he asked, nodding at the car. When I told him I hadn't, he sighed. 'Ah, you young fellows are greedy. You drink it all up. You drink it all up, all up—up!' he kept chewing it over."

Cavenaugh paused and looked embarrassed again. "The thing that was most unpleasant is difficult to explain. The old man sat there by the fire and leered at me with a silly sort of admiration that was—well, more than humiliating. 'Gay boy, gay dog!' he would mutter, and when he grinned he showed his teeth, worn and yellow—shells. I remembered that it was better to talk casually to insane people; so I remarked carelessly that I had been out with a party and got stuck.

"'Oh yes, I remember,' he said, 'Flora and Lottie and Maybelle and Marcelline, and poor Kate.'

"He had named them correctly; so I began to think I had been hitting the bright waters too hard.

"Things I drank never had seemed to make me woody; but you can never tell when trouble is going to hit you. I pulled my hat down and tried to look as uncommunicative as possible; but he kept croaking on from time to time, like this: 'Poor Kate! Splendid arms, but dope got her. She took up with Eastern religions after she had her hair dyed. Got to going to a Swami's joint, and smoking opium. Temple of the Lotus, it was called, and the police raided it.'

"This was nonsense, of course; the young woman was in the pink of condition. I let him rave, but I decided that if something didn't come out for me pretty soon, I'd foot it across Long Island. There wasn't room enough for the two of us. I got up and took another try at my car. He hopped right after me.

"'Good car,' he wheezed, 'better than the little Ford.'

"I'd had a Ford before, but so has everybody; that was a safe guess.

"'Still,' he went on, 'that run in from Huntington Bay in the rain wasn't bad. Arrested for speeding, he-he.'

"It was true I had made such a run, under rather unusual circumstances, and had been arrested. When at last I heard my life-boat snorting up the road, my visitor got up, sighed, and stepped back into the shadow of the trees. I didn't wait to see what became of him, you may believe. That was visitation number one. What do you think of it?"

Cavenaugh looked at his host defiantly. Eastman smiled.

"I think you'd better change your mode of life, Cavenaugh. Had many returns?" he inquired.

"Too many, by far." The young man took a turn about the room and came back to the fire. Standing by the mantel he lit another cigarette before going on with his story:

"The second visitation happened in the street, early in the evening, about eight o'clock. I was held up in a traffic block before the Plaza. My chauffeur was driving. Old Nibbs steps up out of the crowd, opens the door of my car, gets in and sits down beside me. He had on wilted evening clothes, same as before, and there was some sort of heavy scent about him. Such an unpleasant old party! A thorough-going rotter; you knew it at once. This time he wasn't talkative, as he had been when I first saw him. He leaned back in the car as if he owned it, crossed his hands on his stick and looked out at the crowd—sort of hungrily.

"I own I really felt a loathing compassion for him. We got down the avenue slowly. I kept looking out at the mounted police. But what could I do? Have him pulled? I was afraid to. I was awfully afraid of getting him into the papers.

"'I'm going to the New Astor,' I said at last. 'Can I take you anywhere?'

"'No, thank you,' says he. 'I get out when you do. I'm due on West 44th. I'm dining to-night with Marcelline—all that is left of her!'

"He put his hand to his hat brim with a grewsome salute. Such a scandalous, foolish old face as he had! When we pulled up at the Astor, I stuck my hand in my pocket and asked him if he'd like a little loan.

"'No, thank you, but'—he leaned over and whispered, ugh!—'but save a little, save a little. Forty years from now—a little—comes in handy. Save a little.'

"His eyes fairly glittered as he made his remark. I jumped out. I'd have jumped into the North River. When he tripped off, I asked my chauffeur if he'd noticed the man who got into the car with me. He said he knew someone was with me, but he hadn't noticed just when he got in. Want to hear any more?"

Cavenaugh dropped into his chair again. His plump cheeks were a trifle more flushed than usual, but he was perfectly calm. Eastman felt that the young man believed what he was telling him.

"Of course I do. It's very interesting. I don't see quite where you are coming out though."

Cavenaugh sniffed. "No more do I. I really feel that I've been put upon. I haven't deserved it any more than any other fellow of my kind. Doesn't it impress you disagreeably?"

"Well, rather so. Has anyone else seen your friend?"

"You saw him."

"We won't count that. As I said, there's no certainty that you and I saw the same person in the court that night. Has anyone else had a look in?"

"People sense him rather than see him. He usually crops up when I'm alone or in a crowd on the street. He never approaches me when I'm with people I know, though I've seen him hanging about the doors of theatres when I come out with a party; loafing around the stage exit, under a wall; or across the street, in a doorway. To be frank, I'm not anxious to introduce him. The third time, it was I who came upon him. In November my driver, Harry, had a sudden attack of appendicitis. I took him to the Presbyterian Hospital in the car, early in the evening. When I came home, I found the old villain in my rooms. I offered him a drink, and he sat down. It was the first time I had seen him in a steady light, with his hat off.

"His face is lined like a railway map, and as to color—Lord, what a liver! His scalp grows tight to his skull, and his hair is dyed until it's perfectly dead, like a piece of black cloth."

Cavenaugh ran his fingers through his own neatly trimmed thatch, and seemed to forget where he was for a moment.

"I had a twin brother, Brian, who died when we were sixteen. I have a photograph of him on my wall, an enlargement from a kodak of him, doing a high jump, rather good thing, full of action. It seemed to annoy the old gentleman. He kept looking at it and lifting his eyebrows, and finally he got up, tip-toed across the room, and turned the picture to the wall.

"'Poor Brian! Fine fellow, but died young,' says he.

"Next morning, there was the picture, still reversed."

"Did he stay long?" Eastman asked interestedly.

"Half an hour, by the clock."

"Did he talk?"

"Well, he rambled."

"What about?"

Cavenaugh rubbed his pale eyebrows before answering.

"About things that an old man ought to want to forget. His conversation is highly objectionable. Of course he knows me like a book; everything I've ever done or thought. But when he recalls them, he throws a bad light on them, somehow. Things that weren't much off color, look rotten. He doesn't leave one a shred of self-respect, he really doesn't. That's the amount of it." The young man whipped out his handkerchief and wiped his face.

"You mean he really talks about things that none of your friends know?"

"Oh, dear, yes! Recalls things that happened in school. Anything disagreeable. Funny thing, he always turns Brian's picture to the wall."

"Does he come often?"

"Yes, oftener, now. Of course I don't know how he gets in down-stairs. The hall boys never see him. But he has a key to my door. I don't know how he got it, but I can hear him turn it in the lock."

"Why don't you keep your driver with you, or telephone for me to come down?"

"He'd only grin and go down the fire escape as he did before. He's often done it when Harry's come in suddenly. Everybody has to be alone sometimes, you know. Besides, I don't want anybody to see him. He has me there."

"But why not? Why do you feel responsible for him?"

Cavenaugh smiled wearily. "That's rather the point, isn't it? Why do I? But I absolutely do. That identifies him, more than his knowing all about my life and my affairs."

Eastman looked at Cavenaugh thoughtfully. "Well, I should advise you to go in for something altogether different and new, and go in for it hard; business, engineering, metallurgy, something this old fellow wouldn't be interested in. See if you can make him remember logarithms."

Cavenaugh sighed. "No, he has me there, too. People never really change; they go on being themselves. But I would never make much trouble. Why can't they let me alone, damn it! I'd never hurt anybody, except, perhaps——"

"Except your old gentleman, eh?" Eastman laughed. "Seriously, Cavenaugh, if you want to shake him, I think a year on a ranch would do it. He would never be coaxed far from his favorite haunts. He would dread Montana."

Cavenaugh pursed up his lips. "So do I!"

"Oh, you think you do. Try it, and you'll find out. A gun and a horse beats all this sort of thing. Besides losing your haunt, you'd be putting ten years in the bank for yourself. I know a good ranch where they take people, if you want to try it."

"Thank you. I'll consider. Do you think I'm batty?"

"No, but I think you've been doing one sort of thing too long. You need big horizons. Get out of this."

Cavenaugh smiled meekly. He rose lazily and yawned behind his hand. "It's late, and I've taken your whole evening." He strolled over to the window and looked out. "Queer place, New York; rough on the little fellows. Don't you feel sorry for them, the girls especially? I do. What a fight they put up for a little fun! Why, even that old goat is sorry for them, the only decent thing he kept."

Eastman followed him to the door and stood in the hall, while Cavenaugh waited for the elevator. When the car came up Cavenaugh extended his pink, warm hand. "Good night."

The cage sank and his rosy countenance disappeared, his round-eyed smile being the last thing to go.

Weeks passed before Eastman saw Cavenaugh again. One morning, just as he was starting for Washington to argue a case before the Supreme Court, Cavenaugh telephoned him at his office to ask him about the Montana ranch he had recommended; said he meant to take his advice and go out there for the spring and summer.

When Eastman got back from Washington, he saw dusty trunks, just up from the trunk room, before Cavenaugh's door. Next morning, when he stopped to see what the young man was about, he found Cavenaugh in his shirt sleeves, packing.

"I'm really going; off to-morrow night. You didn't think it of me, did you?" he asked gaily.

"Oh, I've always had hopes of you!" Eastman declared. "But you are in a hurry, it seems to me."

"Yes, I am in a hurry." Cavenaugh shot a pair of leggings into one of the open trunks. "I telegraphed your ranch people, used your name, and they said it would be all right. By the way, some of my crowd are giving a little dinner for me at Rector's to-night. Couldn't you be persuaded, as it's a farewell occasion?" Cavenaugh looked at him hopefully.

Eastman laughed and shook his head. "Sorry, Cavenaugh, but that's too gay a world for me. I've got too much work lined up before me. I wish I had time to stop and look at your guns, though. You seem to know something about guns. You've more than you'll need, but nobody can have too many good ones." He put down one of the revolvers regretfully. "I'll drop in to see you in the morning, if you're up."

"I shall be up, all right. I've warned my crowd that I'll cut away before midnight."

"You won't, though," Eastman called back over his shoulder as he hurried down-stairs.

The next morning, while Eastman was dressing, Rollins came in greatly excited.

"I'm a little late, sir. I was stopped by Harry, Mr. Cavenaugh's driver. Mr. Cavenaugh shot himself last night, sir."

Eastman dropped his vest and sat down on his shoe-box. "You're drunk, Rollins," he shouted. "He's going away to-day!"

"Yes, sir. Harry found him this morning. Ah, he's quite dead, sir. Harry's telephoned for the coroner. Harry don't know what to do with the ticket."

Eastman pulled on his coat and ran down the stairway. Cavenaugh's trunks were strapped and piled before the door. Harry was walking up and down the hall with a long green railroad ticket in his hand and a look of complete stupidity on his face.

"What shall I do about this ticket, Mr. Eastman?" he whispered. "And what about his trunks? He had me tell the transfer people to come early. They may be here any minute. Yes, sir. I brought him home in the car last night, before twelve, as cheerful as could be."

"Be quiet, Harry. Where is he?"

"In his bed, sir."

Eastman went into Cavenaugh's sleeping-room. When he came back to the sitting-room, he looked over the writing table; railway folders, time-tables, receipted bills, nothing else. He looked up for the photograph of Cavenaugh's twin brother. There it was, turned to the wall. Eastman took it down and looked at it; a boy in track clothes, half lying in the air, going over the string shoulders first, above the heads of a crowd of lads who were running and cheering. The face was somewhat blurred by the motion and the bright sunlight. Eastman put the picture back, as he found it. Had Cavenaugh entertained his visitor last night, and had the old man been more convincing than usual? "Well, at any rate, he's seen to it that the old man can't establish identity. What a soft lot they are, fellows like poor Cavenaugh!" Eastman thought of his office as a delightful place.

McClure's, November 1915

The Bookkeeper's Wife

Nobody but the janitor was stirring about the offices of the Remsen Paper Company, and still Percy Bixby sat at his desk, crouched on his high stool and staring out at the tops of the tall buildings flushed with the winter sunset, at the hundreds of windows, so many rectangles of white electric light, flashing against the broad waves of violet that ebbed across the sky. His ledgers were all in their places, his desk was in order, his office coat on its peg, and yet Percy's smooth, thin face wore the look of anxiety and strain which usually meant that he was behind in his work. He was trying to persuade himself to accept a loan from the company without the company's knowledge. As a matter of fact, he had already accepted it. His books were fixed, the money, in a black-leather bill-book, was already inside his waistcoat pocket.

He had still time to change his mind, to rectify the false figures in his ledger, and to tell Stella Brown that they couldn't possibly get married next month. There he always halted in his reasoning, and went back to the beginning.

The Remsen Paper Company was a very wealthy concern, with easy, old-fashioned working methods. They did a longtime credit business with safe customers, who never thought of paying up very close on their large indebtedness. From the payments on these large accounts Percy had taken a hundred dollars here and two hundred there until he had made up the thousand he needed. So long as he stayed by the books himself and attended to the mail-orders he couldn't possibly be found out. He could move these little shortages about from account to account indefinitely. He could have all the time he needed to pay back the deficit, and more time than he needed.

Although he was so far along in one course of action, his mind still clung resolutely to the other. He did not believe he was going to do it. He was the least of a sharper in the world. Being scrupulously honest even in the most trifling matters was a pleasure to him. He was the sort of young man that Socialists hate more than they hate capitalists. He loved his desk, he loved his books, which had no handwriting in them but his own. He never thought of resenting the fact that he had written away in those books the good red years between twenty-one and twenty-seven. He would have hated to let any one else put so much as a pen-scratch in them. He liked all the boys about the office; his desk, worn smooth by the sleeves of his alpaca coat; his rulers and inks and pens and calendars. He had a great pride in working economics, and he always got so far ahead when supplies were distributed that he had drawers full of pencils and pens and rubber bands against a rainy day.

Percy liked regularity: to get his work done on time, to have his half-day off every Saturday, to go to the theater Saturday night, to buy a new necktie twice a month, to appear in a new straw hat on the right day in May, and to know what was going on in New York. He read the morning and evening papers coming and going on the elevated, and preferred journals of approximate reliability. He got excited about ballgames and elections and business failures, was not above an interest in murders and divorce scandals, and he checked the news off as neatly as he checked his mail-orders. In short, Percy Bixby was like the model pupil who is satisfied with his lessons and his teachers and his holidays, and who would gladly go to school all his life. He had never wanted anything outside his routine until he wanted Stella Brown to marry him, and that had upset everything.

It wasn't, he told himself for the hundredth time, that she was extravagant. Not a bit of it. She was like all girls. Moreover, she made good money, and why should she marry unless she could better herself? The trouble was that he had lied to her about his salary. There were a lot of fellows rushing Mrs. Brown's five daughters, and they all seemed to have fixed on Stella as first choice and this or that one of the sisters as second. Mrs. Brown thought it proper to drop an occasional hint in the presence of these young men to the effect that she expected Stella to "do well." It went without saying that hair and complexion like Stella's could scarcely be expected to do poorly. Most of the boys who went to the house and took the girls out in a bunch to dances and movies seemed to realize this. They merely wanted a whirl with Stella before they settled down to one of her sisters. It was tacitly understood that she came too high for them. Percy had sensed all this through those slumbering instincts which awake in us all to befriend us in love or in danger.

But there was one of his rivals, he knew, who was a man to be reckoned with. Charley Greengay was a young salesman who wore tailor-made clothes and spotted waistcoats, and had a necktie for every day in the month. His air was that of a young man who is out for things that come high and who is going to get them. Mrs. Brown was ever and again dropping a word before Percy about how the girl that took Charley would have her flat furnished by the best furniture people, and her china-closet stocked with the best ware, and would have nothing to worry about but nicks and scratches. It was because he felt himself pitted against this pulling power of Greengay's that Percy had brazenly lied to Mrs. Brown, and told her that his salary had been raised to fifty a week, and that now he wanted to get married.

When he threw out this challenge to Mother Brown, Percy was getting thirty-five dollars a week, and he knew well enough that there were several hundred thousand young men in New York who would do his work as well as he did for thirty.

These were the factors in Percy's present situation. He went over them again and again as he sat stooping on his tall stool. He had quite lost track of time when he heard the janitor call good night to the watchman. Without thinking what he was doing, he slid into his overcoat, caught his hat, and rushed out to the elevator, which was waiting for the janitor. The moment the car dropped, it occurred to him that the thing was decided without his having made up his mind at all. The familiar floors passed him, ten, nine, eight, seven. By the time he reached the fifth, there was no possibility of going back; the click of the drop-lever seemed to settle that. The money was in his pocket. Now, he told himself as he hurried out into the exciting clamor of the street, he was not going to worry about it any more.

When Percy reached the Browns' flat on 123d Street that evening he felt just the slightest chill in Stella's greeting. He could make that all right, he told himself, as he kissed her lightly in the dark three-by-four entrance-hall. Percy's courting had been prosecuted mainly in the Bronx or in winged pursuit of a Broadway car. When he entered the crowded sitting-room he greeted Mrs. Brown respectfully and the four girls playfully. They were all piled on one couch, reading the continued story in the evening paper, and they didn't think it necessary to assume more formal attitudes for Percy. They looked up over the smeary pink sheets of paper, and handed him, as Percy said, the same old jolly:

"Hullo, Perc'! Come to see me, ain't you? So flattered!"

"Any sweet goods on you, Perc'? Anything doing in the bong-bong line to-night?"

"Look at his new neckwear! Say, Perc', remember me. That tie would go lovely with my new tailored waist."

"Quit your kiddin', girls!" called Mrs. Brown, who was drying shirt-waists on the dining-room radiator. "And, Percy, mind the rugs when you're steppin' round among them gum-drops."

Percy fired his last shot at the recumbent figures, and followed Stella into the dining-room, where the table and two large easy-chairs formed, in Mrs. Brown's estimation, a proper background for a serious suitor.

"I say, Stell'," he began as he walked about the table with his hands in his pockets, "seems to me we ought to begin buying our stuff." She brightened perceptibly. "Ah," Percy thought, "so that *was* the trouble!" "To-morrow's Saturday; why can't we make an afternoon of it?" he went on cheerfully. "Shop till we're tired, then go to Houtin's for dinner, and end up at the theater."

As they bent over the lists she had made of things needed, Percy glanced at her face. She was very much out of her sisters' class and out of his, and he kept congratulating himself on his nerve. He was going in for something much too handsome and expensive and distinguished for him, he felt, and it took courage to be a plunger. To begin with, Stella was the sort of girl who had to be well dressed. She had pale primrose hair, with bluish tones in it, very soft and fine, so that it lay smooth however she dressed it, and pale-blue eyes, with blond eyebrows and long, dark lashes. She would have been a little too remote and languid even for the fastidious Percy had it not been for her hard, practical mouth, with lips that always kept their pink even when the rest of her face was pale. Her employers, who at first might be struck by her indifference, understood that anybody with that sort of mouth would get through the work.

After the shopping-lists had been gone over, Percy took up the question of the honeymoon. Stella said she had been thinking of Atlantic City. Percy met her with firmness. Whatever happened, he couldn't leave his books now.

"I want to do my traveling right here on Forty-second Street, with a high-price show every night," he declared. He made out an itinerary, punctuated by theaters and restaurants, which Stella consented to accept as a substitute for Atlantic City.

"They give your fellows a week off when they're married, don't they?" she asked.

"Yes, but I'll want to drop into the office every morning to look after my mail. That's only businesslike."

"I'd like to have you treated as well as the others, though." Stella turned the rings about on her pale hand and looked at her polished finger-tips.

"I'll look out for that. What do you say to a little walk, Stell'?" Percy put the question coaxingly. When Stella was pleased with him she went to walk with him, since that was the only way in which Percy could ever see her alone. When she was displeased, she said she was too tired to go out. To-night she smiled at him incredulously, and went to put on her hat and gray fur piece.

Once they were outside, Percy turned into a shadowy side street that was only partly built up, a dreary waste of derricks and foundation holes, but comparatively solitary. Stella liked Percy's steady, sympathetic silences; she was not a chatterbox herself. She often wondered why she was going to marry Bixby instead of Charley Greengay. She knew that Charley would go further in the world. Indeed, she had often coolly told herself that Percy would never go very far. But, as she admitted with a shrug, she was "weak to Percy." In the capable New York stenographer, who estimated values coldly and got the most for the least outlay, there was something left that belonged to another kind of woman—something that liked the very things in Percy that were not good business assets. However much she dwelt upon the effectiveness of Greengay's dash and color and assurance, her mind always came back to Percy's neat little head, his clean-cut face, and warm, clear, gray eyes, and she liked them better than Charley's fullness and blurred floridness. Having reckoned up their respective chances with no doubtful result, she opposed a mild obstinacy to her own good sense. "I guess I'll take Percy, *anyway*," she said simply, and that was all the good her clever business brain did her.

Percy spent a night of torment, lying tense on his bed in the dark, and figuring out how long it would take him to pay back the money he was advancing to himself. Any fool could do it in five years, he reasoned, but he was going to do it in three. The trouble was that his expensive courtship had taken every penny of his salary. With competitors like Charley Greengay, you had to spend money or drop out. Certain birds, he reflected ruefully, are supplied with more attractive plumage when they are courting, but nature hadn't been so thoughtful for men. When Percy reached the office in the morning he climbed on his tall stool and leaned his arms on his ledger. He was so glad to feel it there that he was faint and weak-kneed.

Oliver Remsen, Junior, had brought new blood into the Remsen Paper Company. He married shortly after Percy Bixby did, and in the five succeeding years he had considerably enlarged the company's business and profits. He had been particularly successful in encouraging efficiency and loyalty in the employees. From the time he came into the office he had stood for shorter hours, longer holidays, and a generous consideration of men's necessities. He came out of college on the wave of economic reform, and he continued to read and think a good deal about how the machinery of labor is operated. He knew more about the men who worked for him than their mere office records.

Young Remsen was troubled about Percy Bixby because he took no summer vacations—always asked for the two weeks' extra pay instead.

Other men in the office had skipped a vacation now and then, but Percy had stuck to his desk for five years, had tottered to his stool through attacks of grippe and tonsilitis. He seemed to have grown fast to his ledger, and it was to this that Oliver objected. He liked his men to stay men, to look like men and live like men. He remembered how alert and wide-awake Bixby had seemed to him when he himself first came into the office. He had picked Bixby out as the most intelligent and interested of his father's employees, and since then had often wondered why he never seemed to see chances to forge ahead. Promotions, of course, went to the men who went after them. When Percy's baby died, he went to the funeral, and asked Percy to call on him if he needed money. Once when he chanced to sit down by Bixby on the elevated and found him reading Bryce's "American Commonwealth," he asked him to make use of his own large office library. Percy thanked him, but he never came for any books. Oliver wondered whether his bookkeeper really tried to avoid him.

One evening Oliver met the Bixbys in the lobby of a theater. He introduced Mrs. Remsen to them, and held them for some moments in conversation. When they got into their motor, Mrs. Remsen said:

"Is that little man afraid of you, Oliver? He looked like a scared rabbit."

Oliver snapped the door, and said with a shade of irritation:

"I don't know what's the matter with him. He's the fellow I've told you about who never takes a vacation. I half believe it's his wife. She looks pitiless enough for anything."

"She's very pretty of her kind," mused Mrs. Remsen, "but rather chilling. One can see that she has ideas about elegance."

"Rather unfortunate ones for a bookkeeper's wife. I surmise that Percy felt she was overdressed, and that made him awkward with me. I've always suspected that fellow of good taste."

After that, when Remsen passed the counting-room and saw Percy screwed up over his ledger, he often remembered Mrs. Bixby, with her cold, pale eyes and long lashes, and her expression that was something between indifference and discontent. She rose behind Percy's bent shoulders like an apparition.

One spring afternoon Remsen was closeted in his private office with his lawyer until a late hour. As he came down the long hall in the dusk he glanced through the glass partition into the counting-room, and saw Percy Bixby huddled up on his tall stool, though it was too dark to work. Indeed, Bixby's ledger was closed, and he sat with his two arms resting on the brown cover. He did not move a muscle when young Remsen entered.

"You are late, Bixby, and so am I," Oliver began genially as he crossed to the front of the room and looked out at the lighted windows of other tall buildings. "The fact is, I've been doing something that men have a foolish way of putting off. I've been making my will."

"Yes, sir." Percy brought it out with a deep breath.

"Glad to be through with it," Oliver went on. "Mr. Melton will bring the paper back to-morrow, and I'd like to ask you to be one of the witnesses."

"I'd be very proud, Mr. Remsen."

"Thank you, Bixby. Good night." Remsen took up his hat just as Percy slid down from his stool.

"Mr. Remsen, I'm told you're going to have the books gone over."

"Why, yes, Bixby. Don't let that trouble you. I'm taking in a new partner, you know, an old college friend. Just because he is a friend, I insist upon all the usual formalities. But it is a formality, and I'll guarantee the expert won't make a scratch on your books. Good night. You'd better be coming, too." Remsen had reached the door when he heard "Mr. Remsen!" in a desperate voice behind him. He turned, and saw Bixby standing uncertainly at one end of the desk, his hand still on his ledger, his uneven shoulders drooping forward and his head hanging as if he were seasick. Remsen came back and stood at the other end of the long desk. It was too dark to see Bixby's face clearly.

"What is it, Bixby?"

"Mr. Remsen, five years ago, just before I was married, I falsified the books a thousand dollars, and I used the money." Percy leaned forward against his desk, which took him just across the chest.

"What's that, Bixby?" Young Remsen spoke in a tone of polite surprise. He felt painfully embarrassed.

"Yes, sir. I thought I'd get it all paid back before this. I've put back three hundred, but the books are still seven hundred out of true. I've played the shortages about from account to account these five years, but an expert would find 'em in twenty-four hours."

"I don't just understand how—" Oliver stopped and shook his head.

"I held it out of the Western remittances, Mr. Remsen. They were coming in heavy just then. I was up against it. I hadn't saved anything to marry on, and my wife thought I was getting more money than I was. Since we've been married, I've never had the nerve to tell her. I could have paid it all back if it hadn't been for the unforeseen expenses."

Remsen sighed.

"Being married is largely unforeseen expenses, Percy. There's only one way to fix this up: I'll give you seven hundred dollars in cash to-morrow, and you can give me your personal note, with the understanding that I hold ten dollars a week out of your pay-check until it is paid. I think you ought to tell your wife exactly how you are fixed, though. You can't expect her to help you much when she doesn't know."

That night Mrs. Bixby was sitting in their flat, waiting for her husband. She was dressed for a bridge party, and often looked with impatience from her paper to the Mission clock, as big as a coffin and with nothing but two weights dangling in its hollow framework. Percy had been loath to buy the clock when they got their furniture, and he had hated it ever since. Stella had changed very little since she came into the flat a bride. Then she wore her hair in a Floradora pompadour; now she wore it hooded close about her head like a scarf, in a rather smeary manner, like an Impressionist's brush-work. She heard her husband come in and close the door softly. While he was taking off his hat in the narrow tunnel of a hall, she called to him:

"I hope you've had something to eat down-town. You'll have to dress right away." Percy came in and sat down. She looked up from the evening paper she was reading. "You've no time to sit down. We must start in fifteen minutes."

He shaded his eyes from the glaring overhead light.

"I'm afraid I can't go anywhere to-night. I'm all in."

Mrs. Bixby rattled her paper, and turned from the theatrical page to the fashions.

"You'll feel better after you dress. We won't stay late."

Her even persistence usually conquered her husband. She never forgot anything she had once decided to do. Her manner of following it up grew more chilly, but never weaker. To-night there was no spring in Percy. He closed his eyes and replied without moving:

"I can't go. You had better telephone the Burks we aren't coming. I have to tell you something disagreeable."

Stella rose.

"I certainly am not going to disappoint the Burks and stay at home to talk about anything disagreeable."

"You're not very sympathetic, Stella."

She turned away.

"If I were, you'd soon settle down into a pretty dull proposition. We'd have no social life now if I didn't keep at you."

Percy roused himself a little.

"Social life? Well, we'll have to trim that pretty close for a while. I'm in debt to the company. We've been living beyond our means ever since we were married."

"We can't live on less than we do," Stella said quietly. "No use in taking that up again."

Percy sat up, clutching the arms of his chair.

"We'll have to take it up. I'm seven hundred dollars short, and the books are to be audited to-morrow. I told young Remsen and he's going to take my note and hold the money out of my pay-checks. He could send me to jail, of course."

Stella turned and looked down at him with a gleam of interest.

"Oh, you've been playing solitaire with the books, have you? And he's found you out! I hope I'll never see that man again. Sugar face!" She said this with intense acrimony. Her forehead flushed delicately, and her eyes were full of hate. Young Remsen was not her idea of a "business man."

Stella went into the other room. When she came back she wore her evening coat and carried long gloves and a black scarf. This she began to arrange over her hair before the mirror above the false fireplace. Percy lay inert in the Morris chair and watched her. Yes, he understood; it was very difficult for a woman with hair like that to be shabby and to go without things. Her hair made her conspicuous, and it had to be lived up to. It had been the deciding factor in his fate.

Stella caught the lace over one ear with a large gold hairpin. She repeated this until she got a good effect. Then turning to Percy, she began to draw on her gloves.

"I'm not worrying any, because I'm going back into business," she said firmly. "I meant to, anyway, if you didn't get a raise the first of the year. I have the offer of a good position, and we can live in an apartment hotel."

Percy was on his feet in an instant.

"I won't have you grinding in any office. That's flat."

Stella's lower lip quivered in a commiserating smile. "Oh, I won't lose my health. Charley Greengay's a partner in his concern now, and he wants a private secretary."

Percy drew back.

"You can't work for Greengay. He's got too bad a reputation. You've more pride than that, Stella."

The thin sweep of color he knew so well went over Stella's face.

"His business reputation seems to be all right," she commented, working the kid on with her left hand.

"What if it is?" Percy broke out. "He's the cheapest kind of a skate. He gets into scrapes with the girls in his own office. The last one got into the newspapers, and he had to pay the girl a wad."

"He don't get into scrapes with his books, anyway, and he seems to be able to stand getting into the papers. I excuse Charley. His wife's a pill."

"I suppose you think he'd have been all right if he'd married you," said Percy, bitterly.

"Yes, I do." Stella buttoned her glove with an air of finishing something, and then looked at Percy without animosity. "Charley and I both have sporty tastes, and we like excitement. You might as well live in Newark if you're going to sit at home in the evening. You oughtn't to have married a business woman; you need somebody domestic. There's nothing in this sort of life for either of us."

"That means, I suppose, that you're going around with Greengay and his crowd?"

"Yes, that's my sort of crowd, and you never did fit into it. You're too intellectual. I've always been proud of you, Percy. You're better style than Charley, but that gets tiresome. You will never burn much red fire in New York, now, will you?"

Percy did not reply. He sat looking at the minute-hand of the eviscerated Mission clock. His wife almost never took the trouble to argue with him.

"You're old style, Percy," she went on. "Of course everybody marries and wishes they hadn't, but nowadays people get over it. Some women go ahead on the quiet, but I'm giving it to you straight. I'm going to work for Greengay. I like his line of business, and I meet people well. Now I'm going to the Burks'."

Percy dropped his hands limply between his knees.

"I suppose," he brought out, "the real trouble is that you've decided my earning power is not very great."

"That's part of it, and part of it is you're old-fashioned." Stella paused at the door and looked back. "What made you rush me, anyway, Percy?"

she asked indulgently. "What did you go and pretend to be a spender and get tied up with me for?"

"I guess everybody wants to be a spender when he's in love," Percy replied.

Stella shook her head mournfully.

"No, you're a spender or you're not. Greengay has been broke three times, fired, down and out, black-listed. But he's always come back, and he always will. You will never be fired, but you'll always be poor." She turned and looked back again before she went out.

Six months later Bixby came to young Oliver Remsen one afternoon and said he would like to have twenty dollars a week held out of his pay until his debt was cleared off.

Oliver looked up at his sallow employee and asked him how he could spare as much as that.

"My expenses are lighter," Bixby replied. "My wife has gone into business with a ready-to-wear firm. She is not living with me any more."

Oliver looked annoyed, and asked him if nothing could be done to readjust his domestic affairs. Bixby said no; they would probably remain as they were.

"But where are you living, Bixby? How have you arranged things?" the young man asked impatiently.

"I'm very comfortable. I live in a boarding-house and have my own furniture. There are several fellows there who are fixed the same way. Their wives went back into business, and they drifted apart."

With a baffled expression Remsen stared at the uneven shoulders under the skin-fitting alpaca desk coat as his bookkeeper went out. He had meant to do something for Percy, but somehow, he reflected, one never did do anything for a fellow who had been stung as hard as that.

Century, May 1916

Ardessa

The grand-mannered old man who sat at a desk in the reception-room of "The Outcry" offices to receive visitors and incidentally to keep the time-book of the employees, looked up as Miss Devine entered at ten minutes past ten and condescendingly wished him good morning. He bowed profoundly as she minced past his desk, and with an indifferent air took her course down the corridor that led to the editorial offices. Mechanically he opened the flat, black book at his elbow and placed his finger on D, running his eye along the line of figures after the name Devine. "It's banker's hours she keeps, indeed," he muttered. What was the use of entering so capricious a record? Nevertheless, with his usual preliminary flourish he wrote 10:10 under this, the fourth day of May.

The employee who kept banker's hours rustled on down the corridor to her private room, hung up her lavender jacket and her trim spring hat, and readjusted her side combs by the mirror inside her closet door. Glancing at her desk, she rang for an office boy, and reproved him because he had not dusted more carefully and because there were lumps in her paste. When he disappeared with the paste-jar, she sat down to decide which of her employer's letters he should see and which he should not.

Ardessa was not young and she was certainly not handsome. The coquettish angle at which she carried her head was a mannerism surviving from a time when it was more becoming. She shuddered at the cold candor of the new business woman, and was insinuatingly feminine.

Ardessa's employer, like young Lochinvar, had come out of the West, and he had done a great many contradictory things before he became proprietor and editor of "The Outcry." Before he decided to go to New York and make the East take notice of him, O'Mally had acquired a punctual, reliable silver-mine in South Dakota. This silent friend in the background made his journalistic success comparatively easy. He had figured out, when he was a rich nobody in Nevada, that the quickest way to cut into the known world was through the printing-press. He arrived in New York, bought a highly respectable publication, and turned it into a red-hot magazine of protest, which he called "The Outcry." He knew what the West wanted, and it proved to be what everybody secretly wanted. In six years he had done the thing that had hitherto seemed impossible: built up a national weekly, out on the news-stands the same day in New York and San Francisco; a magazine the people howled for, a moving-picture film of their real tastes and interests.

O'Mally bought "The Outcry" to make a stir, not to make a career, but he had got built into the thing more than he ever intended. It had made him a public man and put him into politics. He found the publicity game diverting, and it held him longer than any other game had ever done. He had built up about him an organization of which he was somewhat afraid and with which he was vastly bored. On his staff there were five famous men, and he had made every one of them. At first it amused him to manufacture celebrities. He found he could take an average reporter from the daily press, give him a "line" to follow, a trust to fight, a vice to expose, — this was all in that good time when people were eager to read about their own wickedness, — and in two years the reporter would be recognized as an authority. Other people—Napoleon, Disraeli, Sarah Bernhardt—had discovered that advertising would go a long way; but Marcus O'Mally discovered that in America it would go all the way—as far as you wished to pay its passage. Any human countenance, plastered in three-sheet posters from sea to sea, would be revered by the American people. The strangest thing was that the owners of these grave countenances, staring at their own faces on newsstands and billboards, fell to venerating themselves; and even he, O'Mally, was more or less constrained by these reputations that he had created out of cheap paper and cheap ink.

Constraint was the last thing O'Mally liked. The most engaging and unusual thing about the man was that he couldn't be fooled by the success of his own methods, and no amount of "recognition" could make a stuffed shirt of him. No matter how much he was advertised as a great medicine-man in the councils of the nation, he knew that he was a born gambler and a soldier of fortune. He left his dignified office to take care of itself for a good many months of the year while he played about on the outskirts of social order. He liked being a great man from the East in rough-and-tumble Western cities where he had once been merely an unconsidered spender.

O'Mally's long absences constituted one of the supreme advantages of Ardessa Devine's position. When he was at his post her duties were not heavy, but when he was giving balls in Goldfield, Nevada, she lived an ideal life. She came to the office every day, indeed, to forward such of O'Mally's letters as she thought best, to attend to his club notices and tradesmen's bills, and to taste the sense of her high connections. The great men of the staff were all about her, as contemplative as Buddhas in their private offices, each meditating upon the particular trust or form of vice confided to his care. Thus surrounded, Ardessa had a pleasant sense of being at the heart of things. It was like a mental massage, exercise without exertion. She read and she embroidered. Her room was pleasant, and she liked to be seen at ladylike tasks and to feel herself a graceful contrast to the crude girls in the advertising and circulation departments across the hall. The younger stenographers, who had to get through with the enormous office correspondence, and who rushed about from one editor to another with wire baskets full of letters, made faces as they passed Ardessa's door and saw her cool and cloistered, daintily plying her needle. But no matter how hard the other stenographers were driven, no one, not even one of the five oracles of the staff, dared dictate so much as a letter to Ardessa. Like a sultan's bride, she was inviolate in her lord's absence; she had to be kept for him.

Naturally the other young women employed in "The Outcry" offices disliked Miss Devine. They were all competent girls, trained in the exacting methods of modern business, and they had to make good every day in the week, had to get through with a great deal of work or lose their position. O'Mally's private secretary was a mystery to them. Her exemptions and privileges, her patronizing remarks, formed an exhaustless subject of conversation at the lunch-hour. Ardessa had, indeed, as they knew she must have, a kind of "purchase" on her employer.

When O'Mally first came to New York to break into publicity, he engaged Miss Devine upon the recommendation of the editor whose ailing publication he bought and rechristened. That editor was a conservative, scholarly gentleman of the old school, who was retiring because he felt out of place in the world of brighter, breezier magazines that had been flowering since the new century came in. He believed that in this vehement world young O'Mally would make himself heard and that Miss Devine's training in an editorial office would be of use to him.

When O'Mally first sat down at a desk to be an editor, all the cards that were brought in looked pretty much alike to him. Ardessa was at his elbow. She had long been steeped in literary distinctions and in the social distinctions which used to count for much more than they do now. She knew all the great men, all the nephews and clients of great men. She knew which must be seen, which must be made welcome, and which could safely be sent away. She could give O'Mally on the instant the former rating in magazine offices of nearly every name that was brought in to him. She could give him an idea of the man's connections, of the price his work commanded, and insinuate whether he ought to be met with the old punctiliousness or with the new joviality. She was useful in explaining to her employer the significance of various invitations, and the standing of clubs and associations. At first she was virtually the social mentor of the bullet-headed young Westerner who wanted to break into everything, the solitary person about the office of the humming new magazine who knew anything about the editorial traditions of the eighties and nineties which, antiquated as they now were, gave an editor, as O'Mally said, a background.

Despite her indolence, Ardessa was useful to O'Mally as a social reminder. She was the card catalogue of his ever-changing personal relations. O'Mally went in for everything and got tired of everything; that was why he made a good editor. After he was through with people, Ardessa was very skilful in covering his retreat. She read and answered the letters of admirers who had begun to bore him. When great authors, who had been dined and fêted the month before, were suddenly left to cool their heels in the reception-room, thrown upon the suave hospitality of the grand old man at the desk, it was Ardessa who went out and made soothing and plausible explanations as to why the editor could not see them. She was the brake that checked the too-eager neophyte, the emollient that eased the severing of relationships, the gentle extinguisher of the lights that failed. When there were no longer messages of hope and cheer to be sent to ardent young writers and reformers, Ardessa delivered, as sweetly as possible, whatever messages were left.

In handling these people with whom O'Mally was quite through, Ardessa had gradually developed an industry which was immensely gratifying to her own vanity. Not only did she not crush them; she even fostered them a little. She continued to advise them in the reception-room and "personally" received their manuscripts long after O'Mally had declared that he would never read another line they wrote. She let them outline their plans for stories and articles to her, promising to bring these suggestions to the editor's attention. She denied herself to nobody, was gracious even to the Shakspere-Bacon man, the perpetual-motion man, the travel-article man, the ghosts which haunt every magazine office. The writers who had had their happy hour of O'Mally's favor kept feeling that Ardessa might reinstate them. She answered their letters of inquiry in her most polished and elegant style, and even gave them hints as to the subjects in which the restless editor was or was not interested at the moment: she feared it would be useless to send him an article on "How to Trap Lions," because he had just bought an article on "Elephant-Shooting in Majuba Land," etc.

So when O'Mally plunged into his office at 11:30 on this, the fourth day of May, having just got back from three-days' fishing, he found Ardessa in the reception-room, surrounded by a little court of discards. This was annoying, for he always wanted his stenographer at once. Telling the office boy to give her a hint that she was needed, he threw off his hat and topcoat and began to race through the pile of letters Ardessa had put on his desk.

When she entered, he did not wait for her polite inquiries about his trip, but broke in at once.

"What is that fellow who writes about phossy jaw still hanging round here for? I don't want any articles on phossy jaw, and if I did, I wouldn't want his."

"He has just sold an article on the match industry to 'The New Age,' Mr. O'Mally," Ardessa replied as she took her seat at the editor's right.

"Why does he have to come and tell us about it? We've nothing to do with 'The New Age.' And that prison-reform guy, what's he loafing about for?"

Ardessa bridled.

"You remember, Mr. O'Mally, he brought letters of introduction from Governor Harper, the reform Governor of Mississippi."

O'Mally jumped up, kicking over his waste-basket in his impatience.

"That was months ago. I went through his letters and went through him, too. He hasn't got anything we want. I've been through with Governor Harper a long while. We're asleep at the switch in here. And let me tell you, if I catch sight of that causes-of-blindness-in-babies woman around here again, I'll do something violent. Clear them out, Miss Devine! Clear them out! We need a traffic policeman in this office. Have you got that article on 'Stealing Our National Water Power' ready for me?"

"Mr. Gerrard took it back to make modifications. He gave it to me at noon on Saturday, just before the office closed. I will have it ready for you to-morrow morning, Mr. O'Mally, if you have not too many letters for me this afternoon," Ardessa replied pointedly.

"Holy Mike!" muttered O'Mally, "we need a traffic policeman for the staff, too. Gerrard's modified that thing half a dozen times already. Why don't they get accurate information in the first place?"

He began to dictate his morning mail, walking briskly up and down the floor by way of giving his stenographer an energetic example. Her indolence and her ladylike deportment weighed on him. He wanted to take her by the elbows and run her around the block. He didn't mind that she loafed when he was away, but it was becoming harder and harder to speed her up when he was on the spot. He knew his correspondence was not enough to keep her busy, so when he was in town he made her type his own breezy editorials and various articles by members of his staff.

Transcribing editorial copy is always laborious, and the only way to make it easy is to farm it out. This Ardessa was usually clever enough to do. When she returned to her own room after O'Mally had gone out to lunch, Ardessa rang for an office boy and said languidly, "James, call Becky, please."

In a moment a thin, tense-faced Hebrew girl of eighteen or nineteen came rushing in, carrying a wire basket full of typewritten sheets. She was as gaunt as a plucked spring chicken, and her cheap, gaudy clothes might have been thrown on her. She looked as if she were running to catch a train and in mortal dread of missing it. While Miss Devine examined the pages in the basket, Becky stood with her shoulders drawn up and her elbows drawn in, apparently trying to hide herself in her insufficient open-work waist. Her wild, black eyes followed Miss Devine's hands desperately. Ardessa sighed.

"This seems to be very smeary copy again, Becky. You don't keep your mind on your work, and so you have to erase continually."

Becky spoke up in wailing self-vindication.

"It ain't that, Miss Devine. It's so many hard words he uses that I have to be at the dictionary all the time. Look! Look!" She produced a bunch of manuscript faintly scrawled in pencil, and thrust it under Ardessa's eyes. "He don't write out the words at all. He just begins a word, and then makes waves for you to guess."

"I see you haven't always guessed correctly, Becky," said Ardessa, with a weary smile. "There are a great many words here that would surprise Mr. Gerrard, I am afraid."

"And the inserts," Becky persisted. "How is anybody to tell where they go, Miss Devine? It's mostly inserts; see, all over the top and sides and back."

Ardessa turned her head away.

"Don't claw the pages like that, Becky. You make me nervous. Mr. Gerrard has not time to dot his i's and cross his t's. That is what we keep copyists for. I will correct these sheets for you,—it would be terrible if Mr. O'Mally saw them,—and then you can copy them over again. It must be done by to-morrow morning, so you may have to work late. See that your hands are clean and dry, and then you will not smear it."

"Yes, ma'am. Thank you, Miss Devine. Will you tell the janitor, please, it's all right if I have to stay? He was cross because I was here Saturday afternoon doing this. He said it was a holiday, and when everybody else was gone I ought to—"

"That will do, Becky. Yes, I will speak to the janitor for you. You may go to lunch now."

Becky turned on one heel and then swung back.

"Miss Devine," she said anxiously, "will it be all right if I get white shoes for now?"

Ardessa gave her kind consideration.

"For office wear, you mean? No, Becky. With only one pair, you could not keep them properly clean; and black shoes are much less conspicuous. Tan, if you prefer."

Becky looked down at her feet. They were too large, and her skirt was as much too short as her legs were too long.

"Nearly all the girls I know wear white shoes to business," she pleaded.

"They are probably little girls who work in factories or department stores, and that is quite another matter. Since you raise the question, Becky, I ought to speak to you about your new waist. Don't wear it to the office again, please. Those cheap open-work waists are not appropriate in an office like this. They are all very well for little chorus girls."

"But Miss Kalski wears expensive waists to business more open than this, and jewelry—"

Ardessa interrupted. Her face grew hard.

"Miss Kalski," she said coldly, "works for the business department. You are employed in the editorial offices. There is a great difference. You see, Becky, I might have to call you in here at any time when a scientist or a great writer or the president of a university is here talking over editorial matters, and such clothes as you have on to-day would make a bad impression. Nearly all our connections are with important people of that kind, and we ought to be well, but quietly, dressed."

"Yes, Miss Devine. Thank you," Becky gasped and disappeared. Heaven knew she had no need to be further impressed with the greatness of "The Outcry" office. During the year and a half she had been there she had never ceased to tremble. She knew the prices all the authors got as well as Miss Devine did, and everything seemed to her to be done on a magnificent scale. She hadn't a good memory for long technical words, but she never forgot dates or prices or initials or telephone numbers.

Becky felt that her job depended on Miss Devine, and she was so glad to have it that she scarcely realized she was being bullied. Besides, she was grateful for all that she had learned from Ardessa; Ardessa had taught her to do most of the things that she was supposed to do herself. Becky wanted to learn, she had to learn; that was the train she was always running for. Her father, Isaac Tietelbaum, the tailor, who pressed Miss Devine's skirts and kept her ladylike suits in order, had come to his client two years ago and told her he had a bright girl just out of a commercial high school. He implored Ardessa to find some office position for his daughter. Ardessa told an appealing story to O'Mally, and brought Becky into the office, at a salary of six dollars a week, to help with the copying and to learn business routine. When Becky first came she was as ignorant as a young savage. She was rapid at her shorthand and typing, but a Kafir girl would have known as much about the English language. Nobody ever wanted to learn more than Becky. She fairly wore the dictionary out. She dug up her old school grammar and worked over it at night. She faithfully mastered Miss Devine's fussy system of punctuation.

There were eight children at home, younger than Becky, and they were all eager to learn. They wanted to get their mother out of the three dark rooms behind the tailor shop and to move into a flat up-stairs, where they could, as Becky said, "live private." The young Tietelbaums doubted their father's ability to bring this change about, for the more things he declared himself ready to do in his window placards, the fewer were brought to him to be done. "Dyeing, Cleaning, Ladies' Furs Remodeled"—it did no good.

Rebecca was out to "improve herself," as her father had told her she must. Ardessa had easy way with her. It was one of those rare relationships from which both persons profit. The more Becky could learn from Ardessa, the happier she was; and the more Ardessa could unload on Becky, the greater was her contentment. She easily broke Becky of the gum-chewing habit, taught her to walk quietly, to efface herself at the proper moment, and to hold her tongue. Becky had been raised to eight dollars a week; but she didn't care half so much about that as she did about her own increasing efficiency. The more work Miss Devine handed over to her the happier she was, and the faster she was able to eat it up. She tested and tried herself in every possible way. She now had full confidence that she would surely one day be a high-priced stenographer, a real "business woman."

Becky would have corrupted a really industrious person, but a bilious temperament like Ardessa's couldn't make even a feeble stand against such willingness. Ardessa had grown soft and had lost the knack of turning out work. Sometimes, in her importance and serenity, she shivered. What if O'Mally should die, and she were thrust out into the world to work in competition with the brazen, competent young women she saw about her everywhere? She believed herself indispensable, but she knew that in such a mischanceful world as this the very powers of darkness might rise to separate her from this pearl among jobs.

When Becky came in from lunch she went down the long hall to the wash-room, where all the little girls who worked in the advertising and circulation departments kept their hats and jackets. There were shelves and shelves of bright spring hats, piled on top of one another, all as stiff as sheet-iron and trimmed with gay flowers. At the marble wash-stand stood Rena Kalski, the right bower of the business manager, polishing her diamond rings with a nail-brush.

"Hullo, kid," she called over her shoulder to Becky. "I've got a ticket for you for Thursday afternoon."

Becky's black eyes glowed, but the strained look on her face drew tighter than ever.

"I'll never ask her, Miss Kalski," she said rapidly. "I don't dare. I have to stay late to-night again; and I know she'd be hard to please after, if I was to try to get off on a week-day. I thank you, Miss Kalski, but I'd better not."

Miss Kalski laughed. She was a slender young Hebrew, handsome in an impudent, Tenderloin sort of way, with a small head, reddish-brown almond eyes, a trifle tilted, a rapacious mouth, and a beautiful chin.

"Ain't you under that woman's thumb, though! Call her bluff. She isn't half the prima donna she thinks she is. On my side of the hall we know who's who about this place."

The business and editorial departments of "The Outcry" were separated by a long corridor and a great contempt. Miss Kalski dried her rings with tissue-paper and studied them with an appraising eye.

"Well, since you're such a 'fraidy-calf,'" she went on, "maybe I can get a rise out of her myself. Now I've got you a ticket out of that shirt-front, I want you to go. I'll drop in on Devine this afternoon."

When Miss Kalski went back to her desk in the business manager's private office, she turned to him familiarly, but not impertinently.

"Mr. Henderson, I want to send a kid over in the editorial stenographers' to the Palace Thursday afternoon. She's a nice kid, only she's scared out of her skin all the time. Miss Devine's her boss, and she'll be just mean enough not to let the young one off. Would you say a word to her?"

The business manager lit a cigar.

"I'm not saying words to any of the high-brows over there. Try it out with Devine yourself. You're not bashful."

Miss Kalski shrugged her shoulders and smiled.

"Oh, very well." She serpentined out of the room and crossed the Rubicon into the editorial offices. She found Ardessa typing O'Mally's letters and wearing a pained expression.

"Good afternoon, Miss Devine," she said carelessly. "Can we borrow Becky over there for Thursday afternoon? We're short."

Miss Devine looked piqued and tilted her head.

"I don't think it's customary, Miss Kalski, for the business department to use our people. We never have girls enough here to do the work. Of course if Mr. Henderson feels justified—"

"Thanks awfully, Miss Devine,"—Miss Kalski interrupted her with the perfectly smooth, good-natured tone which never betrayed a hint of the scorn every line of her sinuous figure expressed,—"I will tell Mr. Henderson. Perhaps we can do something for you some day." Whether this was a threat, a kind wish, or an insinuation, no mortal could have told. Miss Kalski's face was always suggesting insolence without being quite insolent. As she returned to her own domain she met the cashier's head clerk in the hall. "That Devine woman's a crime," she murmured. The head clerk laughed tolerantly.

That afternoon as Miss Kalski was leaving the office at 5:15, on her way down the corridor she heard a typewriter clicking away in the empty, echoing editorial offices. She looked in, and found Becky bending forward over the machine as if she were about to swallow it.

"Hello, kid. Do you sleep with that?" she called. She walked up to Becky and glanced at her copy. "What do you let 'em keep you up nights over that stuff for?" she asked contemptuously. "The world wouldn't suffer if that stuff never got printed."

Rebecca looked up wildly. Not even Miss Kalski's French pansy hat or her ear-rings and landscape veil could loosen Becky's tenacious mind from Mr. Gerrard's article on water power. She scarcely knew what Miss Kalski had said to her, certainly not what she meant.

"But I must make progress already, Miss Kalski," she panted.

Miss Kalski gave her low, siren laugh.

"I should say you must!" she ejaculated.

Ardessa decided to take her vacation in June, and she arranged that Miss Milligan should do O'Mally's work while she was away. Miss Milligan was blunt and noisy, rapid and inaccurate. It would be just as well for O'Mally to work with a coarse instrument for a time; he would be more appreciative, perhaps, of certain qualities to which he had seemed insensible of late. Ardessa was to leave for East Hampton on Sunday, and she spent Saturday morning instructing her substitute as to the state of the correspondence. At noon O'Mally burst into her room. All the morning he had been closeted with a new writer of mystery-stories just over from England.

"Can you stay and take my letters this afternoon, Miss Devine? You're not leaving until to-morrow."

Ardessa pouted, and tilted her head at the angle he was tired of.

"I'm sorry, Mr. O'Mally, but I've left all my shopping for this afternoon. I think Becky Tietelbaum could do them for you. I will tell her to be careful."

"Oh, all right." O'Mally bounced out with a reflection of Ardessa's disdainful expression on his face. Saturday afternoon was always a half-holiday, to be sure, but since she had weeks of freedom when he was away—However—

At two o'clock Becky Tietelbaum appeared at his door, clad in the sober office suit which Miss Devine insisted she should wear, her note-book in her hand, and so frightened that her fingers were cold and her lips were pale. She had never taken dictation from the editor before. It was a great and terrifying occasion.

"Sit down," he said encouragingly. He began dictating while he shook from his bag the manuscripts he had snatched away from the amazed English author that morning. Presently he looked up.

"Do I go too fast?"

"No, sir," Becky found strength to say.

At the end of an hour he told her to go and type as many of the letters as she could while he went over the bunch of stuff he had torn from the Englishman. He was with the Hindu detective in an opium den in Shanghai when Becky returned and placed a pile of papers on his desk.

"How many?" he asked, without looking up.

"All you gave me, sir."

"All, so soon? Wait a minute and let me see how many mistakes." He went over the letters rapidly, signing them as he read. "They seem to be all right. I thought you were the girl that made so many mistakes."

Rebecca was never too frightened to vindicate herself.

"Mr. O'Mally, sir, I don't make mistakes with letters. It's only copying the articles that have so many long words, and when the writing isn't plain, like Mr. Gerrard's. I never make many mistakes with Mr. Johnson's articles, or with yours I don't."

O'Mally wheeled round in his chair, looked with curiosity at her long, tense face, her black eyes, and straight brows.

"Oh, so you sometimes copy articles, do you? How does that happen?"

"Yes, sir. Always Miss Devine gives me the articles to do. It's good practice for me."

"I see." O'Mally shrugged his shoulders. He was thinking that he could get a rise out of the whole American public any day easier than he could get a rise out of Ardessa. "What editorials of mine have you copied lately, for instance?"

Rebecca blazed out at him, reciting rapidly:

"Oh, 'A Word about the Rosenbaums,' 'Useless Navy-Yards,' 'Who Killed Cock Robin' — "

"Wait a minute." O'Mally checked her flow. "What was that one about — Cock Robin?"

"It was all about why the secretary of the interior dismissed — "

"All right, all right. Copy those letters, and put them down the chute as you go out. Come in here for a minute on Monday morning."

Becky hurried home to tell her father that she had taken the editor's letters and had made no mistakes. On Monday she learned that she was to do O'Mally's work for a few days. He disliked Miss Milligan, and he was annoyed with Ardessa for trying to put her over on him when there was better material at hand. With Rebecca he got on very well; she was impersonal, unreproachful, and she fairly panted for work. Everything was done almost before he told her what he wanted. She raced ahead with him; it was like riding a good modern bicycle after pumping along on an old hard tire.

On the day before Miss Devine's return O'Mally strolled over for a chat with the business office.

"Henderson, your people are taking vacations now, I suppose? Could you use an extra girl?"

"If it's that thin black one, I can."

O'Mally gave him a wise smile.

"It isn't. To be honest, I want to put one over on you. I want you to take Miss Devine over here for a while and speed her up. I can't do anything. She's got the upper hand of me. I don't want to fire her, you understand, but she makes my life too difficult. It's my fault, of course. I've pampered her. Give her a chance over here; maybe she'll come back. You can be firm with 'em, can't you?"

Henderson glanced toward the desk where Miss Kalski's lightning eye was skimming over the printing-house bills that he was supposed to verify himself.

"Well, if I can't, I know who can," he replied, with a chuckle.

"Exactly," O'Mally agreed. "I'm counting on the force of Miss Kalski's example. Miss Devine's all right, Miss Kalski, but she needs regular exercise. She owes it to her complexion. I can't discipline people."

Miss Kalski's only reply was a low, indulgent laugh.

O'Mally braced himself on the morning of Ardessa's return. He told the waiter at his club to bring him a second pot of coffee and to bring it hot. He was really afraid of her. When she presented herself at his office at 10:30 he complimented her upon her tan and asked about her vacation. Then he broke the news to her.

"We want to make a few temporary changes about here, Miss Devine, for the summer months. The business department is short of help. Henderson is going to put Miss Kalski on the books for a while to figure out some economies for him, and he is going to take you over. Meantime I'll get Becky broken in so that she could take your work if you were sick or anything."

Ardessa drew herself up.

"I've not been accustomed to commercial work, Mr. O'Mally. I've no interest in it, and I don't care to brush up in it."

"Brushing up is just what we need, Miss Devine." O'Mally began tramping about his room expansively. "I'm going to brush everybody up. I'm going to brush a few people out; but I want you to stay with us, of course. You belong here. Don't be hasty now. Go to your room and think it over."

Ardessa was beginning to cry, and O'Mally was afraid he would lose his nerve. He looked out of the window at a new sky-scraper that was building, while she retired without a word.

At her own desk Ardessa sat down breathless and trembling. The one thing she had never doubted was her unique value to O'Mally. She had, as she told herself, taught him everything. She would say a few things to Becky Tietelbaum, and to that pigeon-breasted tailor, her father, too! The worst of it was that Ardessa had herself brought it all about; she could see that clearly now. She had carefully trained and qualified her successor. Why had she ever civilized Becky? Why had she taught her manners and deportment,

158 | A Collection Of Stories

broken her of the gum-chewing habit, and made her presentable? In her original state O'Mally would never have put up with her, no matter what her ability.

Ardessa told herself that O'Mally was notoriously fickle; Becky amused him, but he would soon find out her limitations. The wise thing, she knew, was to humor him; but it seemed to her that she could not swallow her pride. Ardessa grew yellower within the hour. Over and over in her mind she bade O'Mally a cold adieu and minced out past the grand old man at the desk for the last time. But each exit she rehearsed made her feel sorrier for herself. She thought over all the offices she knew, but she realized that she could never meet their inexorable standards of efficiency.

While she was bitterly deliberating, O'Mally himself wandered in, rattling his keys nervously in his pocket. He shut the door behind him.

"Now, you're going to come through with this all right, aren't you, Miss Devine? I want Henderson to get over the notion that my people over here are stuck up and think the business department are old shoes. That's where we get our money from, as he often reminds me. You'll be the best-paid girl over there; no reduction, of course. You don't want to go wandering off to some new office where personality doesn't count for anything." He sat down confidentially on the edge of her desk. "Do you, now, Miss Devine?"

Ardessa simpered tearfully as she replied.

"Mr. O'Mally," she brought out, "you'll soon find that Becky is not the sort of girl to meet people for you when you are away. I don't see how you can think of letting her."

"That's one thing I want to change, Miss Devine. You're too soft-handed with the has-beens and the never-was-ers. You're too much of a lady for this rough game. Nearly everybody who comes in here wants to sell us a gold-brick, and you treat them as if they were bringing in wedding presents. Becky is as rough as sandpaper, and she'll clear out a lot of dead wood." O'Mally rose, and tapped Ardessa's shrinking shoulder. "Now, be a sport and go through with it, Miss Devine. I'll see that you don't lose. Henderson thinks you'll refuse to do his work, so I want you to get moved in there before he comes back from lunch. I've had a desk put in his office for you. Miss Kalski is in the bookkeeper's room half the time now."

Rena Kalski was amazed that afternoon when a line of office boys entered, carrying Miss Devine's effects, and when Ardessa herself coldly followed them. After Ardessa had arranged her desk, Miss Kalski went over to her and told her about some matters of routine very good-naturedly. Ardessa looked pretty badly shaken up, and Rena bore no grudges.

"When you want the dope on the correspondence with the paper men, don't bother to look it up. I've got it all in my head, and I can save time for you. If he wants you to go over the printing bills every week, you'd better let me help you with that for a while. I can stay almost any afternoon. It's quite a trick to figure out the plates and over-time charges till you get used to it. I've worked out a quick method that saves trouble."

When Henderson came in at three he found Ardessa, chilly, but civil, awaiting his instructions. He knew she disapproved of his tastes and his manners, but he didn't mind. What interested and amused him was that Rena Kalski, whom he had always thought as cold-blooded as an adding-machine, seemed to be making a hair-mattress of herself to break Ardessa's fall.

At five o'clock, when Ardessa rose to go, the business manager said breezily:

"See you at nine in the morning, Miss Devine. We begin on the stroke."

Ardessa faded out of the door, and Miss Kalski's slender back squirmed with amusement.

"I never thought to hear such words spoken," she admitted; "but I guess she'll limber up all right. The atmosphere is bad over there. They get moldy."

After the next monthly luncheon of the heads of departments, O'Mally said to Henderson, as he feed the coat-boy:

"By the way, how are you making it with the bartered bride?"

Henderson smashed on his Panama as he said:

"Any time you want her back, don't be delicate."

But O'Mally shook his red head and laughed.

"Oh, I'm no Indian giver!"

Century, May 1918

Her Boss

Paul Wanning opened the front door of his house in Orange, closed it softly behind him, and stood looking about the hall as he drew off his gloves.

Nothing was changed there since last night, and yet he stood gazing about him with an interest which a long-married man does not often feel in his own reception hall. The rugs, the two pillars, the Spanish tapestry chairs, were all the same. The Venus di Medici stood on her column as usual and there, at the end of the hall (opposite the front door), was the full-length portrait of Mrs. Wanning, maturely blooming forth in an evening gown, signed with the name of a French painter who seemed purposely to have made his signature indistinct. Though the signature was largely what one paid for, one couldn't ask him to do it over.

In the dining room the colored man was moving about the table set for dinner, under the electric cluster. The candles had not yet been lighted. Wanning watched him with a homesick feeling in his heart. They had had Sam a long while, twelve years, now. His warm hall, the lighted dining-room, the drawing room where only the flicker of the wood fire played upon the shining surfaces of many objects—they seemed to Wanning like a haven of refuge. It had never occurred to him that his house was too full of things. He often said, and he believed, that the women of his household had "perfect taste." He had paid for these objects, sometimes with difficulty, but always with pride. He carried a heavy life-insurance and permitted himself to spend most of the income from a good law practise. He wished, during his life-time, to enjoy the benefits of his wife's discriminating extravagance.

Yesterday Wanning's doctor had sent him to a specialist. Today the specialist, after various laboratory tests, had told him most disconcerting things about the state of very necessary, but hitherto wholly uninteresting, organs of his body.

The information pointed to something incredible; insinuated that his residence in this house was only temporary; that he, whose time was so full, might have to leave not only his house and his office and his club, but a world with which he was extremely well satisfied—the only world he knew anything about.

Wanning unbuttoned his overcoat, but did not take it off. He stood folding his muffler slowly and carefully. What he did not understand was, how he could go while other people stayed. Sam would be moving about the table like this, Mrs. Wanning and her daughters would be dressing upstairs, when he would not be coming home to dinner any more; when he would not, indeed, be dining anywhere.

Sam, coming to turn on the parlor lights, saw Wanning and stepped behind him to take his coat.

"Good evening, Mr. Wanning, sah, excuse me. You entahed so quietly, sah, I didn't heah you."

The master of the house slipped out of his coat and went languidly upstairs.

He tapped at the door of his wife's room, which stood ajar.

"Come in, Paul," she called from her dressing table.

She was seated, in a violet dressing gown, giving the last touches to her coiffure, both arms lifted. They were firm and white, like her neck and shoulders. She was a handsome woman of fifty-five,—still a woman, not an old person, Wanning told himself, as he kissed her cheek. She was heavy in figure, to be sure, but she had kept, on the whole, presentable outlines. Her complexion was good, and she wore less false hair than either of her daughters.

Wanning himself was five years older, but his sandy hair did not show the gray in it, and since his mustache had begun to grow white he kept it clipped so short that it was unobtrusive. His fresh skin made him look younger than he was. Not long ago he had overheard the stenographers in his law office discussing the ages of their employers. They had put him down at fifty, agreeing that his two partners must be considerably older than he—which was not the case. Wanning had an especially kindly feeling for the little new girl, a copyist, who had exclaimed that "Mr. Wanning couldn't be fifty; he seemed so boyish!"

Wanning lingered behind his wife, looking at her in the mirror.

"Well, did you tell the girls, Julia?" he asked, trying to speak casually.

Mrs. Wanning looked up and met his eyes in the glass. "The girls?"

She noticed a strange expression come over his face.

"About your health, you mean? Yes, dear, but I tried not to alarm them. They feel dreadfully. I'm going to have a talk with Dr. Seares myself. These specialists are all alarmists, and I've often heard of his frightening people."

She rose and took her husband's arm, drawing him toward the fireplace.

"You are not going to let this upset you, Paul? If you take care of yourself, everything will come out all right. You have always been so strong. One has only to look at you."

"Did you," Wanning asked, "say anything to Harold?"

"Yes, of course. I saw him in town today, and he agrees with me that Seares draws the worst conclusions possible. He says even the young men are always being told the most terrifying things. Usually they laugh at the doctors and do as they please. You certainly don't look like a sick man, and you don't feel like one, do you?"

She patted his shoulder, smiled at him encouragingly, and rang for the maid to come and hook her dress.

When the maid appeared at the door, Wanning went out through the bathroom to his own sleeping chamber. He was too much dispirited to put on a dinner coat, though such remissness was always noticed. He sat down and waited for the sound of the gong, leaving his door open, on the chance that perhaps one of his daughters would come in.

When Wanning went down to dinner he found his wife already at her chair, and the table laid for four.

"Harold," she explained, "is not coming home. He has to attend a first night in town."

A moment later their two daughters entered, obviously "dressed." They both wore earrings and masses of hair. The daughters' names were Roma and Florence,—Roma, Firenze, one of the young men who came to the house often, but not often enough, had called them. Tonight they were going to a rehearsal of "The Dances of the Nations,"—a benefit performance in which Miss Roma was to lead the Spanish dances, her sister the Grecian.

The elder daughter had often been told that her name suited her admirably. She looked, indeed, as we are apt to think the unrestrained beauties of later Rome must have looked,—but as their portrait busts emphatically declare they did not. Her head was massive, her lips full and crimson, her eyes large and heavy-lidded, her forehead low. At costume balls and in living pictures she was always Semiramis, or Poppea, or Theodora. Barbaric accessories brought out something cruel and even rather brutal in her handsome face. The men who were attracted to her were somehow afraid of her.

Florence was slender, with a long, graceful neck, a restless head, and a flexible mouth—discontent lurked about the corners of it. Her shoulders were pretty, but her neck and arms were too thin. Roma was always struggling to keep within a certain weight—her chin and upper arms grew persistently more solid—and Florence was always striving to attain a certain weight. Wanning used sometimes to wonder why these disconcerting fluctuations could not go the other way; why Roma could not melt away as easily as did her sister, who had to be sent to Palm Beach to save the precious pounds.

"I don't see why you ever put Rickie Allen in charge of the English country dances," Florence said to her sister, as they sat down. "He knows the figures, of course, but he has no real style."

Roma looked annoyed. Rickie Allen was one of the men who came to the house almost often enough.

"He is absolutely to be depended upon, that's why," she said firmly.

"I think he is just right for it, Florence," put in Mrs. Wanning. "It's remarkable he should feel that he can give up the time; such a busy man. He must be very much interested in the movement."

Florence's lip curled drolly under her soup spoon. She shot an amused glance at her mother's dignity.

"Nothing doing," her keen eyes seemed to say.

Though Florence was nearly thirty and her sister a little beyond, there was, seriously, nothing doing. With so many charms and so much preparation, they never, as Florence vulgarly said, quite pulled it off. They had been rushed, time and again, and Mrs. Wanning had repeatedly steeled herself to bear the blow. But the young men went to follow a career in Mexico or the Philippines, or moved to Yonkers, and escaped without a mortal wound.

Roma turned graciously to her father.

"I met Mr. Lane at the Holland House today, where I was lunching with the Burtons, father. He asked about you, and when I told him you were not so well as usual, he said he would call you up. He wants to tell you about some doctor he discovered in Iowa, who cures everything with massage and hot water. It sounds freakish, but Mr. Lane is a very clever man, isn't he?"

"Very," assented Wanning.

"I should think he must be!" sighed Mrs. Wanning. "How in the world did he make all that money, Paul? He didn't seem especially promising years ago, when we used to see so much of them."

"Corporation business. He's attorney for the P. L. and G.," murmured her husband.

"What a pile he must have!" Florence watched the old negro's slow movements with restless eyes. "Here is Jenny, a Contessa, with a glorious palace in Genoa that her father must have bought her. Surely Aldrini had nothing. Have you seen the baby count's pictures, Roma? They're very cunning. I should think you'd go to Genoa and visit Jenny."

"We must arrange that, Roma. It's such an opportunity." Though Mrs. Wanning addressed her daughter, she looked at her husband. "You would get on so well among their friends. When Count Aldrini was here you spoke Italian much better than poor Jenny. I remember when we entertained him, he could scarcely say anything to her at all."

Florence tried to call up an answering flicker of amusement upon her sister's calm, well-bred face. She thought her mother was rather outdoing herself tonight,—since Aldrini had at least managed to say the one important thing to Jenny, somehow, somewhere. Jenny Lane had been Roma's friend and schoolmate, and the Count was an ephemeral hope in Orange. Mrs. Wanning was one of the first matrons to declare that she had no prejudices against foreigners, and at the dinners that were given for the Count, Roma was always put next him to act as interpreter.

Roma again turned to her father.

"If I were you, dear, I would let Mr. Lane tell me about his doctor. New discoveries are often made by queer people."

Roma's voice was low and sympathetic; she never lost her dignity.

Florence asked if she might have her coffee in her room, while she dashed off a note, and she ran upstairs humming "Bright Lights" and wondering how she was going to stand her family until the summer scattering. Why could Roma never throw off her elegant reserve and call things by their names? She sometimes thought she might like her sister, if she would only come out in the open and howl about her disappointments.

Roma, drinking her coffee deliberately, asked her father if they might have the car early, as they wanted to pick up Mr. Allen and Mr. Rydberg on their way to rehearsal.

Wanning said certainly. Heaven knew he was not stingy about his car, though he could never quite forget that in his day it was the young men who used to call for the girls when they went to rehearsals.

"You are going with us, Mother?" Roma asked as they rose.

"I think so dear. Your father will want to go to bed early, and I shall sleep better if I go out. I am going to town tomorrow to pour tea for Harold. We must get him some new silver, Paul. I am quite ashamed of his spoons."

Harold, the only son, was a playwright—as yet "unproduced"—and he had a studio in Washington Square.

A half-hour later, Wanning was alone in his library. He would not permit himself to feel aggrieved. What was more commendable than a mother's interest in her children's pleasures? Moreover, it was his wife's way of following things up, of never letting die grass grow under her feet, that had helped to push him along in the world. She was more ambitious than he,—that had been good for him. He was naturally indolent, and Julia's childlike desire to possess material objects, to buy what other people were buying, had been the spur that made him go after business. It had, moreover, made his house the attractive place he believed it to be.

"Suppose," his wife sometimes said to him when the bills came in from Céleste or Mme. Blanche, "suppose you had homely daughters; how would you like that?"

He wouldn't have liked it. When he went anywhere with his three ladies, Wanning always felt very well done by. He had no complaint to make about them, or about anything. That was why it seemed so unreasonable— He felt along his back incredulously with his hand. Harold, of course, was a trial; but among all his business friends, he knew scarcely one who had a promising boy.

The house was so still that Wanning could hear a faint, metallic tinkle from the butler's pantry. Old Sam was washing up the silver, which he put away himself every night.

Wanning rose and walked aimlessly down the hall and out through the dining-room.

"Any Apollinaris on ice, Sam? I'm not feeling very well tonight."

The old colored man dried his hands.

"Yessah, Mistah Wanning. Have a little rye with it, sah?"

"No, thank you, Sam. That's one of the things I can't do any more. I've been to see a big doctor in the city, and he tells me there's something seriously wrong with me. My kidneys have sort of gone back on me."

It was a satisfaction to Wanning to name the organ that had betrayed him, while all the rest of him was so sound.

Sam was immediately interested. He shook his grizzled head and looked full of wisdom.

"Don't seem like a gen'leman of such a temperate life ought to have anything wrong thar, sah."

"No, it doesn't, does it?"

Wanning leaned against the china closet and talked to Sam for nearly half an hour. The specialist who condemned him hadn't seemed half so much interested. There was not a detail about the examination and the laboratory tests in which Sam did not show the deepest concern. He kept asking Wanning if he could remember "straining himself" when he was a young man.

"I've knowed a strain like that to sleep in a man for yeahs and yeahs, and then come back on him, 'deed I have," he said, mysteriously. "An' again, it might be you got a floatin' kidney, sah. Aftah dey once teah loose, dey sometimes don't make no trouble for quite a while."

When Wanning went to his room he did not go to bed. He sat up until he heard the voices of his wife and daughters in the hall below. His own bed somehow frightened him. In all the years he had lived in this house he had never before looked about his room, at that bed, with the thought that he might one day be trapped there, and might not get out again. He had been ill, of course, but his room had seemed a particularly pleasant place for a sick man; sunlight, flowers,—agreeable, well-dressed women coming in and out.

Now there was something sinister about the bed itself, about its position, and its relation to the rest of the furniture.

II

The next morning, on his way downtown, Wanning got off the subway train at Astor Place and walked over to Washington Square. He climbed three flights of stairs and knocked at his son's studio. Harold, dressed, with his stick and gloves in his hand, opened the door. He was just going over to the Brevoort for breakfast. He greeted his father with the cordial familiarity practised by all the "boys" of his set, clapped him on the shoulder and said in his light, tonsilitis voice:

"Come in, Governor, how delightful! I haven't had a call from you in a long time."

He threw his hat and gloves on the writing table. He was a perfect gentleman, even with his father.

Florence said the matter with Harold was that he had heard people say he looked like Byron, and stood for it.

What Harold would stand for in such matters was, indeed, the best definition of him. When he read his play "The Street Walker" in drawing rooms and one lady told him it had the poetic symbolism of Tchekhov, and another said that it suggested the biting realism of Brieux, he never, in his most secret thoughts, questioned the acumen of either lady. Harold's speech, even if you heard it in the next room and could not see him, told you that he had no sense of the absurd, — a throaty staccato, with never a downward inflection, trustfully striving to please.

"Just going out?" his father asked. "I won't keep you. Your mother told you I had a discouraging session with Seares?"

"So awfully sorry you've had this bother, Governor; just as sorry as I can be. No question about it's coming out all right, but it's a downright nuisance, your having to diet and that sort of thing. And I suppose you ought to follow directions, just to make us all feel comfortable, oughtn't you?" Harold spoke with fluent sympathy.

Wanning sat down on the arm of a chair and shook his head. "Yes, they do recommend a diet, but they don't promise much from it."

Harold laughed precipitately. "Delicious! All doctors are, aren't they? So profound and oracular! The medicine-man; it's quite the same idea, you see; with tom-toms."

Wanning knew that Harold meant something subtle, — one of the subtleties which he said were only spoiled by being explained — so he came bluntly to one of the issues he had in mind.

"I would like to see you settled before I quit the harness, Harold."

Harold was absolutely tolerant.

He took out his cigarette case and burnished it with his handkerchief.

"I perfectly understand your point of view, dear Governor, but perhaps you don't altogether get mine. Isn't it so? I am settled. What you mean by being settled, would unsettle me, completely. I'm cut out for just such an existence as this; to live four floors up in an attic, get my own breakfast, and have a charwoman to do for me. I should be awfully bored with an establishment. I'm quite content with a little diggings like this."

Wanning's eyes fell. Somebody had to pay the rent of even such modest quarters as contented Harold, but to say so would be rude, and Harold himself was never rude. Wanning did not, this morning, feel equal to hearing a statement of his son's uncommercial ideals.

"I know," he said hastily. "But now we're up against hard facts, my boy. I did not want to alarm your mother, but I've had a time limit put on me, and it's not a very long one."

Harold threw away the cigarette he had just lighted in a burst of indignation.

"That's the sort of thing I consider criminal, Father, absolutely criminal! What doctor has a right to suggest such a thing? Seares himself may be knocked out tomorrow. What have laboratory tests got to do with a man's will to live? The force of that depends upon his entire personality, not on any organ or pair of organs."

Harold thrust his hands in his pockets and walked up and down, very much stirred. "Really, I have a very poor opinion of scientists. They ought to be made serve an apprenticeship in art, to get some conception of the power of human motives. Such brutality!"

Harold's plays dealt with the grimmest and most depressing matters, but he himself was always agreeable, and he insisted upon high cheerfulness as the correct tone of human intercourse.

Wanning rose and turned to go. There was, in Harold, simply no reality, to which one could break through. The young man took up his hat and gloves.

"Must you go? Let me step along with you to the sub. The walk will do me good."

Harold talked agreeably all the way to Astor Place. His father heard little of what he said, but he rather liked his company and his wish to be pleasant.

Wanning went to his club for luncheon, meaning to spend the afternoon with some of his friends who had retired from business and who read the papers there in the empty hours between two and seven. He got no satisfaction, however. When he tried to tell these men of his present predicament, they began to describe ills of their own in which he could not feel interested. Each one of them had a treacherous organ of which he spoke with animation, almost with pride, as if it were a crafty business competitor whom he was constantly outwitting. Each had a doctor, too, for whom he was ardently soliciting business. They wanted either to telephone their doctor and make an appointment for Wanning, or to take him then and there to the consulting room. When he did not accept these invitations, they lost interest in him and remembered engagements. He called a taxi and returned to the offices of McQuiston, Wade, and Wanning.

Settled at his desk, Wanning decided that he would not go home to dinner, but would stay at the office and dictate a long letter to an old college friend who lived in Wyoming. He could tell Douglas Brown things that he had not succeeded in getting to any one else. Brown, out in the Wind River mountains, couldn't defend himself, couldn't slap Wanning on the back and tell him to gather up the sunbeams.

He called up his house in Orange to say that he would not be home until late. Roma answered the telephone. He spoke mournfully, but she was not disturbed by it.

"Very well, Father. Don't get too tired," she said in her well modulated voice.

When Wanning was ready to dictate his letter, he looked out from his private office into the reception room and saw that his stenographer in her hat and gloves, and furs of the newest cut, was just leaving.

"Goodnight, Mr. Wanning," she said, drawing down her dotted veil.

Had there been important business letters to be got off on the night mail, he would have felt that he could detain her, but not for anything personal. Miss Doane was an expert legal stenographer, and she knew her value. The slightest delay in dispatching office business annoyed her. Letters that were not signed until the next morning awoke her deepest contempt. She was scrupulous in professional etiquette, and Wanning felt that their relations, though pleasant, were scarcely cordial.

As Miss Doane's trim figure disappeared through the outer door, little Annie Wooley, the copyist, came in from the stenographers' room. Her hat was pinned over one ear, and she was scrambling into her coat as she came, holding her gloves in her teeth and her battered handbag in the fist that was already through a sleeve.

"Annie, I wanted to dictate a letter. You were just leaving, weren't you?"

"Oh, I don't mind!" she answered cheerfully, and pulling off her old coat, threw it on a chair. "I'll get my book."

She followed him into his room and sat down by a table,—though she wrote with her book on her knee.

Wanning had several times kept her after office hours to take his private letters for him, and she had always been good-natured about it. On each occasion, when he gave her a dollar to get her dinner, she protested, laughing, and saying that she could never eat so much as that.

She seemed a happy sort of little creature, didn't pout when she was scolded, and giggled about her own mistakes in spelling. She was plump and undersized, always dodging under the elbows of taller people and clattering about on high heels, much run over. She had bright black eyes and fuzzy black hair in which, despite Miss Doane's reprimands, she often stuck her pencil. She was the girl who couldn't believe that Wanning was fifty, and he had liked her ever since he overheard that conversation.

Tilting back his chair—he never assumed this position when he dictated to Miss Doane—Wanning began: "To Mr. D. E. Brown, South Forks, Wyoming."

He shaded his eyes with his hand and talked off a long letter to this man who would be sorry that his mortal frame was breaking up. He recalled to him certain fine months they had spent together on the Wind River when they were young men, and said he sometimes wished that like D. E. Brown, he had claimed his freedom in a big country where the wheels did not grind a man as hard as they did in New York. He had spent all these years hustling about and getting ready to live the way he wanted to live, and now he had a puncture the doctors couldn't mend. What was the use of it?

Wanning's thoughts were fixed on the trout streams and the great silver-firs in the canyons of the Wind River Mountains, when he was disturbed by a soft, repeated sniffling. He looked out between his fingers. Little Annie, carried away by his eloquence, was fairly panting to make dots and dashes fast enough, and she was sopping her eyes with an unpresentable, end-of-the-day handkerchief.

Wanning rambled on in his dictation. Why was she crying? What did it matter to her? He was a man who said good-morning to her, who sometimes took an hour of the precious few she had left at the end of the day and then complained about her bad spelling. When the letter was finished, he handed her a new two dollar bill.

"I haven't got any change tonight; and anyhow, I'd like you to eat a whole lot. I'm on a diet, and I want to see everybody else eat."

Annie tucked her notebook under her arm and stood looking at the bill which she had not taken up from the table.

"I don't like to be paid for taking letters to your friends, Mr. Wanning," she said impulsively. "I can run personal letters off between times. It ain't as if I needed the money," she added carelessly.

"Get along with you! Anybody who is eighteen years old and has a sweet tooth needs money, all they can get."

Annie giggled and darted out with the bill in her hand.

Wanning strolled aimlessly after her into the reception room.

"Let me have that letter before lunch tomorrow, please, and be sure that nobody sees it." He stopped and frowned. "I don't look very sick, do I?"

"I should say you don't!" Annie got her coat on after considerable tugging. "Why don't you call in a specialist? My mother called a specialist for my father before he died."

"Oh, is your father dead?"

"I should say he is! He was a painter by trade, and he fell off a seventy-foot stack into the East River. Mother couldn't get anything out of the company, because he wasn't buckled. He lingered for four months, so I know all about taking care of sick people. I was attending business college then, and sick as he was, he used to give me dictation for practise. He made us all go into professions; the girls, too. He didn't like us to just run."

Wanning would have liked to keep Annie and hear more about her family, but it was nearly seven o'clock, and he knew he ought, in mercy, to let her go. She was the only person to whom he had talked about his illness who had been frank and honest with him, who had looked at him with eyes that concealed nothing. When he broke the news of his condition to his partners that morning, they shut him off as if he were uttering indecent ravings. All day they had met him with a hurried, abstracted manner. McQuiston and Wade went out to lunch together, and he knew what they were thinking, perhaps talking, about. Wanning had brought into the firm valuable business, but he was less enterprising than either of his partners.

III

In the early summer Wanning's family scattered. Roma swallowed her pride and sailed for Genoa to visit the Contessa Jenny. Harold went to Cornish to be in an artistic atmosphere. Mrs. Wanning and Florence took a cottage at York Harbor where Wanning was supposed to join them whenever he could get away from town. He did not often get away. He felt most at ease among his accustomed surroundings. He kept his car in the city and went back and forth from his office to the club where he was living. Old Sam, his butler, came in from Orange every night to put his clothes in order and make him comfortable.

Wanning began to feel that he would not tire of his office in a hundred years. Although he did very little work, it was pleasant to go down town every morning when the streets were crowded, the sky clear, and the sunshine bright. From the windows of his private office he could see the harbor and watch the ocean liners come down the North River and go out to sea.

While he read his mail, he often looked out and wondered why he had been so long indifferent to that extraordinary scene of human activity and hopefulness. How had a short-lived race of beings the energy and courage valiantly to begin enterprises which they could follow for only a few years; to throw up towers and build sea-monsters and found great businesses, when the frailest of the materials with which they worked, the paper upon which they wrote, the ink upon their pens, had more permanence in this world than they? All this material rubbish lasted. The linen clothing and cosmetics of the Egyptians had lasted. It was only the human flame that certainly, certainly went out. Other things had a fighting chance; they might meet with mishap and be destroyed, they might not. But the human creature who gathered and shaped and hoarded and foolishly loved these things, he had no chance—absolutely none. Wanning's cane, his hat, his topcoat, might go from beggar to beggar and knock about in this world for another fifty years or so; but not he.

In the late afternoon he never hurried to leave his office now. Wonderful sunsets burned over the North River, wonderful stars trembled up among the towers; more wonderful than anything he could hurry away to. One of his windows looked directly down upon the spire of Old Trinity, with the green churchyard and the pale sycamores far below. Wanning often dropped into the church when he was going out to lunch; not because he was trying to make his peace with Heaven, but because the church was old and restful and familiar, because it and its gravestones had sat in the same place for a long while. He bought flowers from the street boys and kept them on his desk, which his partners thought strange behavior, and which Miss Doane considered a sign that he was failing.

But there were graver things than bouquets for Miss Doane and the senior partner to ponder over.

The senior partner, McQuiston, in spite of his silvery hair and mustache and his important church connections, had rich natural taste for scandal.— After Mr. Wade went away for his vacation, in May, Wanning took Annie Wooley out of the copying room, put her at a desk in his private office, and raised her pay to eighteen dollars a week, explaining to McQuiston that for the summer months he would need a secretary. This explanation satisfied neither McQuiston nor Miss Doane.

Annie was also paid for overtime, and although Wanning attended to very little of the office business now, there was a great deal of overtime. Miss Doane was, of course, 'above' questioning a chit like Annie; but what was he doing with his time and his new secretary, she wanted to know?

If anyone had told her that Wanning was writing a book, she would have said bitterly that it was just like him. In his youth Wanning had hankered for the pen. When he studied law, he had intended to combine that profession with some tempting form of authorship. Had he remained a bachelor, he would have been an unenterprising literary lawyer to the end of his days. It was his wife's restlessness and her practical turn of mind that had made him a money-getter. His illness seemed to bring back to him the illusions with which he left college.

As soon as his family were out of the way and he shut up the Orange house, he began to dictate his autobiography to Annie Wooley. It was not only the story of his life, but an expression of all his theories and opinions, and a commentary on the fifty years of events which he could remember.

Fortunately, he was able to take great interest in this undertaking. He had the happiest convictions about the clear-cut style he was developing and his increasing felicity in phrasing. He meant to publish the work handsomely, at his own expense and under his own name. He rather enjoyed the thought of how greatly disturbed Harold would be. He and Harold differed in their estimates of books. All the solid works which made up Wanning's library, Harold considered beneath contempt. Anybody, he said, could do that sort of thing.

When Wanning could not sleep at night, he turned on the light beside his bed and made notes on the chapter he meant to dictate the next day.

When he returned to the office after lunch, he gave instructions that he was not to be interrupted by telephone calls, and shut himself up with his secretary.

After he had opened all the windows and taken off his coat, he fell to dictating. He found it a delightful occupation, the solace of each day. Often he had sudden fits of tiredness; then he would lie down on the leather sofa and drop asleep, while Annie read "The Leopard's Spots" until he awoke.

Like many another business man Wanning had relied so long on stenographers that the operation of writing with a pen had become laborious to him. When he undertook it, he wanted to cut everything short. But walking up and down his private office, with the strong afternoon sun pouring in at his windows, a fresh air stirring, all the people and boats moving restlessly down there, he could say things he wanted to say. It was like living his life over again.

He did not miss his wife or his daughters. He had become again the mild, contemplative youth he was in college, before he had a profession and a family to grind for, before the two needs which shape our destiny had made of him pretty much what they make of every man.

At five o'clock Wanning sometimes went out for a cup of tea and took Annie along. He felt dull and discouraged as soon as he was alone. So long as Annie was with him, he could keep a grip on his own thoughts. They talked about what he had just been dictating to her. She found that he liked to be questioned, and she tried to be greatly interested in it all.

After tea, they went back to the office. Occasionally Wanning lost track of time and kept Annie until it grew dark. He knew he had old McQuiston guessing, but he didn't care. One day the senior partner came to him with a reproving air.

"I am afraid Miss Doane is leaving us, Paul. She feels that Miss Wooley's promotion is irregular."

"How is that any business of hers, I'd like to know? She has all my legal work. She is always disagreeable enough about doing anything else."

McQuiston's puffy red face went a shade darker.

"Miss Doane has a certain professional pride; a strong feeling for office organization. She doesn't care to fill an equivocal position. I don't know that I blame her. She feels that there is something not quite regular about the confidence you seem to place in this inexperienced young woman."

Wanning pushed back his chair.

"I don't care a hang about Miss Doane's sense of propriety. I need a stenographer who will carry out my instructions. I've carried out Miss Doane's long enough. I've let that schoolma'am hector me for years. She can go when she pleases."

That night McQuiston wrote to his partner that things were in a bad way, and they would have to keep an eye on Wanning. He had been seen at the theatre with his new stenographer.

That was true. Wanning had several times taken Annie to the Palace on Saturday afternoon. When all his acquaintances were off motoring or playing golf, when the down-town offices and even the streets were deserted, it amused him to watch a foolish show with a delighted, cheerful little person beside him.

Beyond her generosity, Annie had no shining merits of character, but she had the gift of thinking well of everything, and wishing well. When she was there Wanning felt as if there were someone who cared whether this was a good or a bad day with him. Old Sam, too, was like that. While the old black man put him to bed and made him comfortable, Wanning could talk to him as he talked to little Annie. Even if he dwelt upon his illness, in plain terms, in detail, he did not feel as if he were imposing on them.

People like Sam and Annie admitted misfortune,—admitted it almost cheerfully. Annie and her family did not consider illness or any of its hard facts vulgar or indecent. It had its place in their scheme of life, as it had not in that of Wanning's friends.

Annie came out of a typical poor family of New York. Of eight children, only four lived to grow up. In such families the stream of life is broad enough, but runs shallow. In the children, vitality is exhausted early. The roots do not go down into anything very strong. Illness and deaths and funerals, in her own family and in those of her friends, had come at frequent intervals in Annie's life. Since they had to be, she and her sisters made the best of them. There was something to be got out of funerals, even, if they were managed right. They kept people in touch with old friends who had moved uptown, and revived kindly feelings.

Annie had often given up things she wanted because there was sickness at home, and now she was patient with her boss. What he paid her for overtime work by no means made up to her what she lost.

Annie was not in the least thrifty, nor were any of her sisters. She had to make a living, but she was not interested in getting all she could for her time, or in laying up for the future. Girls like Annie know that the future is a very uncertain thing, and they feel no responsibility about it. The present is what they have—and it is all they have. If Annie missed a chance to go sailing with the plumber's son on Saturday afternoon, why, she missed it. As for the two dollars her boss gave her, she handed them over to her mother. Now that Annie was getting more money, one of her sisters quit a job she didn't like and was staying at home for a rest. That was all promotion meant to Annie.

The first time Annie's boss asked her to work on Saturday afternoon, she could not hide her disappointment. He suggested that they might knock off early and go to a show, or take a run in his car, but she grew tearful and said it would be hard to make her family understand. Wanning thought perhaps he could explain to her mother. He called his motor and took Annie home.

When his car stopped in front of the tenement house on Eighth Avenue, heads came popping out of the windows for six storys up, and all the neighbor women, in dressing sacks and wrappers, gazed down at the machine and at the couple alighting from it. A motor meant a wedding or the hospital.

The plumber's son, Willy Steen, came over from the corner saloon to see what was going on, and Annie introduced him at the doorstep.

Mrs. Wooley asked Wanning to come into the parlor and invited him to have a chair of ceremony between the folding bed and the piano.

Annie, nervous and tearful, escaped to the dining-room—the cheerful spot where the daughters visited with each other and with their friends. The parlor was a masked sleeping chamber and store room.

The plumber's son sat down on the sofa beside Mrs. Wooley, as if he were accustomed to share in the family councils. Mrs. Wooley waited expectant and kindly. She looked the sensible, hard-working woman that she was, and one could see she hadn't lived all her life on Eighth Avenue without learning a great deal.

Wanning explained to her that he was writing a book which he wanted to finish during the summer months when business was not so heavy. He was ill and could not work regularly. His secretary would have to take his dictation when he felt able to give it; must, in short, be a sort of companion to him. He would like to feel that she could go out in his car with him, or even to the theater, when he felt like it. It might have been better if he had engaged a young man for this work, but since he had begun it with Annie, he would like to keep her if her mother was willing.

Mrs. Wooley watched him with friendly, searching eyes. She glanced at Willy Steen, who, wise in such distinctions, had decided that there was nothing shady about Annie's boss. He nodded his sanction.

"I don't want my girl to conduct herself in any such way as will prejudice her, Mr. Wanning," she said thoughtfully. "If you've got daughters, you know how that is. You've been liberal with Annie, and it's a good position for her. It's right she should go to business every day, and I want her to do her work right, but I like to have her home after working hours. I always think a young girl's time is her own after business hours, and I try not to burden them when they come home. I'm willing she should do your work as suits you, if it's her wish; but I don't like to press her. The good times she misses now, it's not you nor me, sir, that can make them up to her. These young things has their feelings."

"Oh, I don't want to press her, either," Wanning said hastily. "I simply want to know that you understand the situation. I've made her a little present in my will as a recognition that she is doing more for me than she is paid for."

"That's something above me, sir. We'll hope there won't be no question of wills for many years yet," Mrs. Wooley spoke heartily. "I'm glad if my girl can be of any use to you, just so she don't prejudice herself."

The plumber's son rose as if the interview were over.

"It's all right, Mama Wooley, don't you worry," he said.

He picked up his canvas cap and turned to Wanning. "You see, Annie ain't the sort of girl that would want to be spotted circulating around with a monied party her folks didn't know all about. She'd lose friends by it."

After this conversation Annie felt a great deal happier. She was still shy and a trifle awkward with poor Wanning when they were outside the office building, and she missed the old freedom of her Saturday afternoons. But she did the best she could, and Willy Steen tried to make it up to her.

In Annie's absence he often came in of an afternoon to have a cup of tea and a sugar-bun with Mrs. Wooley and the daughter who was "resting." As they sat at the dining-room table, they discussed Annie's employer, his peculiarities, his health, and what he had told Mrs. Wooley about his will.

Mrs. Wooley said she sometimes felt afraid he might disinherit his children, as rich people often did, and make talk; but she hoped for the best. Whatever came to Annie, she prayed it might not be in the form of taxable property.

IV

Late in September Wanning grew suddenly worse. His family hurried home, and he was put to bed in his house in Orange. He kept asking the doctors when he could get back to the office, but he lived only eight days.

The morning after his father's funeral, Harold went to the office to consult Wanning's partners and to read the will. Everything in the will was as it should be. There were no surprises except a codicil in the form of a letter to Mrs. Wanning, dated July 8th, requesting that out of the estate she should pay the sum of one thousand dollars to his stenographer, Annie Wooley, "in recognition of her faithful services."

"I thought Miss Doane was my father's stenographer," Harold exclaimed.

Alec McQuiston looked embarrassed and spoke in a low, guarded tone.

"She was, for years. But this spring,—" he hesitated.

McQuiston loved a scandal. He leaned across his desk toward Harold.

"This spring your father put this little girl, Miss Wooley, a copyist, utterly inexperienced, in Miss Doane's place. Miss Doane was indignant and left us. The change made comment here in the office. It was slightly— No, I will be frank with you, Harold, it was very irregular."

Harold also looked grave. "What could my father have meant by such a request as this to my mother?"

The silver haired senior partner flushed and spoke as if he were trying to break something gently.

"I don't understand it, my boy. But I think, indeed I prefer to think, that your father was not quite himself all this summer. A man like your father does not, in his right senses, find pleasure in the society of an ignorant, common little girl. He does not make a practise of keeping her at the office after hours, often until eight o'clock, or take her to restaurants and to the theater with him; not, at least, in a slanderous city like New York."

Harold flinched before McQuiston's meaning gaze and turned aside in pained silence. He knew, as a dramatist, that there are dark chapters in all men's lives, and this but too clearly explained why his father had stayed in town all summer instead of joining his family.

McQuiston asked if he should ring for Annie Wooley.

Harold drew himself up. "No. Why should I see her? I prefer not to. But with your permission, Mr. McQuiston, I will take charge of this request to my mother. It could only give her pain, and might awaken doubts in her mind."

"We hardly know," murmured the senior partner, "where an investigation would lead us. Technically, of course, I cannot agree with you. But if, as one of the executors of the will, you wish to assume personal responsibility for this bequest, under the circumstances—irregularities beget irregularities."

"My first duty to my father," said Harold, "is to protect my mother."

That afternoon McQuiston called Annie Wooley into his private office and told her that her services would not be needed any longer, and that in lieu of notice the clerk would give her two weeks' salary.

"Can I call up here for references?" Annie asked.

"Certainly. But you had better ask for me, personally. You must know there has been some criticism of you here in the office, Miss Wooley."

"What about?" Annie asked boldly.

"Well, a young girl like you cannot render so much personal service to her employer as you did to Mr. Wanning without causing unfavorable comment. To be blunt with you, for your own good, my dear young lady, your services to your employer should terminate in the office, and at the close of office hours. Mr. Wanning was a very sick man and his judgment was at fault, but you should have known what a girl in your station can do and what she cannot do."

The vague discomfort of months flashed up in little Annie. She had no mind to stand by and be lectured without having a word to say for herself.

"Of course he was sick, poor man!" she burst out. "Not as anybody seemed much upset about it. I wouldn't have given up my half-holidays for anybody if they hadn't been sick, no matter what they paid me. There wasn't anything in it for me."

McQuiston raised his hand warningly.

"That will do, young lady. But when you get another place, remember this: it is never your duty to entertain or to provide amusement for your employer."

He gave Annie a look which she did not clearly understand, although she pronounced him a nasty old man as she hustled on her hat and jacket.

When Annie reached home she found Willy Steen sitting with her mother and sister at the dining-room table. This was the first day that Annie had gone to the office since Wanning's death, and her family awaited her return with suspense.

"Hello yourself," Annie called as she came in and threw her handbag into an empty armchair.

"You're off early, Annie," said her mother gravely. "Has the will been read?"

"I guess so. Yes, I know it has. Miss Wilson got it out of the safe for them. The son came in. He's a pill."

"Was nothing said to you, daughter?"

"Yes, a lot. Please give me some tea, mother." Annie felt that her swagger was failing.

"Don't tantalize us, Ann," her sister broke in. "Didn't you get anything?"

"I got the mit, all right. And some back talk from the old man that I'm awful sore about."

Annie dashed away the tears and gulped her tea.

Gradually her mother and Willy drew the story from her. Willy offered at once to go to the office building and take his stand outside the door and never leave it until he had punched old Mr. McQuiston's face. He rose as if to attend to it at once, but Mrs. Wooley drew him to his chair again and patted his arm.

"It would only start talk and get the girl in trouble, Willy. When it's lawyers, folks in our station is helpless. I certainly believed that man when he sat here; you heard him yourself. Such a gentleman as he looked."

Willy thumped his great fist, still in punching position, down on his knee.

"Never you be fooled again, Mama Wooley. You'll never get anything out of a rich guy that he ain't signed up in the courts for. Rich is tight. There's no exceptions."

Annie shook her head.

"I didn't want anything out of him. He was a nice, kind man, and he had his troubles, I guess. He wasn't tight."

"Still," said Mrs. Wooley sadly, "Mr. Wanning had no call to hold out promises. I hate to be disappointed in a gentleman. You've had confining work for some time, daughter; a rest will do you good."

Smart Set, October 1919

Part II
Reviews and Essays

Mark Twain

If there is anything which should make an American sick and disgusted at the literary taste of his country, and almost swerve his allegiance to his flag it is that controversy between Mark Twain and Max O'Rell, in which the Frenchman proves himself a wit and a gentleman and the American shows himself little short of a clown and an all around tough. The squabble arose apropos of Paul Bourget's new book on America, "Outre Mer," a book which deals more fairly and generously with this country than any book yet written in a foreign tongue. Mr. Clemens did not like the book, and like all men of his class, and limited mentality, he cannot criticise without becoming personal and insulting. He cannot be scathing without being a blackguard. He tried to demolish a serious and well considered work by publishing a scurrilous, slangy and loosely written article about it. In this article Mr. Clemens proves very little against Mr. Bourget and a very great deal against himself. He demonstrates clearly that he is neither a scholar, a reader or a man of letters and very little of a gentleman. His ignorance of French literature is something appalling. Why, in these days it is as necessary for a literary man to have a wide knowledge of the French masterpieces as it is for him to have read Shakespeare or the Bible. What man who pretends to be an author can afford to neglect those models of style and composition. George Meredith, Thomas Hardy and Henry James excepted, the great living novelists are Frenchmen.

Mr. Clemens asks what the French sensualists can possibly teach the great American people about novel writing or morality? Well, it would not seriously hurt the art of the classic author of "Puddin' Head Wilson" to study Daudet, De Maupassant, Hugo and George Sand, whatever it might do to his morals. Mark Twain is a humorist of a kind. His humor is always rather broad, so broad that the polite world can justly call it coarse. He is not a reader nor a thinker nor a man who loves art of any kind. He is a clever Yankee who has made a "good thing" out of writing. He has been published in the North American Review and in the Century, but he is not and never will be a part of literature. The association and companionship of cultured men has given Mark Twain a sort of professional veneer, but it could not give him fine instincts or nice discriminations or elevated tastes. His works are pure and suitable for children, just as the work of most shallow and mediocre fellows. House dogs and donkeys make the most harmless and chaste companions for young innocence in the world. Mark Twain's humor is of the kind that teamsters use in bantering with each other, and his laugh is the gruff "haw-haw" of the backwoodsman. He is still the rough, awkward, good-natured boy who swore at the deck hands on the river steamer and chewed uncured tobacco when he was three years old. Thoroughly likeable as a good fellow, but impossible as a man of letters. It is an unfortunate feature of American literature that a hostler with some natural cleverness and a great deal of assertion receives the same recognition as a standard American author that a man like Lowell does. The French academy is a good thing after all. It at least divides the sheep from the goats and gives a sheep the consolation of knowing that he is a sheep.

It is rather a pity that Paul Bourget should have written "Outre Mer," thoroughly creditable book though it is. Mr. Bourget is a novelist, and he should not content himself with being an essayist, there are far too many of them in the world already. He can develop strong characters, invent strong situations, he can write the truth and he should not drift into penning opinions and platitudes. When God has made a man a creator, it is a great mistake for him to turn critic. It is rather an insult to God and certainly a very great wrong to man.

Nebraska State Journal, May 5, 1895

I got a letter last week from a little boy just half-past seven who had just read "Huckleberry Finn" and "Tom Sawyer." He said: "If there are any more books like them in the world, send them to me quick." I had to humbly confess to him that if there were any others I had not the good fortune to know of them. What a red-letter-day it is to a boy, the day he first opens "Tom Sawyer." I would rather sail on the raft down the Missouri again with "Huck" Finn and Jim than go down the Nile in December or see Venice from a gondola in May. Certainly Mark Twain is much better when he writes of his Missouri boys than when he makes sickley romances about Joan of

Arc. And certainly he never did a better piece of work than "Prince and Pauper." One seems to get at the very heart of old England in that dearest of children's books, and in its pages the frail boy king, and his gloomy sister Mary who in her day wrought so much woe for unhappy England, and the dashing Princess Elizabeth who lived to rule so well, seem to live again. A friend of Mr. Clemens' once told me that he said he wrote that book so that when his little daughters grew up they might know that their tired old jester of a father could be serious and gentle sometimes.

The Home Monthly, May 1897

William Dean Howells

Certainly now in his old age Mr. Howells is selecting queer titles for his books. A while ago we had that feeble tale, "The Coast of Bohemia," and now we have "My Literary Passions." "Passions," literary or otherwise, were never Mr. Howells' forte and surely no man could be further from even the coast of Bohemia.

Apropos of "My Literary Passions" which has so long strung out in the Ladies' Home Journal along with those thrilling articles about how Henry Ward Beecher tied his necktie and what kind of coffee Mrs. Hall Cain likes, why did Mr. Howells write it? Doesn't Mr. Howells know that at one time or another every one raves over Don Quixote, imitates Heine, worships Tourgueneff and calls Tolstoi a prophet? Does Mr. Howells think that no one but he ever had youth and enthusiasm and aspirations? Doesn't he know that the only thing that makes the world worth living in at all is that once, when we are young, we all have that great love for books and impersonal things, all reverence and dream? We have all known the time when Porthos, Athos and d'Artagan were vastly more real and important to us than the folks who lived next door. We have all dwelt in that country where Anna Karenina and the Levins were the only people who mattered much. We have all known that intoxicating period when we thought we "understood life," because we had read Daudet, Zola and Guy de Maupassant, and like Mr. Howells we all looked back rather fondly upon the time when we believed that books were the truth and art was all. After a while books grow matter of fact like everything else and we always think enviously of the days when they were new and wonderful and strange. That's a part of existence. We lose our first keen relish for literature just as we lose it for ice-cream and confectionery. The taste grows older, wiser and more subdued. We would all wear out of very enthusiasm if it did not. But why should Mr. Howells tell the world this common experience in detail as though it were his and his alone. He might as well write a detailed account of how he had the measles and the whooping cough. It was all right and proper for Mr. Howells to like Heine and Hugo, but, in the words of the circus clown, "We've all been there."

Nebraska State Journal, July 14, 1895

Edgar Allan Poe

My tantalized spirit
Here blandly reposes,
Forgetting, or never
Regretting its roses,
Its old agitations
Of myrtles and roses.

For now, while so quietly
Lying, it fancies
A holier odor
About it, of pansies—
A rosemary odor
Commingled with pansies.
With rue and the beautiful
Puritan pansies.

—Edgar Allan Poe.

The Shakespeare society of New York, which is really about the only useful literary organization in this country, is making vigorous efforts to redress an old wrong and atone for a long neglect. Sunday, Sept. 22, it held a meeting at the Poe cottage on Kingsbridge road near Fordham, for the purpose of starting an organized movement to buy back the cottage, restore it to its original condition and preserve it as a memorial of Poe. So it has come at last. After helping build monuments to Shelley, Keats and Carlyle we have at last remembered this man, the greatest of our poets and the most unhappy. I am glad that this movement is in the hands of American actors, for it was among them that Poe found his best friends and warmest admirers. Some way he always seemed to belong to the strolling Thespians who were his mother's people.

Among all the thousands of life's little ironies that make history so diverting, there is none more paradoxical than that Edgar Poe should have been an American. Look at his face. Had we ever another like it? He must have been a strange figure in his youth, among those genial, courtly Virginians, this handsome, pale fellow, violent in his enthusiasm, ardent in his worship, but spiritually cold in his affections. Now playing heavily for the mere excitement of play, now worshipping at the shrine of a woman old enough to be his mother, merely because her voice was beautiful; now swimming six miles up the James river against a heavy current in the glaring sun of a June midday. He must have seemed to them an unreal figure, a sort of stage man who was wandering about the streets with his mask and buskins on, a theatrical figure who had escaped by some strange mischance into the prosaic daylight. His speech and actions were unconsciously and sincerely dramatic, always as though done for effect. He had that nervous, egotistic, self-centered nature common to stage children who seem to have been dazzled by the footlights and maddened by the applause before they are born. It was in his blood. With the exception of two women who loved him, lived for him, died for him, he went through life friendless, misunderstood, with that dense, complete, hopeless misunderstanding which, as Amiel said, is the secret of that sad smile upon the lips of the great. Men tried to befriend him, but in some way or other he hurt and disappointed them. He tried to mingle and share with other men, but he was always shut from them by that shadow, light as gossamer but unyielding as adamant, by which, from the beginning of the world, art has shielded and guarded and protected her own, that God-concealing mist in which the heroes of old were hidden, immersed in that gloom and solitude which, if we could but know it here, is but the shadow of God's hand as it falls upon his elect.

We lament our dearth of great prose. With the exception of Henry James and Hawthorne, Poe is our only master of pure prose. We lament our dearth of poets. With the exception of Lowell, Poe is our only great poet. Poe found short story writing a bungling makeshift. He left it a perfect art. He wrote the first perfect short stories in the English language. He first gave the short story purpose, method, and artistic form. In a careless reading one can not realize the wonderful literary art, the cunning devices, the masterly effects that those entrancing tales conceal. They are simple and direct enough to delight us when we are children, subtle and artistic enough to be our marvel when we are old. To this day they are the wonder and admiration of the French, who are the acknowledged masters of craft and form. How in his wandering, laborious life, bound to the hack work of the press and crushed by an ever-growing burden of want and debt, did he ever come upon all this deep and mystical lore, this knowledge of all history, of all languages, of all art, this penetration into the hidden things of the East? As Steadman says, "The self training of genius is always a marvel." The past is spread before us all and most of us spend our lives in learning those things which we do not need to know, but genius reaches out instinctively and takes only the vital detail, by some sort of spiritual gravitation goes directly to the right thing.

Poe belonged to the modern French school of decorative and discriminating prose before it ever existed in France. He rivalled Gautier, Flaubert and de Maupassant before they were born. He clothed his tales in a barbaric splendor and persuasive unreality never before heard of in English. No such profusion of color, oriental splendor of detail, grotesque combinations and mystical effects had ever before been wrought into language. There are tales as grotesque, as monstrous, unearthly as the stone griffens and gargoyles that are cut up among the unvisited niches and towers of Notre Dame, stories as poetic and delicately beautiful as the golden lace work chased upon an Etruscan ring. He fitted his words together as the Byzantine jewelers fitted priceless stones. He found the inner harmony and kinship of words. Where lived another man who could blend the beautiful and the horrible, the gorgeous and the grotesque in such intricate and inexplicable fashion? Who could delight you with his noun and disgust you with his verb, thrill you with his adjective and chill you with his adverb, make you run the whole gamut of human emotions in a single sentence? Sitting in that miserable cottage at Fordham he wrote of the splendor of dream palaces beyond the dreams of art. He hung those grimy walls with dream tapestries, paved those narrow halls with black marble and polished onyx, and into those low-roofed chambers he brought all the treasured imagery of fancy, from the "huge carvings of untutored Egypt" to "mingled and conflicting perfumes, reeking up from strange convolute censers, together with multitudinous, flaring and flickering tongues of purple and violet fire." Hungry and ragged he wrote of Epicurean feasts and luxury that would have beggared the purpled pomp of pagan Rome and put Nero and his Golden House to shame.

And this mighty master of the organ of language, who knew its every stop and pipe, who could awaken at will the thin silver tones of its slenderest reeds or the solemn cadence of its deepest thunder, who could make it sing like a flute or roar like a cataract, he was born into a country without a literature. He was of that ornate school which usually comes last in a national literature, and he came first. American taste had been vitiated by men like Griswold and N. P. Willis until it was at the lowest possible ebb. Willis was considered a genius, that is the worst that could possibly be said. In the North a new race of great philosophers was growing up, but Poe had neither their friendship nor encouragement. He went indeed, sometimes, to the chilly *salon* of Margaret Fuller, but he was always a discord there. He was a mere artist and he had no business with philosophy, he had no theories as to the "higher life" and the "true happiness." He had only his unshapen dreams that battled with him in dark places, the unborn that struggled in his brain for birth. What time has an artist to learn the multiplication table or to talk philosophy? He was not afraid of them. He laughed at Willis, and flung Longfellow's lie in his teeth, the lie the rest of the world was twenty years in finding. He scorned the obtrusive learning of the transcendentalists and he disliked their hard talkative women. He left them and went back to his dream women, his *Berenice*, his *Ligeia*, his *Marchesa Aphrodite*, pale and cold as the mist maidens of the North, sad as the Norns who weep for human woe.

The tragedy of Poe's life was not alcohol, but hunger. He died when he was forty, when his work was just beginning. Thackeray had not touched his great novels at forty, George Eliot was almost unknown at that age. Hugo, Goethe, Hawthorne, Lowell and Dumas all did their great work after they were forty years old. Poe never did his great work. He could not endure the hunger. This year the Drexel Institute has put over sixty thousand dollars into a new edition of Poe's poems and stories. He himself never got six thousand for them altogether. If one of the great and learned institutions of the land had invested one tenth of that amount in the living author forty years ago we should have had from him such works as would have made the name of this nation great. But he sold "The Masque of the Red Death" for a few dollars, and now the Drexel Institute pays a publisher thousands to publish it beautifully. It is enough to make Satan laugh until his ribs ache, and all the little devils laugh and heap on fresh coals. I don't wonder they hate humanity. It's so dense, so hopelessly stupid.

Only a few weeks before Poe's death he said he had never had time or opportunity to make a serious effort. All his tales were merely experiments, thrown off when his day's work as a journalist was over, when he should have been asleep. All those voyages into the mystical unknown, into the gleaming, impalpable kingdom of pure romance from which he brought back such splendid trophies, were but experiments. He was only getting his tools into shape getting ready for his great effort, the effort that never came.

Bread seems a little thing to stand in the way of genius, but it can. The simple sordid facts were these, that in the bitterest storms of winter Poe seldom wrote by a fire, that after he was twenty-five years old he never knew what it was to have enough to eat without dreading tomorrow's hunger. Chatterton had only himself to sacrifice, but Poe saw the woman he loved die of want before his very eyes, die smiling and begging him not to give up his work. They saw the depths together in those long winter nights when she lay in that cold room, wrapped in Poe's only coat, he, with one hand holding hers, and with the other dashing off some of the most perfect masterpieces of English prose. And when he would wince and turn white at her coughing, she would always whisper: "Work on, my poet, and when you have finished read it to me. I am happy when I listen." O, the devotion of women and the madness of art! They are the two most awesome things on earth, and surely this man knew both to the full.

I have wondered so often how he did it. How he kept his purpose always clean and his taste always perfect. How it was that hard labor never wearied nor jaded him, never limited his imagination, that the jarring clamor about him never drowned the fine harmonies of his fancy. His discrimination remained always delicate, and from the constant strain of toil his fancy always rose strong and unfettered. Without encouragement or appreciation of any sort, without models or precedents he built up that pure style of his that is without peer in the language, that style of which every sentence is a drawing by Vedder. Elizabeth Barrett and a few great artists over in France knew what he was doing, they knew that in literature he was making possible a new heaven and a new earth. But he never knew that they knew it. He died without the assurance that he was or ever would be understood. And yet through all this, with the whole world of art and letters against him, betrayed by his own people, he managed to keep that lofty ideal of perfect work. What he suffered never touched or marred his work, but it wrecked his character. Poe's character was made by his necessity. He was a liar and an egotist; a man who had to beg for bread at the hands of his publishers and critics could be nothing but a liar, and had he not had the insane egotism and conviction of genius, he would have broken down and written the drivelling trash that his countrymen delighted to read. Poe lied to his publishers sometimes, there is no doubt of that, but there were two to whom he was never false, his wife and his muse. He drank sometimes too, when for very ugly and relentless reasons he could not eat. And then he forgot what he suffered. For Bacchus is the kindest of the gods after all. When Aphrodite has fooled us and left us and Athene has betrayed us in battle, then poor tipsy Bacchus, who covers his head with vine leaves where the curls are getting thin, holds out his cup to us and says, "forget." It's poor consolation, but he means it well.

The Transcendentalists were good conversationalists, that in fact was their principal accomplishment. They used to talk a great deal of genius, that rare and capricious spirit that visits earth so seldom, that is wooed by so many, and won by so few. They had grand theories that all men should be poets, that the visits of that rare spirit should be made as frequent and universal as afternoon calls. O, they had plans to make a whole generation of little geniuses. But she only laughed her scornful laughter, that deathless lady of the immortals, up in her echoing chambers that are floored with dawn and roofed with the spangled stars. And she snatched from them the only man of their nation she had ever deigned to love, whose lips she had touched with music and whose soul with song. In his youth she had shown him the secrets of her beauty and his manhood had been one pursuit of her, blind to all else, like Anchises, who on the night that he knew the love of Venus, was struck sightless, that he might never behold the face of a mortal woman. For Our Lady of Genius has no care for the prayers and groans of mortals, nor for their hecatombs sweet of savor. Many a time of old she has foiled the plans of seers and none may entreat her or take her by force. She favors no one nation or clime. She takes one from the millions, and when she gives herself unto a man it is without his will or that of his fellows, and he pays for it, dear heaven, he pays!

> "The sun comes forth and many reptiles spawn,
>
> He sets and each ephemeral insect then
>
> Is gathered unto death without a dawn,
>
> And the immortal stars awake again."

Yes, "and the immortal stars awake again." None may thwart the unerring justice of the gods, not even the Transcendentalists. What matter that one man's life was miserable, that one man was broken on the wheel? His work lives and his crown is eternal. That the work of his age was undone, that is the pity, that the work of his youth was done, that is the glory. The man is nothing. There are millions of men. The work is everything. There is so little perfection. We lament our dearth of poets when we let Poe starve. We are like the Hebrews who stoned their prophets and then marvelled that the voice of God was silent. We will wait a long time for another. There are Griswold and N. P. Willis, our chosen ones, let us turn to them. Their names are forgotten. God is just. They are,

> "Gathered unto death without a dawn.
>
> And the immortal stars awake again."

The Courier, October 12, 1895

You can afford to give a little more care and attention to this imaginative boy of yours than to any of your other children. His nerves are more finely strung and all his life he will need your love more than the others. Be careful to get him the books he likes and see that they are good ones. Get him a volume of Poe's short stories. I know many people are prejudiced against Poe because of the story that he drank himself to death. But that myth has been exploded long ago. Poe drank less than even the average man of his time. No, the most artistic of all American story tellers did not die because he drank too much, but because he ate too little. And yet we, his own countrymen who should be so proud of him, are not content with having starved him and wronged him while he lived, we must even go on slandering him after he has been dead almost fifty years. But get his works for this imaginative boy of yours and he will tell you how great a man the author of "The Gold Bug" and "The Masque of the Red Death" was. Children are impartial critics and sometimes very good ones. They do not reason about a book, they just like it or dislike it intensely, and after all that is the conclusion of the whole matter. I am very sure that "The Fall of the House of Usher," "The Pit and the Pendulum" and "The Black Cat" will give this woolgathering lad of yours more pleasure than a new bicycle could.

The Home Monthly, May 1897

Walt Whitman

Speaking of monuments reminds one that there is more talk about a monument to Walt Whitman, "the good, gray poet." Just why the adjective good is always applied to Whitman it is difficult to discover, probably because people who could not understand him at all took it for granted that he meant well. If ever there was a poet who had no literary ethics at all beyond those of nature, it was he. He was neither good nor bad, any more than are the animals he continually admired and envied. He was a poet without an exclusive sense of the poetic, a man without the finer discriminations, enjoying everything with the unreasoning enthusiasm of a boy. He was the poet of the dung hill as well as of the mountains, which is admirable in theory but excruciating in verse. In the same paragraph he informs you that, "The pure contralto sings in the organ loft," and that "The malformed limbs are tied to the table, what is removed drop horribly into a pail." No branch of surgery is poetic, and that hopelessly prosaic word "pail" would kill a whole volume of sonnets. Whitman's poems are reckless rhapsodies over creation in general, some times sublime, some times ridiculous. He declares that the ocean with its "imperious waves, commanding" is beautiful, and that the fly-specks on the walls are also beautiful. Such catholic taste may go in science, but in poetry their results are sad. The poet's task is usually to select the poetic. Whitman never bothers to do that, he takes everything in the universe from fly-specks to the fixed stars. His "Leaves of Grass" is a sort of dictionary of the English language, and in it is the name of everything in creation set down with great reverence but without any particular connection.

But however ridiculous Whitman may be there is a primitive elemental force about him. He is so full of hardiness and of the joy of life. He looks at all nature in the delighted, admiring way in which the old Greeks and the primitive poets did. He exults so in the red blood in his body and the strength in his arms. He has such a passion for the warmth and dignity of all that is natural. He has no code but to be natural, a code that this complex world has so long outgrown. He is sensual, not after the manner of Swinbourne and Gautier, who are always seeking for perverted and bizarre effects on the senses, but in the frank fashion of the old barbarians who ate and slept and married and smacked their lips over the mead horn. He is rigidly limited to the physical, things that quicken his pulses, please his eyes or delight his nostrils. There is an element of poetry in all this, but it is by no means the highest. If a joyous elephant should break forth into song, his lay would probably be very much like Whitman's famous "song of myself." It would have just about as much delicacy and deftness and discriminations. He says:

"I think I could turn and live with the animals. They are so placid and self-contained, I stand and look at them long and long. They do not sweat and whine about their condition. They do not lie awake in the dark and weep for their sins. They do not make me sick discussing their duty to God. Not one is dissatisfied nor not one is demented with the mania of many things. Not one kneels to another nor to his kind that lived thousands of years ago. Not one is respectable or unhappy, over the whole earth." And that is not irony on nature, he means just that, life meant no more to him. He accepted the world just as it is and glorified it, the seemly and unseemly, the good and the bad. He had no conception of a difference in people or in things. All men had bodies and were alike to him, one about as good as another. To live was to fulfil all natural laws and impulses. To be comfortable was to be happy. To be happy was the ultimatum. He did not realize the existence of a conscience or a responsibility. He had no more thought of good or evil than the folks in Kipling's Jungle book.

And yet there is an undeniable charm about this optimistic vagabond who is made so happy by the warm sunshine and the smell of spring fields. A sort of good fellowship and whole-heartedness in every line he wrote. His veneration for things physical and material, for all that is in water or air or land, is so real that as you read him you think for the moment that you would rather like to live so if you could. For the time you half believe that a sound body and a strong arm are the greatest things in the world. Perhaps no book shows so much as "Leaves of Grass" that keen senses do not make a poet. When you read it you realize how spirited a thing poetry really is and how great a part spiritual perceptions play in apparently sensuous verse, if only to select the beautiful from the gross.

Nebraska State Journal, January 19, 1896

Henry James

Their mania for careless and hasty work is not confined to the lesser men. Howells and Hardy have gone with the crowd. Now that Stevenson is dead I can think of but one English speaking author who is really keeping his self-respect and sticking for perfection. Of course I refer to that mighty master of language and keen student of human actions and motives, Henry James. In the last four years he has published, I believe, just two small volumes, "The Lesson of the Master" and "Terminations," and in those two little volumes of short stories he who will may find out something of what it means to be really an artist. The framework is perfect and the polish is absolutely without flaw. They are sometimes a little hard, always calculating and dispassionate, but they are perfect. I wish James would write about modern society, about "degeneracy" and the new woman and all the rest of it. Not that he would throw any light on it. He seldom does; but he would say such awfully clever things about it, and turn on so many side-lights. And then his sentences! If his character novels were all wrong one could read him forever for the mere beauty of his sentences. He never lets his phrases run away with him. They are never dull and never too brilliant. He subjects them to the general tone of his sentence and has his whole paragraph partake of the same predominating color. You are never startled, never surprised, never thrilled or never enraptured; always delighted by that masterly prose that is as correct, as classical, as calm and as subtle as the music of Mozart.

The Courier, November 16, 1895

It is strange that from "Felicia" down, the stage novel has never been a success. Henry James' "Tragic Muse" is the only theatrical novel that has a particle of the real spirit of the stage in it, a glimpse of the enthusiasm, the devotion, the exaltation and the sordid, the frivolous and the vulgar which are so strangely and inextricably blended in that life of the green room. For although Henry James cannot write plays he can write passing well of the people who enact them. He has put into one book all those inevitable attendants of the drama, the patronizing theatre goer who loves it above all things and yet feels so far superior to it personally; the old tragedienne, the queen of a dying school whose word is law and whose judgments are to a young actor as the judgments of God; and of course there is the girl, the aspirant, the tragic muse who beats and beats upon those brazen doors that guard the unapproachable until one fine morning she beats them down and comes into her kingdom, the kingdom of unborn beauty that is to live through her. It is a great novel, that book of the master's, so perfect as a novel that one does not realize what a masterly study it is of the life and ends and aims of the people who make plays live.

Nebraska State Journal, March 29, 1896

Harold Frederic

"THE MARKET-PLACE." Harold Frederic. $1.50. New York: F. A. Stokes & Co. Pittsburg: J. R. Weldin & Co.

Unusual interest is attached to the posthumous work of that great man whose career ended so prematurely and so tragically. The story is a study in the ethics and purposes of money-getting, in the romantic element in modern business. In it finance is presented not as being merely the province of shrewdness, or greediness, or petty personal gratification, but of great projects, of great brain-battles, a field for the exercising of talent, daring, imagination, appealing to the strength of a strong man, filling the same place in men's lives that was once filled by the incentives of war, kindling in man the desire for the leadership of men. The hero of the story, "Joel Thorpe," is one of those men, huge of body, keen of brain, with cast iron nerves, as sound a heart as most men, and a magnificent capacity for bluff. He has lived and risked and lost in a dozen countries, been almost within reach of fortune a dozen times, and always missed her until, finally, in London, by promoting a great rubber syndicate he becomes a multi-millionaire. He marries the most beautiful and one of the most impecunious peeresses in England and retires to his country estate. There, as a gentleman of leisure, he loses his motive in life, loses power for lack of opportunity, and grows less commanding even in the eyes of his wife, who misses the uncompromising, barbaric strength which took her by storm and won her. Finally he evolves a gigantic philanthropic scheme of spending his money as laboriously as he made it.

Mr. Frederic says:

> "Napoleon was the greatest man of his age—one of the greatest men of all ages—not only in war but in a hundred other ways. He spent the last six years of his life at St. Helena in excellent health, with companions that he talked freely to, and in all the extraordinarily copious reports of his conversations there, we don't get a single sentence worth repeating. The greatness had entirely evaporated from him the moment he was put on an island where he had nothing to do."

It is very fitting that Mr. Frederic's last book should be in praise of action, the thing that makes the world go round; of force, however misspent, which is the sum of life as distinguished from the inertia of death. In the forty-odd years of his life he wrote almost as many pages as Balzac, most of it mere newspaper copy, it is true, read and forgotten, but all of it vigorous and with the stamp of a strong man upon it. And he played just as hard as he worked—alas, it was the play that killed him! The young artist who illustrated the story gave to the pictures of "Joel Thorpe" very much the look of Harold Frederic himself, and they might almost stand for his portraits. I fancy the young man did not select his model carelessly. In this big, burly adventurer who took fortune and women by storm, who bluffed the world by his prowess and fought his way to the front with battle-ax blows, there is a great deal of Harold Frederic, the soldier of fortune, the Utica milk boy who fought his way from the petty slavery of a provincial newspaper to the foremost ranks of the journalists of the world and on into literature, into literature worth the writing. The man won his place in England much as his hero won his, by defiance, by strong shoulder blows, by his self-sufficiency and inexhaustible strength, and when he finished his book he did not know that his end would be so much less glorious than his hero's, that it would be his portion not to fall manfully in the thick of the combat and the press of battle, but to die poisoned in the tent of Chryseis. For who could foresee a tragedy so needless, so blind, so brutal in its lack of dignity, or know that such strength could perish through such insidious weakness, that so great a man could be stung to death by a mania born in little minds?

In point of execution and literary excellence, both "The Market Place" and "Gloria Mundi" are vastly inferior to "The Damnation of Theron Ware," or that exquisite London idyl, "March Hares." The first 200 pages of "Theron Ware" are as good as anything in American fiction, much better than most of it. They are not so much the work of a literary artist as of a vigorous thinker, a man of strong opinions and an intimate and comprehensive knowledge of men. The whole work, despite its irregularities and indifference to form, is full of brain stuff, the kind of active, healthful, masterful intellect that some men put into politics, some into science and a few, a very few, into literature. Both "Gloria Mundi" and "The Market Place" bear unmistakable evidences of the slack rein and the hasty hand. Both of them contain considerable padding, the stamp of the space writer. They are imperfectly developed, and are not packed with ideas like his earlier novels. Their excellence is in flashes; it is not the searching, evenly distributed light which permeates his more careful work. There were, as we know too well, good reasons why Mr. Frederic should work hastily. He needed a large income and he worked heroically, writing many thousands of words a day to obtain it. From the experience of the ages we have learned to expect to find, coupled with great strength, a proportionate weakness, and usually it devours the greater part, as the seven lean kine devoured the seven fat in Pharaoh's vision. Achilles was a god in all his nobler parts, but his feet were of the earth and to the earth they held him down, and he died stung by an arrow in the heel.

Pittsburg Leader, June 10, 1899

Kate Chopin

"THE AWAKENING." Kate Chopin. $1.25. Chicago:
H. S. Stone & Co. Pittsburg: J. R. Weldin & Co.

ACreole "Bovary" is this little novel of Miss Chopin's. Not that the heroine is a creole exactly, or that Miss Chopin is a Flaubert—save the mark!—but the theme is similar to that which occupied Flaubert. There was, indeed, no need that a second "Madame Bovary" should be written, but an author's choice of themes is frequently as inexplicable as his choice of a wife. It is governed by some innate temperamental bias that cannot be diagrammed. This is particularly so in women who write, and I shall not attempt to say why Miss Chopin has devoted so exquisite and sensitive, well-governed a style to so trite and sordid a theme. She writes much better than it is ever given to most people to write, and hers is a genuinely literary style; of no great elegance or solidity; but light, flexible, subtle and capable of producing telling effects directly and simply. The story she has to tell in the present instance is new neither in matter nor treatment. "Edna Pontellier," a Kentucky girl, who, like "Emma Bovary," had been in love with innumerable dream heroes before she was out of short skirts, married "Leonce Pontellier" as a sort of reaction from a vague and visionary passion for a tragedian whose unresponsive picture she used to kiss. She acquired the habit of liking her husband in time, and even of liking her children. Though we are not justified in presuming that she ever threw articles from her dressing table at them, as the charming "Emma" had a winsome habit of doing, we are told that "she would sometimes gather them passionately to her heart, she would sometimes forget them." At a creole watering place, which is admirably and deftly sketched by Miss Chopin, "Edna" met "Robert Lebrun," son of the landlady, who dreamed of a fortune awaiting him in Mexico while he occupied a petty clerical position in New Orleans. "Robert" made it his business to be agreeable to his mother's boarders, and "Edna," not being a creole, much against his wish and will, took him seriously. "Robert" went to Mexico but found that fortunes were no easier to make there than in New Orleans. He returns and does not even call to pay his respects to her. She encounters him at the home of a friend and takes him home with her. She wheedles him into staying for dinner, and we are told she sent the maid off "in search of some delicacy she had not thought of for herself, and she recommended great care in the dripping of the coffee and having the omelet done to a turn."

Only a few pages back we were informed that the husband, "M. Pontellier," had cold soup and burnt fish for his dinner. Such is life. The lover of course disappointed her, was a coward and ran away from his responsibilities before they began. He was afraid to begin a chapter with so serious and limited a woman. She remembered the sea where she had first met "Robert." Perhaps from the same motive which threw "Anna Keraninna" under the engine wheels, she threw herself into the sea, swam until she was tired and then let go.

> "She looked into the distance, and for a moment the old terror flamed up, then sank again. She heard her father's voice, and her sister Margaret's. She heard the barking of an old dog that was chained to the sycamore tree. The spurs of the cavalry officer clanged as he walked across the porch. There was a hum of bees, and the musky odor of pinks filled the air."

"Edna Pontellier" and "Emma Bovary" are studies in the same feminine type; one a finished and complete portrayal, the other a hasty sketch, but the theme is essentially the same. Both women belong to a class, not large, but forever clamoring in our ears, that demands more romance out of life than God put into it. Mr. G. Barnard Shaw would say that they are the victims of the over-idealization of love. They are the spoil of the poets, the Iphigenias of sentiment. The unfortunate feature of their disease is that it attacks only women of brains, at least of rudimentary brains, but whose development is one-sided; women of strong and fine intuitions, but without the faculty of observation, comparison, reasoning about things. Probably, for emotional people, the most convenient thing about being able to think is that it occasionally gives them a rest from feeling. Now with women of the "Bovary" type, this relaxation and recreation is impossible. They are not critics of life, but, in the most personal sense, partakers of life. They receive impressions through the fancy. With them everything begins with fancy, and passions rise in the brain rather than in the blood, the poor, neglected, limited one-sided brain that might do so much better things than badgering itself into frantic endeavors to love. For these are the people who pay with their blood for the fine ideals of the poets, as Marie Delclasse paid for Dumas' great creation, "Marguerite Gauthier." These people really expect the passion of love to fill and gratify every need of life, whereas nature only intended that it should meet one of many demands. They insist upon making it stand for all the emotional pleasures of life and art, expecting an individual and self-limited passion to yield infinite variety, pleasure and distraction, to contribute to their lives what the arts and the pleasurable exercise of the intellect gives to less limited and less intense idealists. So this passion, when set up against Shakespeare, Balzac, Wagner, Raphael, fails them. They have staked everything on one hand, and they lose. They have driven the blood until it will drive no further, they have played their nerves up to the point where any relaxation short of absolute annihilation is impossible. Every idealist abuses his nerves, and every sentimentalist brutally abuses them. And in the end, the nerves get even. Nobody ever cheats them, really. Then "the awakening" comes. Sometimes it comes in the form of arsenic, as it came to "Emma Bovary," sometimes it is carbolic acid taken covertly in the police station, a goal to which unbalanced idealism not infrequently leads. "Edna Pontellier," fanciful and romantic to the last, chose the sea on a summer night and went down with the sound of her first lover's spurs in her ears, and the scent of pinks about her. And next time I hope that Miss Chopin will devote that flexible, iridescent style of hers to a better cause.

Pittsburg Leader, July 8, 1899

Stephen Crane

"WAR IS KIND." Stephen Crane. $2.50. New York: F.
A. Stokes & Co. Pittsburg: J. R. Weldin & Co.

This truly remarkable book is printed on dirty gray blotting paper, on each page of which is a mere dot of print over a large I of vacancy. There are seldom more than ten lines on a page, and it would be better if most of those lines were not there at all. Either Mr. Crane is insulting the public or insulting himself, or he has developed a case of atavism and is chattering the primeval nonsense of the apes. His "Black Riders," uneven as it was, was a casket of polished masterpieces when compared with "War Is Kind." And it is not kind at all, Mr. Crane; when it provokes such verses as these, it is all that Sherman said it was.

The only production in the volume that is at all coherent is the following, from which the book gets its title:

Do not weep, maiden, for war is kind,
Because your lover threw wild hands toward the sky,
And the affrighted steed ran on alone.
Do not weep,
War is kind.

Hoarse booming drums of the regiment,
Little souls who thirst for fight,
These men were born to drill and die.
The unexplained glory flies above them.
Great is the battle-god, great, and his kingdom—
A field where a thousand corpses lie.

Do not weep, babe, for war is kind,
Because your father tumbled in the yellow trenches,
Raged at the breast, gulped and died.
Do not weep,
War is kind.

Swift-blazing flag of the regiment,
Eagle with crest of red and gold,
 These men were born to drill and die.
Point for them the virtue of slaughter,
Make plain to them the excellence of killing,
And a field where a thousand corpses lie.

Mother whose heart hung humble as a button
On the bright, splendid shroud of your son,
Do not weep,
War is kind.

Of course, one may have objections to hearts hanging like humble
buttons, or to buttons being humble at all, but one should not stop to quarrel
about such trifles with a poet who can perpetrate the following:

Thou art my love,
And thou art the beard
On another man's face—
Woe is me.

Thou art my love,
And thou art a temple,
And in this temple is an altar,
And on this temple is my heart—
Woe is me.

Thou art my love,
And thou art a wretch.
Let these sacred love-lies choke thee.
For I am come to where I know your lies as truth
And your truth as lies—
Woe is me.

Now, if you please, is the object of these verses animal, mineral or
vegetable? Is the expression, "Thou art the beard on another man's face,"
intended as a figure, or was it written by a barber? Certainly, after reading
this, "Simple Simon" is a ballade of perfect form, and "Jack and Jill" or
"Hickity, Pickity, My Black Hen," are exquisite lyrics. But of the following
what shall be said:

Now let me crunch you
With full weight of affrighted love.
I doubted you
—I doubted you—
And in this short doubting
My love grew like a genie
For my further undoing.

Beware of my friends,
Be not in speech too civil,
For in all courtesy
My weak heart sees specters,
Mists of desire
Arising from the lips of my chosen;
Be not civil.

This is somewhat more lucid as evincing the bard's exquisite sensitiveness:

Ah, God, the way your little finger moved
As you thrust a bare arm backward.
And made play with your hair
And a comb, a silly gilt comb
—Ah, God, that I should suffer
Because of the way a little finger moved.

Mr. Crane's verselets are illustrated by some Bradley pictures, which are badly drawn, in bad taste, and come with bad grace. The book there are just two lines which seem to completely sum up the efforts of both poet and artist:

"My good friend," said a learned bystander,
"Your operations are mad."

Yet this fellow Crane has written short stories equal to some of Maupassant's.

Pittsburg Leader, June 3, 1899

After reading such a delightful newspaper story as Mr. Frank Norris' "Blix," it is with assorted sensations of pain and discomfort that one closes the covers of another newspaper novel, "Active Service," by Stephen Crane. If one happens to have some trifling regard for pure English, he does not come forth from the reading of this novel unscathed. The hero of this lurid tale is a newspaper man, and he edits the Sunday edition of the New York "Eclipse," and delights in publishing "stories" about deformed and sightless infants. "The office of the 'Eclipse' was at the top of an immense building on Broadway. It was a sheer mountain to the heights of which the interminable thunder of the streets rose faintly. The Hudson was a broad path of silver in the distance." This leaves little doubt as to the fortunate journal which had secured Rufus Coleman as its Sunday editor. Mr. Coleman's days were spent in collecting yellow sensations for his paper, and we are told that he "planned for each edition as for a campaign." The following elevating passage is one of the realistic paragraphs by which Mr. Crane makes the routine of Coleman's life known to us:

> Suddenly there was a flash of light and a cage of bronze, gilt and steel dropped magically from above. Coleman yelled "Down!" A door flew open. Coleman stepped upon the elevator. "Well, Johnnie," he said cheerfully to the lad who operated the machine, "is business good?" "Yes, sir, pretty good," answered the boy, grinning. The little cage sank swiftly. Floor after floor seemed to be rising with marvelous speed; the whole building was winging straight into the sky. There was soaring lights, figures and the opalescent glow of ground glass doors marked with black inscriptions. Other lights were springing heavenward. All the lofty corridors rang with cries. "Up!" "Down!" "Down!" "Up!!" The boy's hand grasped a lever and his machine obeyed his lightest movement with sometimes an unbalancing swiftness.

Later, when Coleman reached the street, Mr. Crane describes the cable cars as marching like panoplied elephants, which is rather far, to say the least. The gentleman's nights were spent something as follows:

> "In the restaurant he first ordered a large bottle of champagne. The last of the wine he finished in somber mood like an unbroken and defiant man who chews the straw that litters his prison house. During his dinner he was continually sending out messenger boys. He was arranging a poker party. Through a window he watched the beautiful moving life of upper Broadway at night, with its crowds and clanging cable cars and its electric signs, mammoth and glittering like the jewels of a giantess.

> "Word was brought to him that poker players were arriving. He arose joyfully, leaving his cheese. In the broad hall, occupied mainly by miscellaneous people and actors, all

deep in leather chairs, he found some of his friends waiting. They trooped upstairs to Coleman's rooms, where, as a preliminary, Coleman began to hurl books and papers from the table to the floor. A boy came with drinks. Most of the men, in order to prepare for the game, removed their coats and cuffs and drew up the sleeves of their shirts. The electric globes shed a blinding light upon the table. The sound of clinking chips arose; the elected banker spun the cards, careless and dextrous."

The atmosphere of the entire novel is just that close and enervating. Every page is like the next morning taste of a champagne supper, and is heavy with the smell of stale cigarettes. There is no fresh air in the book and no sunlight, only the "blinding light shed by the electric globes." If the life of New York newspaper men is as unwholesome and sordid as this, Mr. Crane, who has experienced it, ought to be sadly ashamed to tell it. Next morning when Coleman went for breakfast in the grill room of his hotel he ordered eggs on toast and a pint of champagne for breakfast and discoursed affably to the waiter.

"May be you had a pretty lively time last night, Mr. Coleman?"

"Yes, Pat," answered Coleman. "I did. It was all because of an unrequitted affection, Patrick." The man stood near, a napkin over his arm. Coleman went on impressively. "The ways of the modern lover are strange. Now, I, Patrick, am a modern lover, and when, yesterday, the dagger of disappointment was driven deep into my heart, I immediately played poker as hard as I could, and incidentally got loaded. This is the modern point of view. I understand on good authority that in old times lovers used to languish. That is probably a lie, but at any rate we do not, in these times, languish to any great extent. We get drunk. Do you understand Patrick?"

The waiter was used to a harangue at Coleman's breakfast time. He placed his hand over his mouth and giggled. "Yessir."

"Of course," continued Coleman, thoughtfully. "It might be pointed out by uneducated persons that it is difficult to maintain a high standard of drunkenness for the adequate length of time, but in the series of experiments which I am about to make, I am sure I can easily prove them to be in the wrong."

"I am sure, sir," said the waiter, "the young ladies would not like to be hearing you talk this way."

"Yes; no doubt, no doubt. The young ladies have still quite medieval ideas. They don't understand. They still prefer lovers to languish."

"At any rate, sir, I don't see that your heart is sure enough broken. You seem to take it very easy."

"Broken!" cried Coleman. "Easy? Man, my heart is in fragments. Bring me another small bottle."

After this Coleman went to Greece to write up the war for the "Eclipse," and incidentally to rescue his sweetheart from the hands of the Turks and make "copy" of it. Very valid arguments might be advanced that the lady would have fared better with the Turks. On the voyage Coleman spent all his days and nights in the card room and avoided the deck, since fresh air was naturally disagreeable to him. For all that he saw of Greece or that Mr. Crane's readers see of Greece Coleman might as well have stayed in the card room of the steamer, or in the card room of his New York hotel for that matter. Wherever he goes he carries the atmosphere of the card room with him and the "blinding glare of the electrics." In Greece he makes love when he has leisure, but he makes "copy" much more ardently, and on the whole is quite as lurid and sordid and showy as his worst Sunday editions. Some good bits of battle descriptions there are, of the "Red Badge of Courage" order, but one cannot make a novel of clever descriptions of earthworks and poker games. The book concerns itself not with large, universal interests or principles, but with a yellow journalist grinding out yellow copy in such a wooden fashion that the Sunday "Eclipse" must have been even worse than most. In spite of the fact that Mr. Crane has written some of the most artistic short stories in the English language, I begin to wonder whether, blinded by his youth and audacity, two qualities which the American people love, we have not taken him too seriously. It is a grave matter for a man in good health and with a bank account to have written a book so coarse and dull and charmless as "Active Service." Compared with this "War was kind," indeed.

Pittsburg Leader, November 11, 1899

Frank Norris

Anew and a great book has been written. The name of it is "McTeague, a Story of San Francisco," and the man who wrote it is Mr. Frank Norris. The great presses of the country go on year after year grinding out commonplace books, just as each generation goes on busily reproducing its own mediocrity. When in this enormous output of ink and paper, these thousands of volumes that are yearly rushed upon the shelves of the book stores, one appears which contains both power and promise, the reader may be pardoned some enthusiasm. Excellence always surprises: we are never quite prepared for it. In the case of "McTeague, a Story of San Francisco," it is even more surprising than usual. In the first place the title is not alluring, and not until you have read the book, can you know that there is an admirable consistency in the stiff, uncompromising commonplaceness of that title. In the second place the name of the author is as yet comparatively unfamiliar, and finally the book is dedicated to a member of the Harvard faculty, suggesting that whether it be a story of San Francisco or Dawson City, it must necessarily be vaporous, introspective and chiefly concerned with "literary" impressions. Mr. Norris is, indeed, a "Harvard man," but that he is a good many other kinds of a man is self-evident. His book is, in the language of Mr. Norman Hapgood, the work of "a large human being, with a firm stomach, who knows and loves the people."

In a novel of such high merit as this, the subject matter is the least important consideration. Every newspaper contains the essential material for another "Comedie Humaine." In this case "McTeague," the central figure, happens to be a dentist practicing in a little side street of San Francisco. The novel opens with this description of him:

> "It was Sunday, and, according to his custom on that day, McTeague took his dinner at two in the afternoon at the car conductor's coffee joint on Polk street. He had a thick, gray soup, heavy, underdone meat, very hot, on a cold plate; two kinds of vegetables; and a sort of suet pudding, full of strong butter and sugar. Once in his office, or, as he called it on his sign-board, 'Dental Parlors,' he took off his coat and shoes, unbuttoned his vest, and, having crammed his little stove with coke, he lay back in his operating chair at the

bay window, reading the paper, drinking steam beer, and smoking his huge porcelain pipe while his food digested; crop-full, stupid and warm."

McTeague had grown up in a mining camp in the mountains. He remembered the years he had spent there trundling heavy cars of ore in and out of the tunnel under the direction of his father. For thirteen days out of each fortnight his father was a steady, hard-working shift-boss of the mine. Every other Sunday he became an irresponsible animal, a beast, a brute, crazed with alcohol. His mother cooked for the miners. Her one ambition was that her son should enter a profession. He was apprenticed to a traveling quack dentist and after a fashion, learned the business.

"Then one day at San Francisco had come the news of his mother's death; she had left him some money—not much, but enough to set him up in business; so he had cut loose from the charlatan and had opened his 'Dental Parlors' on Polk street, an 'accommodation street' of small shops in the residence quarter of the town. Here he had slowly collected a clientele of butcher boys, shop girls, drug clerks and car conductors. He made but few acquaintances. Polk street called him the 'doctor' and spoke of his enormous strength. For McTeague was a young giant, carrying his huge shock of blonde hair six feet three inches from the ground; moving his immense limbs, heavy with ropes of muscle, slowly, ponderously. His hands were enormous, red, and covered with a fell of stiff yellow hair; they were as hard as wooden mallets, strong as vices, the hands of the old-time car boy. Often he dispensed with forceps and extracted a refractory tooth with his thumb and finger. His head was square-cut, angular; the jaw salient: like that of the carnivora.

"But for one thing McTeague would have been perfectly contented. Just outside his window was his signboard—a modest affair—that read: 'Doctor McTeague. Dental Parlors. Gas Given;' but that was all. It was his ambition, his dream, to have projecting from that corner window a huge gilded tooth, a molar with enormous prongs, something gorgeous and attractive. He would have it some day, but as yet it was far beyond his means."

Then Mr. Norris launches into a description of the street in which "McTeague" lives. He presents that street as it is on Sunday, as it is on working days; as it is in the early dawn when the workmen are going out with pickaxes on their shoulders, as it is at ten o'clock when the women are out purchasing from the small shopkeepers, as it is at night when the shop girls are out with the soda-fountain tenders and the motor cars dash by full of theatre-goers, and the Salvationists sing before the saloon on the corner. In four pages he reproduces the life in a by-street of a great city, the little tragedy of the small shopkeeper. There are many ways of handling environment—most of them bad. When a young author has very little to say and no story worth telling, he resorts to environment. It is frequently used to disguise a weakness of structure, as ladies who paint landscapes put their cows knee-deep in water to conceal the defective drawing of the legs. But such description as one meets throughout Mr. Norris' book is in itself convincing proof of power, imagination and literary skill. It is a positive and active force, stimulating the reader's imagination, giving him an actual command, a realizing sense of this world into which he is suddenly transplanted. It gives to the book perspective, atmosphere, effects of time and distance, creates the illusion of life. This power of mature, and accurate and comprehensive description is very unusual among the younger American writers. Most of them observe the world through a temperament, and are more occupied with their medium than the objects they see. And temperament is a glass which distorts most astonishingly. But this young man sees with a clear eye, and reproduces with a touch firm and decisive, strong almost to brutalness. Yet this hand that can depict so powerfully the brute strength and brute passions of a "McTeague," can deal very finely and adroitly with the feminine element of his story. This is his portrait of the little Swiss girl, "Trina," whom the dentist marries:

> "Trina was very small and prettily made. Her face was round and rather pale; her eyes long and narrow and blue, like the half-opened eyes of a baby; her lips and the lobes of her tiny ears were pale, a little suggestive of anaemia. But it was to her hair that one's attention was most attracted. Heaps and heaps of blue-black coils and braids, a royal crown of swarthy bands, a veritable sable tiara, heavy, abundant and odorous. All the vitality that should have given color to her face seemed to have been absorbed by that marvelous hair: It was the coiffure of a queen that shadowed the temples of this little bourgeoise."

The tragedy of the story dates from a chance, a seeming stroke of good fortune, one of those terrible gifts of the Danai. A few weeks before her marriage "Trina" drew $5 000 from a lottery ticket. From that moment her passion for hoarding money becomes the dominant theme of the story, takes command of the book and its characters. After their marriage the dentist is disbarred from practice. They move into a garret where she starves her husband and herself to save that precious hoard. She sells even his office furniture, everything but his concertina and his canary bird, with which he stubbornly refuses to part and which are destined to become very important accessories in the property room of the theatre where this drama is played. This removal from their first home is to this story what Gervaise's removal from her shop is to L'Assommoir; it is the fatal episode of the third act, the sacrifice of self-respect, the beginning of the end. From that time the money stands between "Trina" and her husband. Outraged and humiliated, hating her for her meanness, demoralized by his idleness and despair, he begins to abuse her. The story becomes a careful and painful study of the disintegration of this union, a penetrating and searching analysis of the degeneration of these two souls, the woman's corroded by greed, the man's poisoned by disappointment and hate.

And all the while this same painful theme is placed in a lower key. Maria, the housemaid who took care of "McTeague's" dental parlors in his better days, was a half-crazy girl from somewhere in Central America, she herself did not remember just where. But she had a wonderful story about her people owning a dinner service of pure gold with a punch bowl you could scarcely lift, which rang like a church bell when you struck it. On the strength of this story "Zercow," the Jew junk man, marries her, and believing that she knows where this treasure is hidden, bullies and tortures her to force her to disclose her secret. At last "Maria" is found with her throat cut, and "Zercow" is picked up by the wharf with a sack full of rusty tin cans, which in his dementia he must have thought the fabled dinner service of gold.

From this it is a short step to "McTeague's" crime. He kills his wife to get possession of her money, and escapes to the mountains. While he is on his way south, pushing toward Mexico, he is overtaken by his murdered wife's cousin and former suitor. Both men are half mad with thirst, and there in the desert wastes of Death's Valley, they spring to their last conflict. The cousin falls, but before he dies he slips a handcuff over "McTeague's" arm, and so the author leaves his hero in the wastes of Death's Valley, a hundred miles from water, with a dead man chained to his arm. As he stands there the canary bird, the survivor of his happier days, to which he had clung with stubborn affection, begins "chittering feebly in its little gilt prison." It reminds one a little of Stevenson's use of poor "Goddedaal's" canary in "The Wrecker." It is just such sharp, sure strokes that bring out the high lights in a story and separate excellence from the commonplace. They are at once dramatic and revelatory. Lacking them, a novel which may otherwise be a good one, lacks its chief reason for being. The fault with many worthy attempts at fiction lies not in what they are, but in what they are not.

Mr. Norris' model, if he will admit that he has followed one, is clearly no less a person than M. Zola himself. Yet there is no discoverable trace of imitation in his book. He has simply taken a method which has been most successfully applied in the study of French life and applied it in studying American life, as one uses certain algebraic formulae to solve certain problems. It is perhaps the only truthful literary method of dealing with that part of society which environment and heredity hedge about like the walls of a prison. It is true that Mr. Norris now and then allows his "method" to become too prominent, that his restraint savors of constraint, yet he has written a true story of the people, courageous, dramatic, full of matter and warm with life. He has addressed himself seriously to art, and he seems to have no ambition to be clever. His horizon is wide, his invention vigorous and bold, his touch heavy and warm and human. This man is not limited by literary prejudices: he sees the people as they are, he is close to them and not afraid of their unloveliness. He has looked at truth in the depths, among men begrimed by toil and besotted by ignorance, and still found her fair. "McTeague" is an achievement for a young man. It may not win at once the success which it deserves, but Mr. Norris is one of those who can afford to wait.

The Courier, April 8, 1899

If you want to read a story that is all wheat and no chaff, read "Blix." Last winter that brilliant young Californian, Mr. Norris, published a remarkable and gloomy novel, "McTeague," a book deep in insight, rich in promise and splendid in execution, but entirely without charm and as disagreeable as only a great piece of work can be. And now this gentleman, who is not yet thirty, turns around and gives us an idyll that sings through one's brain like a summer wind and makes one feel young enough to commit all manner of indiscretions. It may be that Mr. Norris is desirous of showing us his versatility and that he can follow any suit, or it may have been a process of reaction. I believe it was after M. Zola had completed one of his greatest and darkest novels of Parisian life that he went down to the seaside and wrote "La Reve," a book that every girl should read when she is eighteen, and then again when she is eighty. Powerful and solidly built as "McTeague" is, one felt that there method was carried almost too far, that Mr. Norris was too consciously influenced by his French masters. But "Blix" belongs to no school whatever, and there is not a shadow of pedantry or pride of craft in it from cover to cover. "Blix" herself is the method, the motives and the aim of the book. The story is an exhalation of youth and spring; it is the work of a man who breaks loose and forgets himself. Mr. Norris was married only last summer, and the march from "Lohengrin" is simply sticking out all over "Blix." It is the story of a San Francisco newspaper man and a girl.

The newspaper man "came out" in fiction, so to speak, in the drawing room of Mr. Richard Harding Davis, and has languished under that gentleman's chaperonage until he has come to be regarded as a fellow careful of nothing but his toilet and his dinner. Mr. Davis' reporters all bathed regularly and all ate nice things, but beyond that their tastes were rather colorless. I am glad to see one red-blooded newspaper man, in the person of "Landy Rivers," of San Francisco, break into fiction; a real live reporter with no sentimental loyalty for his "paper," and no Byronic poses about his vices, and no astonishing taste about his clothes, and no money whatever, which is the natural and normal condition of all reporters. "Blix" herself was just a society girl, and "Landy" took her to theatres and parties and tried to make himself believe he was in love with her. But it wouldn't work, for "Landy" couldn't love a society girl, not though she were as beautiful as the morning and terrible as an army with banners, and had "round full arms," and "the skin of her face was white and clean, except where it flushed into a most charming pink upon her smooth, cool cheeks." For while "Landy Rivers" was at college he had been seized with the penchant for writing short stories, and had worshiped at the shrines of Maupassant and Kipling, and when a man is craft mad enough to worship Maupassant truly and know him well, when he has that tingling for technique in his fingers, not Aphrodite herself, new risen from the waves, could tempt him into any world where craft was not lord and king. So it happened that their real love affair never began until one morning when "Landy" had to go down to the wharf to write up a whaleback, and "Blix" went along, and an old sailor told them a story and "Blix" recognized the literary possibilities of it, and they had lunch in a Chinese restaurant, and "Landy" because he was a newspaper man and it was the end of the week, didn't have any change about his clothes, and "Blix" had to pay the bill. And it was in that green old tea house that "Landy" read "Blix" one of his favorite yarns by Kipling, and she in a calm, off-handed way, recognized one of the fine, technical points in it, and "Landy" almost went to pieces for joy of her doing it. That scene in the Chinese restaurant is one of the prettiest bits of color you'll find to rest your eyes upon, and mighty good writing it is. I wonder, though if when Mr. Norris adroitly mentioned the "clack and snarl" of the banjo "Landy" played, he remembered the "silver snarling trumpets" of Keats? After that, things went on as such things will, and "Blix" quit the society racket and went to queer places with "Landy," and got interested in his work, and she broke him of wearing red neckties and playing poker, and she made him work, she did, for she grew to realize how much that meant to him, and she jacked him up when he didn't work, and she suggested an ending for one of his stories that was better than his own; just this big, splendid girl, who had never gone to college to learn how to write novels. And so how, in the name of goodness, could he help loving her? So one morning down by the Pacific, with "Blix" and "The Seven Seas," it all came over "Landy," that "living was better than reading and life was better than literature." And so it is; once, and only once, for each of us; and that is the tune that sings and sings through one's head when one puts the book away.

The Courier, January 13, 1900

An Heir Apparent

Last winter a young Californian, Mr. Frank Norris, published a novel with the unpretentious title, "McTeague: a Story of San Francisco." It was a book that could not be ignored nor dismissed with a word. There was something very unusual about it, about its solidity and mass, the thoroughness and firmness of texture, and it came down like a blow from a sledge hammer among the slighter and more sprightly performances of the hour.

The most remarkable thing about the book was its maturity and compactness. It has none of the ear-marks of those entertaining "young writers" whom every season produces as inevitably as its debutantes, young men who surprise for an hour and then settle down to producing industriously for the class with which their peculiar trick of phrase has found favor. It was a book addressed to the American people and to the critics of the world, the work of a young man who had set himself to the art of authorship with an almighty seriousness, and who had no ambition to be clever. "McTeague" was not an experiment in style nor a pretty piece of romantic folly, it was a true story of the people—having about it, as M. Zola would say, "the smell of the people"—courageous, dramatic, full of matter and warm with life. It was realism of the most uncompromising kind. The theme was such that the author could not have expected sudden popularity for his book, such as sometimes overtakes monstrosities of style in these discouraging days when Knighthood is in Flower to the extent of a quarter of a million copies, nor could he have hoped for pressing commissions from the fire-side periodicals. The life story of a quack dentist who sometimes extracted molars with his fingers, who mistreated and finally murdered his wife, is not, in itself, attractive. But, after all, the theme counts for very little. Every newspaper contains the essential subject matter for another *Comedie Humaine*. The important point is that a man considerably under thirty could take up a subject so grim and unattractive, and that, for the mere love of doing things well, he was able to hold himself down to the task of developing it completely, that he was able to justify this quack's existence in literature, to thrust this hairy, blonde dentist with the "salient jaw of the carnivora," in amongst the immortals.

It was after M. Zola had completed one of the greatest and gloomiest of his novels of Parisian life, that he went down by the sea and wrote "La Reve," that tender, adolescent story of love and purity and youth. So, almost simultaneously with "McTeague," Mr. Norris published "Blix," another San Francisco story, as short as "McTeague" was lengthy, as light as "McTeague" was heavy, as poetic and graceful as "McTeague" was somber and charmless. Here is a man worth waiting on; a man who is both realist and poet, a man who can teach

"Not only by a comet's rush,

But by a rose's birth."

Yet unlike as they are, in both books the source of power is the same, and, for that matter, it was even the same in his first book, "Moran of the Lady Letty." Mr. Norris has dispensed with the conventional symbols that have crept into art, with the trite, half-truths and circumlocutions, and got back to the physical basis of things. He has abjured tea-table psychology, and the analysis of figures in the carpet and subtile dissections of intellectual impotencies, and the diverting game of words and the whole literature of the nerves. He is big and warm and sometimes brutal, and the strength of the soil comes up to him with very little loss in the transmission. His art strikes deep down into the roots of life and the foundation of Things as They Are—not as we tell each other they are at the tea-table. But he is realistic art, not artistic realism. He is courageous, but he is without bravado.

He sees things freshly, as though they had not been seen before, and describes them with singular directness and vividness, not with morbid acuteness, with a large, wholesome joy of life. Nowhere is this more evident than in his insistent use of environment. I recall the passage in which he describes the street in which McTeague lives. He represents that street as it is on Sunday, as it is on working days, as it is in the early dawn when the workmen are going out with pickaxes on their shoulders, as it is at ten o'clock when the women are out marketing among the small shopkeepers, as it is at night when the shop girls are out with the soda fountain tenders and the motor cars dash by full of theater-goers, and the Salvationists sing before the saloon on the corner. In four pages he reproduces in detail the life in a by-street of a great city, the little tragedy of the small shopkeeper. There are many ways of handling environment—most of them bad. When a young author has very little to say and no story worth telling, he resorts to environment. It is frequently used to disguise a weakness of structure, as ladies who paint landscapes put their cows knee-deep in water to conceal the defective drawing of the legs. But such description as one meets throughout Mr. Norris' book is in itself convincing proof of power, imagination and literary skill. It is a positive and active force, stimulating the reader's imagination, giving him an actual command, a realizing sense of this world into which he is suddenly transported. It gives to the book perspective, atmosphere, effects of time and distance, creates the illusion of life. This power of mature and comprehensive description is very unusual among the younger American writers. Most of them observe the world through a temperament, and are more occupied with their medium than the objects they watch. And temperament is a glass which distorts most astonishingly. But this young man sees with a clear eye, and reproduces with a touch, firm and decisive, strong almost to brutalness.

Mr. Norris approaches things on their physical side; his characters are personalities of flesh before they are anything else, types before they are individuals. Especially is this true of his women. His Trina is "very small and prettily made. Her face was round and rather pale; her eyes long and narrow and blue, like the half-opened eyes of a baby; her lips and the lobes of her tiny ears were pale, a little suggestive of anaemia. But it was to her hair that one's attention was most attracted. Heaps and heaps of blue-black coils and braids, a royal crown of swarthy bands, a veritable sable tiara, heavy, abundant and odorous. All the vitality that should have given color to her face seems to have been absorbed by that marvelous hair. It was the coiffure of a queen that shadowed the temples of this little bourgeoise." Blix had "round, full arms," and "the skin of her face was white and clean, except where it flushed into a most charming pink upon her smooth, cool cheeks." In this grasp of the element of things, this keen, clean, frank pleasure at color and odor and warmth, this candid admission of the negative of beauty, which is co-existent with and inseparable from it, lie much of his power and promise. Here is a man catholic enough to include the extremes of physical and moral life, strong enough to handle the crudest colors and darkest shadows. Here is a man who has an appetite for the physical universe, who loves the rank smells of crowded alley-ways, or the odors of boudoirs, or the delicate perfume exhaled from a woman's skin; who is not afraid of Pan, be he ever so shaggy, and redolent of the herd.

Structurally, where most young novelists are weak, Mr. Norris is very strong. He has studied the best French masters, and he has adopted their methods quite simply, as one selects an algebraic formula to solve his particular problem. As to his style, that is, as expression always is, just as vigorous as his thought compels it to be, just as vivid as his conception warrants. If God Almighty has given a man ideas, he will get himself a style from one source or another. Mr. Norris, fortunately, is not a conscious stylist. He has too much to say to be exquisitely vain about his medium. He has the kind of brain stuff that would vanquish difficulties in any profession, that might be put to building battleships, or solving problems of finance, or to devising colonial policies. Let us be thankful that he has put it to literature. Let us be thankful, moreover, that he is not introspective and that his intellect does not devour itself, but feeds upon the great race of man, and, above all, let us rejoice that he is not a "temperamental" artist, but something larger, for a great brain and an assertive temperament seldom dwell together.

There are clever men enough in the field of American letters, and the fault of most of them is merely one of magnitude; they are not large enough; they travel in small orbits, they play on muted strings. They sing neither of the combats of Atriedes nor the labors of Cadmus, but of the tea-table and the Odyssey of the Rialto. Flaubert said that a drop of water contained all the elements of the sea, save one—immensity. Mr. Norris is concerned only with serious things, he has only large ambitions. His brush is bold, his color is taken fresh from the kindly earth, his canvas is large enough to hold American life, the real life of the people. He has come into the court of the troubadours singing the song of Elys, the song of warm, full nature. He has struck the true note of the common life. He is what Mr. Norman Hapgood said the great American dramatist must be: "A large human being, with a firm stomach, who knows and loves the people."

The Courier, April 7, 1900

When I Knew Stephen Crane

It was, I think, in the spring of '94 that a slender, narrow-chested fellow in a shabby grey suit, with a soft felt hat pulled low over his eyes, sauntered into the office of the managing editor of the Nebraska State Journal and introduced himself as Stephen Crane. He stated that he was going to Mexico to do some work for the Bacheller Syndicate and get rid of his cough, and that he would be stopping in Lincoln for a few days. Later he explained that he was out of money and would be compelled to wait until he got a check from the East before he went further. I was a Junior at the Nebraska State University at the time, and was doing some work for the State Journal in my leisure time, and I happened to be in the managing editor's room when Mr. Crane introduced himself. I was just off the range; I knew a little Greek and something about cattle and a good horse when I saw one, and beyond horses and cattle I considered nothing of vital importance except good stories and the people who wrote them. This was the first man of letters I had ever met in the flesh, and when the young man announced who he was, I dropped into a chair behind the editor's desk where I could stare at him without being too much in evidence.

Only a very youthful enthusiasm and a large propensity for hero worship could have found anything impressive in the young man who stood before the managing editor's desk. He was thin to emaciation, his face was gaunt and unshaven, a thin dark moustache straggled on his upper lip, his black hair grew low on his forehead and was shaggy and unkempt. His grey clothes were much the worse for wear and fitted him so badly it seemed unlikely he had ever been measured for them. He wore a flannel shirt and a slovenly apology for a necktie, and his shoes were dusty and worn gray about the toes and were badly run over at the heel. I had seen many a tramp printer come up the Journal stairs to hunt a job, but never one who presented such a disreputable appearance as this story-maker man. He wore gloves, which seemed rather a contradiction to the general slovenliness of his attire, but when he took them off to search his pockets for his credentials, I noticed that his hands were singularly fine; long, white, and delicately shaped, with thin, nervous fingers. I have seen pictures of Aubrey Beardsley's hands that recalled Crane's very vividly.

At that time Crane was but twenty-four, and almost an unknown man. Hamlin Garland had seen some of his work and believed in him, and had introduced him to Mr. Howells, who recommended him to the Bacheller Syndicate. "The Red Badge of Courage" had been published in the State Journal that winter along with a lot of other syndicate matter, and the grammatical construction of the story was so faulty that the managing editor had several times called on me to edit the copy. In this way I had read it very carefully, and through the careless sentence-structure I saw the wonder of that remarkable performance. But the grammar certainly was bad. I remember one of the reporters who had corrected the phrase "it don't" for the tenth time remarked savagely, "If I couldn't write better English than this, I'd quit."

Crane spent several days in the town, living from hand to mouth and waiting for his money. I think he borrowed a small amount from the managing editor. He lounged about the office most of the time, and I frequently encountered him going in and out of the cheap restaurants on Tenth Street. When he was at the office he talked a good deal in a wandering, absent-minded fashion, and his conversation was uniformly frivolous. If he could not evade a serious question by a joke, he bolted. I cut my classes to lie in wait for him, confident that in some unwary moment I could trap him into serious conversation, that if one burned incense long enough and ardently enough, the oracle would not be dumb. I was Maupassant mad at the time, a malady particularly unattractive in a Junior, and I made a frantic effort to get expression of opinion from him on "Le Bonheur." "Oh, you're Moping, are you?" he remarked with a sarcastic grin, and went on reading a little volume of Poe that he carried in his pocket. At another time I cornered him in the Funny Man's room and succeeded in getting a little out of him. We were taught literature by an exceedingly analytical method at the University, and we probably distorted the method, and I was busy trying to find the least common multiple of *Hamlet* and the greatest common divisor of *Macbeth*, and I began asking him whether stories were constructed by cabalistic formulae. At length he sighed wearily and shook his drooping shoulders, remarking:

"Where did you get all that rot? Yarns aren't done by mathematics. You can't do it by rule any more than you can dance by rule. You have to have the itch of the thing in your fingers, and if you haven't,—well, you're damned lucky, and you'll live long and prosper, that's all."—And with that he yawned and went down the hall.

Crane was moody most of the time, his health was bad and he seemed profoundly discouraged. Even his jokes were exceedingly drastic. He went about with the tense, preoccupied, self-centered air of a man who is brooding over some impending disaster, and I conjectured vainly as to what it might be. Though he was seemingly entirely idle during the few days I knew him, his manner indicated that he was in the throes of work that told terribly on his nerves. His eyes I remember as the finest I have ever seen, large and dark and full of lustre and changing lights, but with a profound melancholy always lurking deep in them. They were eyes that seemed to be burning themselves out.

As he sat at the desk with his shoulders drooping forward, his head low, and his long, white fingers drumming on the sheets of copy paper, he was as nervous as a race horse fretting to be on the track. Always, as he came and went about the halls, he seemed like a man preparing for a sudden departure. Now that he is dead it occurs to me that all his life was a preparation for sudden departure. I remember once when he was writing a letter he stopped and asked me about the spelling of a word, saying carelessly, "I haven't time to learn to spell."

Then, glancing down at his attire, he added with an absent-minded smile, "I haven't time to dress either; it takes an awful slice out of a fellow's life."

He said he was poor, and he certainly looked it, but four years later when he was in Cuba, drawing the largest salary ever paid a newspaper correspondent, he clung to this same untidy manner of dress, and his ragged overalls and buttonless shirt were eyesores to the immaculate Mr. Davis, in his spotless linen and neat khaki uniform, with his Gibson chin always freshly shaven. When I first heard of his serious illness, his old throat trouble aggravated into consumption by his reckless exposure in Cuba, I recalled a passage from Maeterlinck's essay, "The Pre-Destined," on those doomed to early death: "As children, life seems nearer to them than to other children. They appear to know nothing, and yet there is in their eyes so profound a certainty that we feel they must know all.—In all haste, but wisely and with minute care do they prepare themselves to live, and this very haste is a sign upon which mothers can scarce bring themselves to look." I remembered, too, the young man's melancholy and his tenseness, his burning eyes, and his way of slurring over the less important things, as one whose time is short.

I have heard other people say how difficult it was to induce Crane to talk seriously about his work, and I suspect that he was particularly averse to discussions with literary men of wider education and better equipment than himself, yet he seemed to feel that this fuller culture was not for him. Perhaps the unreasoning instinct which lies deep in the roots of our lives, and which guides us all, told him that he had not time enough to acquire it.

Men will sometimes reveal themselves to children, or to people whom they think never to see again, more completely than they ever do to their confreres. From the wise we hold back alike our folly and our wisdom, and for the recipients of our deeper confidences we seldom select our equals. The soul has no message for the friends with whom we dine every week. It is silenced by custom and convention, and we play only in the shallows. It selects its listeners willfully, and seemingly delights to waste its best upon the chance wayfarer who meets us in the highway at a fated hour. There are moments too, when the tides run high or very low, when self-revelation is necessary to every man, if it be only to his valet or his gardener. At such a moment, I was with Mr. Crane.

The hoped for revelation came unexpectedly enough. It was on the last night he spent in Lincoln. I had come back from the theatre and was in the Journal office writing a notice of the play. It was eleven o'clock when Crane came in. He had expected his money to arrive on the night mail and it had not done so, and he was out of sorts and deeply despondent. He sat down on the ledge of the open window that faced on the street, and when I had finished my notice I went over and took a chair beside him. Quite without invitation on my part, Crane began to talk, began to curse his trade from the first throb of creative desire in a boy to the finished work of the master. The night was oppressively warm; one of those dry winds that are the curse of that country was blowing up from Kansas. The white, western moonlight threw sharp, blue shadows below us. The streets were silent at that hour, and we could hear the gurgle of the fountain in the Post Office square across the street, and the twang of banjos from the lower verandah of the Hotel Lincoln, where the colored waiters were serenading the guests. The drop lights in the office were dull under their green shades, and the telegraph sounder clicked faintly in the next room. In all his long tirade, Crane never raised his voice; he spoke slowly and monotonously and even calmly, but I have never known so bitter a heart in any man as he revealed to me that night. It was an arraignment of the wages of life, an invocation to the ministers of hate.

Incidentally he told me the sum he had received for "The Red Badge of Courage," which I think was something like ninety dollars, and he repeated some lines from "The Black Riders," which was then in preparation. He gave me to understand that he led a double literary life; writing in the first place the matter that pleased himself, and doing it very slowly; in the second place, any sort of stuff that would sell. And he remarked that his poor was just as bad as it could possibly be. He realized, he said, that his limitations were absolutely impassable. "What I can't do, I can't do at all, and I can't acquire it. I only hold one trump."

He had no settled plans at all. He was going to Mexico wholly uncertain of being able to do any successful work there, and he seemed to feel very insecure about the financial end of his venture. The thing that most interested me was what he said about his slow method of composition. He declared that there was little money in story-writing at best, and practically none in it for him, because of the time it took him to work up his detail. Other men, he said, could sit down and write up an experience while the physical effect of it, so to speak, was still upon them, and yesterday's impressions made to-day's "copy." But when he came in from the streets to write up what he had seen there, his faculties were benumbed, and he sat twirling his pencil and hunting for words like a schoolboy.

I mentioned "The Red Badge of Courage," which was written in nine days, and he replied that, though the writing took very little time, he had been unconsciously working the detail of the story out through most of his boyhood. His ancestors had been soldiers, and he had been imagining war stories ever since he was out of knickerbockers, and in writing his first war story he had simply gone over his imaginary campaigns and selected his favorite imaginary experiences. He declared that his imagination was hide bound; it was there, but it pulled hard. After he got a notion for a story, months passed before he could get any sort of personal contract with it, or feel any potency to handle it. "The detail of a thing has to filter through my blood, and then it comes out like a native product, but it takes forever," he remarked. I distinctly remember the illustration, for it rather took hold of me.

I have often been astonished since to hear Crane spoken of as "the reporter in fiction," for the reportorial faculty of superficial reception and quick transference was what he conspicuously lacked. His first newspaper account of his shipwreck on the filibuster "Commodore" off the Florida coast was as lifeless as the "copy" of a police court reporter. It was many months afterwards that the literary product of his terrible experience appeared in that marvellous sea story "The Open Boat," unsurpassed in its vividness and constructive perfection.

At the close of our long conversation that night, when the copy boy came in to take me home, I suggested to Crane that in ten years he would probably laugh at all his temporary discomfort. Again his body took on that strenuous tension and he clenched his hands, saying, "I can't wait ten years, I haven't time."

The ten years are not up yet, and he has done his work and gathered his reward and gone. Was ever so much experience and achievement crowded into so short a space of time? A great man dead at twenty-nine! That would have puzzled the ancients. Edward Garnett wrote of him in The Academy of December 17, 1899: "I cannot remember a parallel in the literary history of fiction. Maupassant, Meredith, Henry James, Mr. Howells and Tolstoy, were all learning their expression at an age where Crane had achieved his and achieved it triumphantly." He had the precocity of those doomed to die in youth. I am convinced that when I met him he had a vague premonition of the shortness of his working day, and in the heart of the man there was that which said, "That thou doest, do quickly."

At twenty-one this son of an obscure New Jersey rector, with but a scant reading knowledge of French and no training, had rivaled in technique the foremost craftsmen of the Latin races. In the six years since I met him, a stranded reporter, he stood in the firing line during two wars, knew hairbreadth 'scapes on land and sea, and established himself as the first writer of his time in the picturing of episodic, fragmentary life. His friends have charged him with fickleness, but he was a man who was in the preoccupation of haste. He went from country to country, from man to man, absorbing all that was in them for him. He had no time to look backward. He had no leisure for *camaraderie*. He drank life to the lees, but at the banquet table where other men took their ease and jested over their wine, he stood a dark and silent figure, sombre as Poe himself, not wishing to be understood; and he took his portion in haste, with his loins girded, and his shoes on his feet, and his staff in his hand, like one who must depart quickly.

The Library, June 23, 1900

On the Art of Fiction

One is sometimes asked about the "obstacles" that confront young writers who are trying to do good work. I should say the greatest obstacles that writers today have to get over, are the dazzling journalistic successes of twenty years ago, stories that surprised and delighted by their sharp photographic detail and that were really nothing more than lively pieces of reporting. The whole aim of that school of writing was novelty—never a very important thing in art. They gave us, altogether, poor standards—taught us to multiply our ideas instead of to condense them. They tried to make a story out of every theme that occurred to them and to get returns on every situation that suggested itself. They got returns, of a kind. But their work, when one looks back on it, now that the novelty upon which they counted so much is gone, is journalistic and thin. The especial merit of a good reportorial story is that it shall be intensely interesting and pertinent today and shall have lost its point by tomorrow.

Art, it seems to me, should simplify. That, indeed, is very nearly the whole of the higher artistic process; finding what conventions of form and what detail one can do without and yet preserve the spirit of the whole—so that all that one has suppressed and cut away is there to the reader's consciousness as much as if it were in type on the page. Millet had done hundreds of sketches of peasants sowing grain, some of them very complicated and interesting, but when he came to paint the spirit of them all into one picture, "The Sower," the composition is so simple that it seems inevitable. All the discarded sketches that went before made the picture what it finally became, and the process was all the time one of simplifying, of sacrificing many conceptions good in themselves for one that was better and more universal.

Any first rate novel or story must have in it the strength of a dozen fairly good stories that have been sacrificed to it. A good workman can't be a cheap workman; he can't be stingy about wasting material, and he cannot compromise. Writing ought either to be the manufacture of stories for which there is a market demand—a business as safe and commendable as making soap or breakfast foods—or it should be an art, which is always a search for something for which there is no market demand, something new and untried, where the values are intrinsic and have nothing to do with standardized values. The courage to go on without compromise does not come to a writer all at once—nor, for that matter, does the ability. Both are phases of natural development. In the beginning the artist, like his public, is wedded to old forms, old ideals, and his vision is blurred by the memory of old delights he would like to recapture.

The Borzoi, 1920